i

AWAKENING THE HEART

Dear Marisol

May this Book awaken any dreams wit'n you Bursting to get out. Thank you so much. I'm joining the INNER circle! ♡ I look forward to seeing your Beautiful SOUL — EXPAND —

Thank you!

Love, Carolyn Kim

iii

"Carolyn Rim's energy within these stories will ignite a burning fire in your heart. This book will not only awaken your heart, it will possibly even help you dig up your own lost dreams. Just a warning: Reading this book could result in taking massive action in your own life."

—Joseph McClendon III, Ph.D.

AWAKENING THE HEART
by Carolyn Rim

INTRODUCTION

IF YOU ARE HOLDING THIS BOOK, REMEMBER WHO YOU ARE.

This book is in your hands for a reason and a purpose and it serves you. You have the opportunity to allow the stories you read in this book to transform you. Everything you need, and will ever need, is within you. May this book spark you awake and tweeze open your sleeping eyes toward your true greatness. Awakenings are not easy, but I promise, it's worth opening your eyes and seeing the truth. Awaken to your truth. DREAMS DO COME TRUE.

This is a true story. Over 18 months, my life changed dramatically. I quit smoking, I quit my job, my husband left me and I started my own company. I am grateful for Facebook, or this book may not have been written. Over the course of a year, I made hundreds of posts, and spent countless hours posting, blogging and writing. If you are waiting for the perfect moment, the perfect timing to jump in, you will be waiting a long time. You need to jump in with both feet!

I remember leaping into the dark and the freedom I got from finally dancing with my fear! It was liberating, and each time I leaped, right before I hit the ground, a platform would light up, and then another one, and then another one, and another one. I kept leaping into the dark and I realized how powerful I was—how powerful we all are.

I have woken up slowly over the past year. I seemed to be seeing things for the first time, and I had never been more grateful in my whole life. I realized that no house, no car, no amount of money would make me happy. For years, I had been searching for the answer and here I had it within me the whole time!

I realized that I had to be grateful for what I already had in my life, and I had to be happy now! You will never be happy getting what you get if you're not happy now. You can be, do and have whatever you want in this world! You can have a goal, a vision of the future and still be grateful for right now.

That's the secret.

WAKE UP!

Wake up to the beautiful gift you are in this world. The relationship with yourself is the most important relationship you have! Everything that you see around you is a reflection of what is going on within you.

You, yes you, make a difference in the world. Absorb those words. Whether you are on the front page of TIME magazine or a stay-at- home mom, you make a difference. See the gift that you are, and be the light. Be the love. Be compassionate. Be kind. Most important, never give up. No matter what.

May this book transform you. May this book wake you up. May the stories in this book reach the right people who will take massive action to make a difference in the world. May this book awaken your soul to its true original nature. it is possible.

You want what you want for a reason.

I have had a spiritual awakening. Throughout this book, you will see my transformation. You will step into my greatest moments and my darkest moments, as I take you on a roller coaster of actual events that transformed my life over the past 18 months.

You are phenomenal. Do not let anyone in this world, even yourself, make you believe that you are anything but incredible. Allow your heart to lead you. It will never steer you wrong. Your heart and intuition already know what you truly want. Learn to trust yourself. You need to dig deep down and ask yourself, "Who do I want to be?" Not *what*, but *who* do you want to be? Figure out for yourself what makes you happy no matter how crazy it might sound to your teachers, friends, or family. You must think for yourself because it is the only thing over which you

2

have absolute control.

Who will be affected by the actions you take today? There are generations yet unborn whose very lives will be shifted and shaped by the moves you make and the actions you take today. And tomorrow. And the next day. And the next.

Every single thing you do matters. How you do *anything* is how you do *everything*. You are vibrating amazing energy. And if you're reading this sentence right now—there is a reason. You were created in order so you could make a difference in the world. BE THE LOVE.

AWAKEN THE HEART

As you read this book, I double-dog-dare you to ask the universe what you really want. Buckle up, Rockstars. We are going to the moon to dance on stardust. Open yourself up to the divine energy, to the infinite intelligence—a magnificent force you cannot touch, you cannot see, you cannot hear, but a beautiful force you can feel all around you. Breathe in the magic, the energy, the love. Now, my sweet darlings, come follow me into the jungle. Into the magic. Into the light.

Chapter 1
Taking the Leap

"You don't have to be great to start, but you have to start to be great."

—Zig Ziglar

OCTOBER 12, 2014

I sit in my cube, staring at the computer. I am researching bridges to jump off. I have just turned 30 and I realize how much I hate my life—okay, not just my life, I hate myself. All I seem to do is wake up, go to work, eat dinner, and sleep.

Don't get me wrong, there are a few moments that are fun and exciting but most of the time I am miserable. I do not have any big life goals—hell, I don't have any goals. I want to die. The chatter in my mind never ceases. Constantly criticizing, contradicting and abusing me. "You're a joke. You think you can change the world? You are nothing. YOU will be going against the whole world. You will never make it. Look at the past—all you are is a high school graduate with a bad reputation. A whore. Used goods. You are nothing."

I have a good voice and a bad voice in my mind. I cannot help but feel overwhelmed and unhappy most of the time. The bad voice was constant and the good voice tried, without success, to convince me of my inherent worth.

I have been at my job for six years and I have moved up the ladder quickly. Up until about a year ago, I was the firm's number one sales rep four years in a row, but I still feel unfulfilled and unhappy. A year and a half ago, the company took a turn for the worse and my salary went way down. I went from making $120,000 a year to

$50,000 a year in seven months. I have been in a car accident and my neck injury is killing me too. I am going to the doctor every week. I smoke a pack of cigarettes a day. I eat unhealthy foods. I work out a few times per week, but my terrible eating habits and smoking cancel out my efforts to be healthy.

My peers are not encouraging. Anytime I spoke about my dream to be something more than what I am, they would tell me not to do it because it's just safer to stay where you are than to go for it and fail. People around me are not going after *their* dreams. When I told them about this dream I had where I was in front of thousands of people, they would tell me there was no way I could do that. I feel trapped. Stuck. How did I get here?

Back to staring at the screen. The peer group and friends in my life, joke about killing themselves and although of course I don't like that, I joke as well. We have a running joke. "Meet me at the bridge and I'll bring the lipstick." Talk about an unhealthy peer group. But, seriously, I would rather die than have my energy dwarfed and locked in this cube for another 10 years. All my light was trapped within the walls of this grey cube, with nowhere to expand. Hot tears stream down my face. I try desperately to mask my emotions at work. I feel like I am speaking a language that no one can understand; they just say I am weird or crazy.

Then something happens. I snap. I am done. No more. Not another minute do I want to spend on this earth. I stare at the screen, unhappy, unfulfilled, unchallenged. I wait for the phone to ring. I decide I am going do it that day. I am going to kill myself. I hate myself. I decide I am going to jump off a bridge. I close my eyes and visualize leaping into the air and finally being able to spread my wings and fly.

That's always what I wanted to do. Fly. Fly into the air, soar like an eagle, even if only for a few seconds. I would feel the wind against my face and plunge to my death, away from pain. No mean voice could reach me. No taunting, horrible memories of my past could reach me. No more of this feeling like I will never be enough.

I am staring at a picture of the Golden Gate Bridge. I would go out there and jump off. No one could get to me out there. I look up the stats on the bridge on how many people jumped from it. I watch the horrible videos of someone actually leaping to his death. Leaping from the bridge and hitting the water at speeds of 70mph is like hitting concrete. They stopped counting the numbers of jumpers.

I think of my little girl, KK, and get tears in my eyes. I think, she is the only reason I am still alive right now.

THE VOICE OF THE HEART

Then I have my first conscious experience with grace, the first time I heard my heart so clearly speak to me. Call it my heart, source, God, divine intervention—whatever it was, it was all around me. I could not see it, hear it, touch it, but I felt a magnificent presence all around me. Almost as if angels were surrounding me. The world around me went into slow motion.

As if my fingers were guided, I stop looking for bridges to jump from and type the name Tony Robbins into YouTube. I watch two minutes of a video of him at one of his seminars and I see the people in slow motion jumping up and down, smiling. Real smiles. Not this fake-smile peanut-butter-fluff I saw from others all day long. These people were authentically happy from within their beautiful souls. I realized at that moment that I needed to go see this man.

I quickly call the number. It rings three times and then a woman answers. "Hi, thank you for calling Tony Robbins Company. My name is Kelly Phillips. How can I help you today?"

I clear my throat, "Hi, my name is Carolyn Rim and I want a front row seat to see Tony Robbins. How much will that be?"

"A front row Diamond Premier seat is $2,997. The next event is 12 days away and almost sold out," she says. I hesitate and think for a moment. I don't have $3,000. Sensing my hesitation, Kelly said, "I also have a few general admission seats available for $500." I think about it. I could take the $500 general admission ticket however I am anything but general. I am Diamond Premier all the way. I say to Kelly, "Hold that Diamond Premier ticket. I will call you back in an hour."

I hang up the phone. I pull up my bank account online to see how much money I have. I stare at the number on the screen. $36. A measly $36. How the hell am I going to pull this off? I close my eyes for a moment. I take a long inhale in through my nose and a long exhale out through my mouth.

I call my sister Marie, who had gone to an Unleash the Power Within seminar years before and said how amazing it was. She had been texting me that day to see how I am. She knows I am struggling but she also knows I am meant for greatness. I text her and tell her what I am planning to do. She texted back, all in caps, "NOW IS THE TIME. GO FOR IT, KID."

That is all I need. I don't call my husband, who I know would talk me out of it. I don't call anyone who will try to talk me out of going. I call the bank and took out a $5,000 loan. For the first time in my life, I am going all-in on me. A magnificent energy streams through me and my heart is racing. I have never done anything like this. A few faxes and signatures later, I have $5,000 transferred into my account.

I call Kelly Phillips back within a half hour and tell her with a smile, "Book my Diamond Premier front row seat, please." I book a flight and a suite at the Aloft hotel in Dallas. Within just a few hours, I am booked for the Unleash The Power Within event with Tony Robbins and 7,000 other souls.

I inhale this beautiful feeling, as if each cell in my body and my soul is awakening. I still feel like something is missing, but in my heart I know I have taken a huge leap of faith, and that ignited something within me. Instead of leaping from the bridge, I have leapt out of my comfort zone with child-like faith into uncertainty. It is the first time in years my heart spoke to me—or maybe it was the first time in years I have listened.

That night I go home and told no one but my little girl, KK. We are snuggling underneath the blankets in her bed, reading with a flashlight. I say, "Baby, Mommy has to go away by herself for a couple of days. Do you think you can take care of Daddy?"

She chuckles at the thought of her taking care of her daddy. She looks at me, "But Mommy, I'm going to miss you."

I place my hand on her heart and then I say, "Remember, all you have to do is put your hand on your heart, think of me and send me love. I will get your message of love-energy, baby, and send a light beam of swirling-twirling-love around you. I love you more than all the stars in the sky and no matter where I am, I am always sending you my love, KK. Mommy has to do this, because for the first time, baby, I am allowing my heart to lead me."

KK smiles her sweet smile and says, "Okay Mommy, I will take care of Daddy while you're gone." We stare at each other for a moment. Looking deeply into my little girl's eyes, I can see the whole universe in them. I instantly feel magic and love when I look at her.

A few days later, I know I need to tell my husband, Mike, before my trip but I am so scared. That night, I tell him I am going away for a few days and he didn't know what to say. "Are you still not happy?" he says. He is upset, but I explain that for me to be happy, I have to do this. He is so

8

mad at me that he refuses to look or talk to me at all. He just is in silence staring at the floor slowly shaking his head at me. Then he says, "Fine. Go. Do what you want."

I tell my family and prepare for take-off toward my destiny. My heart is heavy and sad about Mike but I still know I am on the right road. I stop second-guessing my intuition and decide to start listening to my heart, which says go for it.

OCTOBER 22, 2014

It's the day before the event and I am nervous. I am at work and have not gotten any sales all day so I am stressed, tense and irritated. I am holding back tears in my cell. My cube. This jail. My phone rings and breaks my thought pattern. "Hello," I say, trying my best not to sound like I am on the verge of a breakdown.

"Hey Carolina," my friend says in his usual playful voice. "Hi, Joe," I say and my voice cracks before I can even get out another word. Instantly Joe picks up on my energy and says, "Are you okay?" I tell him I am leaving tomorrow for Dallas to see Tony Robbins and I am nervous and sad and scared all at the same time. He asks me what time I will be at work until. I tell him 5 p.m. "Okay, I will see you at 3 p.m." He hangs up before I can protest. His engagement pictures with his fiancée are today. How could he be thinking about anyone else on this day?

I stop overthinking it and continue to stare at the computer screen and the phone rings. "Thanks for calling Medical Alert, this is Carolyn Rim. How may I help you?" The woman on the phone says, "What? Speak slower, won't you? You young people talk too damn fast." This is my life. I speak to seniors and sell the "Help, I have fallen and I can't get up" buttons." I have been on this call before, 1,000 times before. I feel like it's the rinse and repeat cycle over and over again. I start to get tears in my eyes. My train of thought is interrupted by Brad Lovitz, who stands up in his cube and calls my name.

"Hey Carolyn!" he says. I sit around all men except for a beautiful black woman named Faith who sits behind me, whose smile lights up the room. I stand up. Now if you're looking at this and imagining it in your mind, think of whack-a-mole game—we all stand up in our cubes to talk and then go back down. "Hey, Brad." I tell the few people around me I trust that I am going to a Tony Robbins seminar tomorrow. I have to jump through hoops at work with my boss to even make this possible. I had to get honest and tell my company that I was really depressed, contemplating jumping off a bridge and I needed some time off. They had me fill out a Family Medical Leave Act form. Thank God for FMLA.

Bing. A text message on my phone breaks my train of thought. It's my friend Joe, and he is here. I grab my cigarettes and coat and run out the door to meet him in the parking lot. We instantly give each other a big bear hug. I love this guy. I worked with him 10 years ago in a telemarketing place, and we have been friends ever since. I feel like he understands me more than anyone in the planet some days. I love his wife, too. She understands that Joe and I are friends. They are the most attractive couple I know. I am a bridesmaid in their wedding next year.

A KINDRED SOUL

He hands me a book, *Unlimited Power*, by Tony Robbins. "Joe! I didn't know you liked Tony Robbins!"

"I have been reading and listening to him for years," he says with a smile. I take a cigarette out of my pack and light one up. I take a long drag and watch the paper on the cigarette slowly singe. Joe and I walk around to the smoking area of the office building and find a place to sit. Just being next to him I feel safe.

I say, "I am petrified about tomorrow. Going to Tony Robbins, leaving my family, being in a place I have never been before. Who knows what's in Dallas? I know in my heart that I must go through with this though, no matter how scared I am. I feel like I am called to it. Like almost pulled by a cosmic force I can't explain or see, I can only feel it in my soul. I know one thing is true right now. I just don't want to feel like I am dying anymore."

Our eyes meet, and he says, "You will always succeed, no matter where you go. Think about it. The last place we worked, you were number one booker five years in a row. Then, here, you've been the number one sales rep four years in a row. Everywhere you go and everything you touch, you make better."

I have a hard time taking that compliment and I instantly start to look through the book to deflect his compliment and I realize, he has read the whole book. As I flip through the pages, I see he has carefully underlined passages he's loved, especially certain parts about stepping into the person you want to become. I glance up at him and smile. It doesn't surprise me. He is the smartest person I know, and his wife is the sweetest and the nicest. I am jealous of them sometimes because I see the love between them and I wish that for me and my husband. I get teary and say, "Thank you, Joe. Thank you." He gives me a huge hug and we talk for another 20 minutes.

We get up and start walking back to his car. He is on his way to meet the love of his life for his engagement pictures. He is glowing. He turns and looks at me, "This is just the beginning for you. Call me or Cherie anytime, day or night, doesn't matter, we will be there."

As I watch him get into his car, I realize how grateful I am for his friendship. I run to the car before he pulls out and I knock on his window and get one more hug from him. I tell him to have fun with his beautiful bride-to-be, and I mean it with my whole heart.

I turn and walk back into the office. I have chills. I am holding a book, and tomorrow I am going to see the man who wrote it. My life is going to change tremendously. I am all in, I say to myself. I then say it out loud: "I am all in. I am ready." I feel the presence again in that moment. I feel like I'm not alone. There is a force much greater than me at work behind the scenes here and I feel its grace and love.

FLYING SOLO

That night I lay awake in my bed, feeling like a child on Christmas Eve. I am so excited and scared that I can't fall asleep. I start to wonder about what lies ahead for me tomorrow as I take off toward my destiny, to Love Field in Dallas. I have never been there. Actually, I have never been on a plane by myself.

I lie next to my husband, listening to him breathe. I wish we had more of a connection. Most days I feel like we're shouting at each other from two different worlds and our messages get scrambled along the way. We had fought earlier about my going. He couldn't believe I took out a $5,000 loan. He couldn't believe I am going away for four days. He said he wanted me to make *him* number one. He said he didn't need this "Tony Robbins bullshit."

Our marriage has been one of turmoil. Sure, we have had our amazing moments when things were picture-perfect but somehow we would always end up here, going to bed angry.

I think back to five years earlier where I am putting on my wedding dress. My sister is helping me. I'm looking in the mirror and my sister intuitively knows something is wrong. She is giving me a concerned look. I move away from her and stare out the window, my back turned to her. I stare out the window in my handmade lace wedding gown.

"He isn't the one," I manage to say. "I mean, don't get me wrong. I love him very much, he is great man and we have a little girl together but I feel like my heart is telling me he isn't the one."

My sister says, "Carolyn, you don't have to go through with this. You can cancel everything. People do it all the time."

I turn and look her in the dead in the eyes. "It has to work. We have a child together. Plus, he takes care of me, like no one else I ever met. I will *make* him the one." I walk past her and say, "Come on, let's go get married."

With a small, sad smile on her face, she grabs me and hugs me. She says, "I love you no matter what you decide. I just want you to be happy." I hide a tear that rolls down my face, quickly wiping it away.

"Let's go," I say.

That was five years ago. Mike and I have had many amazing magical moments and many dark moments. I don't think anyone liked us together. Not his family and not my family. And when your family tells you that the person you're with isn't right for you, sometimes they are right. They can see something that you may be blinded to.

The uncertainty of losing my husband and then being alone—well, that is the most frightening thing in the world. I have never just been alone. I have always had some type of boyfriend or someone I was sleeping with or just having sex with.

But I do love Mike immensely. I didn't know love until I met him. He vibrates my soul at times and other times I wonder how we made it this far. I love the man sleeping next to me with my whole heart. We had this sexual synergy that is to the moon and beyond. We were magnets for each other. But, as I prepared to change my life, all he wanted to do was watch TV and chill. I want more. I want to grow, expand, learn and love. I want to fly.

My sister Marie told me a story once. A husband and wife were in a house that was burning down. The man just stood there looking around at the fire and the woman went and found out a way out. She came running back into the house and grabbed the man's hand. He looked at her blankly and sat down on the ground. She said, "What are you doing? Get up! Get up please! I found a way out of the fire." The man stared blankly at the floor and shook his head no. "I do not know what is out there," the man said. "GET UP!" The woman pleaded. "GET UP! PLEASE!" She shouted again and again. She looked at the only exit out of the burning house and then she looked back him and started to cry. She was so in love with him that she sat down beside him with tears flowing. She said, "I would rather die in this fire with you than to go out into the unknown world and face it without you." They held hands as they died in the fire.

I do not want to die in the fire. My mind races with my heart. Why? Why can't Mike understand my dream? I have this burning in my soul that must be satisfied or I will combust. I cannot pretend anymore that I am okay, that things are just fine. That's the problem. I want to be *better* than just fine. I want to unleash my fucking soul. I allow myself to take a few deep breaths.

I am pulled towards a moment from a few hours ago. Mike and I are facing each other in the kitchen. He asks in desperation, "Why can't you just be happy with what you have?"

I take a deep breath before I answer. "I am dying. I can feel my body and my mind and my soul dying. That's why I am going to see Tony Robbins," I say, defending myself.

He still doesn't get it. I can tell from the way he is looking at me. "When was the last time you did something for the first time?" I ask him, desperately wanting him to understand. He glares at me.

He says, "I can tell you exactly how it's going to go down. You are going to lose your job, then stick me with all this debt. It's ridiculous. This is all your fault. All of it. In fact, I want nothing to do with it. Don't ask me to take you to the airport or pick you up."

He turns and walks away. I don't know how to explain what's happening within me. I feel amazing change is coming and if I don't start taking action I will miss this opportunity to unleash and awaken my soul.

I come back to the moment and just *breathe*. I listen to Mike breathe in and out. I finally close my eyes and my racing thoughts slow, sinking into my mind's deep ocean of swirling thoughts until I succumb to the darkness of sleep.

Chapter 2
Unleash the Power Within Event

*"It is in your moments of decision that your
destiny is shaped."*

—*Tony Robbins*

FLYING INTO DESTINY

I awake to someone banging on the door. I open my eyes to the clock
that reads 5:30 a.m. My flight takes off in only two hours! Shit! I run
down the steps and open the door. My sister, Marie, is standing there,
ready to go. "You ready? I've been knocking for, like, 10 minutes."

I'm not even packed yet. My alarm was set for 4 a.m. and I slept right
through it. Self-sabotage is deep. This is deep. Why would I do this to
myself? No time to over-analyze. There's no way I'm going to miss this
flight. I move faster than I ever have, stuff my things into a bag, throw
on jeans and a t-shirt, and grab my sneakers. It is now 6:14 a.m.

I run out to the car and get in the back with my daughter, KK, holding
her hand. She's of course upset I'm leaving. I tell her I have to, to create
a better life for us. I tell her I'm following my heart and I'll be home in
four days to love her up. She hugs me and holds my hand the whole way
there. We pull up to the Philadelphia International Airport at 7:03 a.m.

I give KK one more hug. "I love you more than all the stars in the sky!"

We place our hands over our hearts and give each other that look—that look of love we send each other with our thoughts. This started years ago, when she told me she missed me at lunch in school and wished she could hug me. I told her that anytime she missed me to place her hand over her heart and send me love. I told her I would feel it, and no matter where I was in the world I would put my hand over my heart and send her love back, and it would feel like she was getting a hug from me. She believed this with her whole little heart. We both did.

With tears in my eyes, I run into the airport and run to the front desk and explain my situation. They help me quickly and hand me my ticket. They tell me to run so I oblige.

I run. I run as fast as my legs will carry me. I cannot miss this flight. Please God, I say in my head. Please. Please. I get through security and then I run to gate 14. It's 7:33 a.m. exactly. There's a small line of people by the door. I made it. I smile for the first time in two hours. I breathe. I give them my ticket and I take my seat on the plane. I stare off towards the rising sun and the clouds. I smile as we lift off towards Love Field— lifting off towards my destiny. And then I fall asleep.

When we get to Dallas, I'm anxious to get off the plane since it's been several hours since my last cigarette. As I get outside, I light up. I take a long hard drag in and exhale the smoke. I instantly feel calm. My nerves calm. I have smoked for 15 years, a pack and a half of cigarettes every day. People glare at me as I smoke. Fuck off, I think to myself. Cigarettes have been my best friends for as long as I can remember. I glance in my purse. Five five-hour caffeine shots and six packs of cigarettes.

Here I'm going to a wellness conference to better myself and I have all this junk in my purse. I feel a little guilty and shameful. I feel tense again and decide there's no time to dwell, I have to get moving.

I hail a taxi and drop my bags at my hotel with less than 10 minutes until the seminar. Luckily the event is right across the street. I see people wearing all these different-color necklaces walking in the same direction as me. They're smiling and excited. Now I feel the excitement. It's beaming from everyone. I feel myself opening to the energy within. I feel people in my heart. The necklaces read UPW DALLAS. Some say Diamond Premier. Some say General or VIP and I notice the special Platinum necklace.

As soon as I get into the seminar I can tell that energy-wise, we are in a different space. I feel limitless. There's a long line for General tickets but with my ticket, there are no lines, thankfully.

I walk into the Diamond Premier lounge, and I'm handed my white necklace with red lettering on it, with my name and reading UPW DALLAS DIAMOND PREMIER. I put it on and I feel instant

16

significance, part of something big. I feel like I matter. There is something about this necklace that is pure magic.

I ask the woman usher to please help escort me to my seat. The man behind me says, "Can you help me too?"

He asks me, "Hi. First time here too?" He's standing a little too close and though he seems nice enough, I don't want to give the wrong signals. I chat briefly and then my walls fly up. The woman gestures for us to follow her and as we walk, the man continues to try to chat with me. I have this expression that lets you know I'm done talking with you. He doesn't get it or he gets it and tries anyway, asking me to get a drink with him later that night. I tell him I do not drink and I am here strictly to fall in love with me.

FALLING IN LOVE WITH MYSELF

That's the first time I say it. Fall in love with me. "I want to stop hating me and fall in love with myself," I say out loud again to myself more than to anyone else. The woman escorts us to seats eight rows back from the front row. I want to get away from the man so I move a few seats over.

I tell the woman I thought I would get to sit in the front. There's a section right directly to either side of the stage. I point to it and ask if I may sit there. The woman tells me, "That's CSI. It's only for Tony's special friends and family." Though I decide to not make a big deal out of this and take my seat with a smile, I'm determined to get into that family and friend section.

So, before the woman walks away, I say, "By tomorrow I want to be sitting in the Tony Robbins friends and family section."

She smiles and says, "I'll see what I can do!"

Then, a song starts playing and there's an announcement: "Let's get it started in here!" I jump to my feet and so does everyone else. A team of people comes out to the stage and starts dancing. Everyone is following them. I start clapping, swinging my hips and I can feel this incredible energy in the room. I have never felt anything quite as amazing as this. Now imagine this energy being up. NOW, IMAGINE TURNING IT UP 10 MORE LEVELS.

As Tony Robbins enters, everyone moves forward and is jumping up and down, dancing and screaming! This man, this legend, comes out on stage and is looking right at me, I think. He makes direct eye contact with me and I can feel this unbelievable, amazing energy pouring into me. I soak it up like water into a sponge. I imagine my energy swirled into his.

He tells us to jump up and down. He tells us to massage the person next to us. He tells us to raise our right arm and slap the person's ass in front of us. He tells us about the six human needs: Certainty, Uncertainty, Significance, Love/Connection, Growth, Contribution.

He connects the dots in my mind and explains about the movie *Scrooge*. The ghosts of Christmas Past, Present and Future: If we could take people through a process that would show them exactly what would happen if they didn't stop doing what they were doing, such as smoking for example, the ghost of Christmas Future would show dying a terrible death and leaving children and grandchildren behind.

This makes sense to me. Everything he explains seems like common sense to me. I realize this was exactly what was happening to me! I realized how messed up it was that we were not taught this information in school. Our happiness is so much more important than our grades, history or algebra.

I have a vision flash through me as he is teaching us. I envision myself on stage in front of 7,000 people. I feel the vibrations of the people in the crowd jumping up and down. I feel the energy all the way down to every fiber of my soul.

That's the first time I see through the eyes of myself in the future. It's the first time I have a vision within my heart. I'm transported back to the room and open my eyes. Tony has just walked us through another meditation and now he wants us to celebrate. Tony constantly makes eye contact with me. His energy streams into me when he is looking at me and I never look away. I stream back with just as much energy.

I start to mirror this legend. He bangs on his chest. I bang on mine. He tilts his head back and lifts his head up and I do the same. He roars. I roar louder.

I'm instantly jealous of Tony Robbins. I want to be him; not *really* him, but me. I want to be me, on stage and performing all over the world. I sit on the edge of my seat and absorb energy from this man. He's incredible. It is amazing. I learn about my values and what I want in my life. I create new beliefs for myself.

WOMAN WHO WALKS ON FIRE

Tony spends four hours teaching us how to overcome our fear of walking over fire. We anchor a positive state. He explains NLP (neuro-linguistic programming) and tells us we can change our state at any moment.

"How fast can you change your emotional state?!" he asks.

Then, 7,000 people snap their fingers and yell "Like that!" Being around 7,000 people who are investing in themselves and climbing the success ladder makes me happy.

He raises his hand and asks, "Are you with me? Say I!"

Seven thousand souls raise their hands and shout, "I!" I have never met people just like me, but here people all around me are full of enthusiasm and heart and cheer. I feel transported to my happy place, as if everyone there is connected somehow. Tony Robbins connects us all through emotional bliss. We are in and out of meditations, jumping up and down.

This is better than sex, I think to myself as we go about the day! I feel like howling at the moon! "YOW-OW-OW!!" This is awesome. I feel like I belong. All the years I tried fitting in, and I finally have found a place where I feel right at home. "YES YES YES!" we shout.

And now comes the part where we walk over flaming hot coals.

Tony tells us what to chant as we walk over fire. "Cool moss! Cool moss!" He makes jokes: "Why cool moss? Because it's better than hot moss!" and everyone laughs a nervous laugh. For most of the people here, and for myself, it's our first time walking over fire. We will be walking over coals that are 1,200 degrees; flesh burns at 134 degrees. Just saying.

Needless to say, I am scared.

But I am also excited. Excited to do something that I told myself normally would be impossible. Tony explains how our habitual emotional states are creating our reality. That makes sense to me. He tells me that he will get us into peak emotional state, using anchoring and movement and visualization together.

This has been a long day and it's now 11:30 p.m. and I have been up since 5 a.m.—but the funny thing is that I don't feel tired. I feel alive for the first time in my life.

I feel on fire and energized.

I walk out with my fire buddy, a lovely woman with a London accent who grabs me and we shout and scream YES! YES! YES! YES! We clap and dance and then it's almost our turn. Before I know it one of the Tony Robbins trainers grabs me and says, "STEP UP! YES! YES! YES!"

I've never had a more powerful moment in my whole life. Thousands of people walk outside to walk on coals that are 1,200 degrees. I start to doubt myself and think about how scared I am. My turn to walk over the 1,200 degree coals, the trainer says again, "Step up!"

I say, "YES!" and make my move. I slam my hand on my chest and shout "YES!"

And I walk over the fire with unstoppable confidence and effortless ease. I celebrate and hug my buddy. I jump up and down and feel like I could fly. I feel so strong. So empowered. I feel like I can do *anything*. I breathe in this feeling. I have just conquered what few people get to do. "I have walked on FIRE! I AM OFFICIALLY A FIREWALKER! So. This is Day One," I say out loud to myself. This is my destiny. This is what I flew out here for.

Everyone starts to head back to the main room and grab their stuff, and I see people taking pictures with the people they came with and everyone is talking. I'm grateful I'm alone. I've never had time like this to myself. I send some gratitude into the universe and as I walk out of the main room. I smile a smile that I have never smiled before. I get tears in my eyes.

I'm awakening. This is part of my awakening, a part of my vision. I'm going to become the hero of my life, I decide right now.

Why not me? Why not?

LIMITING BELIEFS TO LIMITLESS GRATITUDE

As I walk back to my hotel room, I light a cigarette. I realize I have not eaten all day. I'm starving. What stops me is how ridiculous this is to be smoking after a day like this.

I think about how lucky I am. I am so grateful. I thank the universe for everything that I have experienced today. I cannot wait to see what tomorrow holds. I have learned how much our beliefs affect us. My limiting beliefs were holding me back. Walking over fire has made me realize that I can do, be, and have anything I want. By the end of the night, I am vibrating joy and energy.

Day One, and I have created a new belief. There are a thousand unseen hands that guide me on my journey. I walk into my hotel room and start to prepare for bed. I brush my teeth, I floss and as I look in the mirror at myself, and I smile. I smile truly at myself for the first time in years. I get into bed and thank the universe for today. I close my eyes, and fall asleep instantly.

OCTOBER 24, 2014

I awake to the sunlight peeking through the window. I watch the sunrise and I feel the excitement for what's coming towards me. I close my eyes and let the warmth of the sun stream onto my face. I see the vision again. I see me helping thousands. I feel the vibrations underneath my feet.

I open my eyes, shower and get dressed quickly. I walk out of my hotel room with a pep in my step—and with more energy than I would have imagined after a night like last night. I walk into the main event room and grab a seat next to a very handsome man. He is young, fresh and he smells nice. I smile at him and instantly he smiles back.

He says, "Hi I'm Ajay Gupta."

"Hi, I'm Carolyn Rim," I say with a wink and smile. He asks, "Is this your first UPW?"

"YES!" I say, with more excitement and enthusiasm than he probably expected. He has an intense look and instantly I realize I have made a friend.

"I like your energy," he says. I get that all the time. I can be calm as hell, but I get it all the time. "I love your energy." I smile at him, and right before I'm about to say thank you, dance music starts playing. It's time.

We both jump up out of our chairs, and the 7,000 other people join us. The dancers come out and get everyone's energy up even more and then Joseph McClendon III comes out on stage. I immediately make eye contact with him and he starts shaking his ass. I run up to the stage and can feel his energy! He is amazing! He is a great dancer, dancing on stage with all the other dancers.

He has us all sit down and says, "So some of you thought you were getting a six-foot-seven white man and got a five-foot-seven black man. I can feel all of you judging me. I know what you're thinking, 'Isn't he *amazing?*'" We all laugh. He *is* amazing.

Ajay and I are partners. I look at the Unleash the Power Within notebook and the questions I am given. What do I love? I can't remember the last time I sat down and actually wrote down what I loved. So I give high fives, I slap asses, I fist-pump. I get into a peak emotional state. I have never felt so good in my life.

LISTENING TO A VOICE OF TRUTH

I have to pee and I need a cigarette. I grab my smokes and run out of the room. I run to the bathroom. And everyone is moving quickly. No one wants to miss anything. I laugh, thinking how funny we all must look racing in and out of the bathrooms. I come out of the bathroom, out of the main room and see a booth, Robbins Coaching.

I decide to give this a go; I get one free session with them anyway. I fill out the paperwork and wait to speak with someone. It only takes a few minutes, but I haven't smoked yet and it's been three hours since my last smoke and I'm bit on edge because I need nicotine. This beautiful blonde woman tells me Scott Chamberlain is available to speak with me now. Scott has white hair and is wearing a sharp gray suit. He looks like he's in the Mafia. Tall, strong and broad. He is in his mid-50s, I guess, and very attractive.

As soon as we start talking, all I can think about is a cigarette. He's asking me, What's my outcome? What goals do I have? Who is the most important person *in* my life?

I answer him on autopilot. I finally tell him I cannot speak with him right now because I want to smoke and I stand up to leave. He looks at me straight in the eyes, and in a tone that demands to be listened to, he says, "Sit down. You can go smoke in a minute."

I sit down again. I listen to him because he speaks with authority. Some women in the booth are clearly eavesdropping. Scott pulls me back to focus.

He tells me to close my eyes and take a deep breath. He says, "Now picture your sweet little girl and you on a pack of cigarettes." I clear my mind and let each of his words seep into my mind and create a mental image. Each word hits me like a brick and takes me deeper and deeper.

He says to picture that cigarette pack in color and very up-close. He says to picture us both smiling and happy. I start to feel a warm wonderful feeling in my heart as I think about KK and me hugging each other.

Without warning, he raises his voice: "NOW RIP YOURSELF OUT OF THERE BECAUSE YOU ARE NOT HERE ANYMORE. YOU CAN CUT YOUR FACE RIGHT OUT OF THAT PICTURE! YOU HURT EVERYONE WITH YOUR SMOKING BUT THE PERSON YOU HURT THE MOST WAS YOURSELF!" He says, "NOW GO SMOKE YOUR DISGUSTING CIGARETTES!"

I'm shaking. My face is hot. It feels like steam's coming off my body, all the toxins leaving my body that instant. Nobody has ever spoken to me like that. I open my eyes, unable to get any words out at first as I blink away tears.

"I don't want to smoke anymore," I say. My voice is quiet at first and steadily gets louder as I start to scream, "I don't want to smoke anymore!"

I look around. The eavesdropping women have their eyes glued to me, as does Scott Chamberlain. They're a bit worried what I will do next. But I smile and high-five every person here. I drop down to the floor with the tears still flowing, a smile on my face and do 10 push-ups as Scott and his staff cheer me on. Scott grabs me and hugs me. I do not know why this man has changed me in an instant—maybe because I have wanted it so badly. I look into his eyes deeply and say a heartfelt, "Thank you." I am done and instead of going outside to smoke, I go back into the main room.

Joseph McClendon is walking everyone through a closed-eye meditation. I run up to my seat in the front. The crew member who sat me yesterday gets my attention. She says she can put me up front, right next to the stage in CSI, special friends and family section. I smile and walk over to the very front row, stage right, in CSI. As I make eye contact with McClendon, he smiles at me and I smile back. There's a connection made. Not sure what it is but I feel it in my soul like I know him. Like I have met him before. Maybe in another life. Something connects deep within my soul.

I sit straight up in my chair and I take only two other breaks for the rest of the 12-hour day! I learn about physiology, assistitude (or, shaking one's ass to bring about positive joyous emotion). I learn about changing my state. I learn about dancing and enjoying life and creating a final outcome. I love the people I meet in the group. I get especially close with a girl named Krissy Richards and a man named Jeffrey Davis. They sell a product called Vi, it's on all their shirts, hats and gear. Cool, I think to myself. Team on a mission! I tell them about quitting smoking an hour ago even though cigarettes had been all I could think about at the moment.

I meet two web designers, Angie and Tony. They are here to set up a deal with Tony Robbins but it fell through since one of their partners got greedy and wanted more money. They told me Tony backed out after that. I explain to them I'm interested in building a website about falling in love with myself and I want to help others fall in love with themselves in the process.

My website will be called 30daystolovemyself.com. I was so mean to myself for so many years, taking a bat to myself inside my mind—I want to help others fall in love with their real selves. They tell me they can help me! I'm so excited! Me?! I thought: Have my own website? How incredible! I also tell them I quit smoking and I do five push-ups in front of them because whenever I need a cigarette I'm going to do five push-ups. We play full-out all day long.

I go back to my hotel room alone and decide to treat myself to a nice dinner. I had not really had a meal in two days, now that I think about it. At the restaurant attached to the conference center, I order wings—10 BBQ wings. I order a drink, my usual a water with lemon. I see Ajay Gupta there with a few people. He calls me over and introduces me to

Taylor Weiss. Ajay tells me they are Tony Robbins sales reps and he introduces me to his team.

Later, while I am mingling in the restaurant, I see everyone from that day in there—the web designers, a couple who was having issues, and a bunch of other people. I start telling my story to everyone. I had $36 in the bank and took out a $5,000 loan to see Tony Robbins and decided to go all in on me for the first time in my life. I play pool and laugh. The wings come and I enjoy each bite. Things taste better now that I'm at UPW. as if I'm transported from the real world into an alternate universe and everyone is nice, passionate and constantly energized and beaming.

Angie and Tony, the web designers, call me over to a table where they are sitting with eight other people. Angie asks me to tell my story again about taking the loan out and quitting smoking. I do and I even do a few push-ups to drive it home. Everyone at the table loves me. I feel like I have finally found people who "get" me. They understand my jokes. My message. My story lines. Amazing things keep happening, I'm thinking that this is exactly where I'm supposed to be. I look around at how everyone is treating me differently. People are respecting me and finally understanding me. Everything is lining up.

On the walk back to my room, I can't stop smiling about what an incredible day this has been—even better than the first.

In my hotel room, I look in my purse. I have five packs of cigarettes left and a few five-hour caffeine shots. I didn't plan on quitting smoking and had brought six packs of cigarettes for a four-day trip. I grab the cigarette packs and carefully put them on the floor. I surprise myself by undressing and keeping just my cowgirl boots on. I start jumping on the cigarette packs! I stomp on them and scream, *"No more! No more! Not one more moment will you steal from me!"* It feels freeing and beautiful. I am crushing the packs under my boots and feeling combustion within my soul. I feel alive for the first time in forever.

I realize I love change and transformation. I'm going to embrace change head-on. I will no longer let the fear of the unknown paralyze me. I will no longer give myself bullshit excuses why I cannot quit smoking or why I cannot go after my dreams or why I have to be stuck in a cube the rest of my life.

I am ready to live out loud. I smile through my tears of relief. My eyes are opening. My heart is beating fast, steady and strong. I have just been ignited. In bed, I feel energized, alive, awakened, ignited. I have never felt a feeling like this before. I feel like I am vibrating. I pray. I cry. I thank God. "Thank you. Thank you. Thank you. Thank you. I'm so grateful." I close my eyes with my heart awakened and open to the gift of life.

DAY 3: "TRANSFORMATION DAY"

I show up early and walk into the event. By this time, I know a ton of people and I walk in giving high fives and laughing and joking with all of Tony's staff and crew members. Everyone keeps whispering, "Its transformation day!" I have no idea what this means as I have already had several transformations since I have been here.

I get to sit in the friends and family section again. The people there save me a seat. They know me by name and when I walk into the front, I can almost feel all eyes on me. I just smile and be me, which makes me feel loved and happy. Someone once told me when I walked into a room, it was really hard not to notice me. They said I was bright and I lit up the room like a bright star in a dim universe. They said, "You don't even have to say a thing, Carolyn. Your energy just illuminates and your happiness and joy for life is contagious."

I think about that as I walk through the crowd of 7,000 people as their eyes turn towards me. I smile at all of them. I lock eyes with Tony Robbins when I get to the front. He smiles at me. I sit down and say hello to everyone.

"Hey, amazing people!" I say with a wink and a smile. Krissy and Jeff, the people from Vi, look at me and smile. I may end up selling the product. It's just so much money to invest—$600 I don't have. But I really want to support them.

Tony Robbins, the amazing legend, breaks my train of thoughts. He tells us to jump up and down and tells everyone to celebrate life.

WOW. What a concept. I wonder when the last time I celebrated life was? I don't remember.

I realize I'm over thinking so I breathe in and out and relax. I enjoy the process. I can feel the vibrations as thousands of feet jump up and down all around me. I can feel the vibrations in their voices as they say hi to me. The camera loves me and I'm put on the big screens so much! People hug me, high-five me. I run to pee and when I come back, I see someone left a little note on my seat that says my smile brightens the room! I decide to put the napkin in my purse as a little keepsake.

Tony takes us through visualizations, in and out. I close my eyes, I take deep breaths, and he takes us in and out of priming. He tells me how I feel is the most important thing. He tells us to be grateful for this moment right here. Right now. Breathe in and out and decide to rise up and step into our greatness. We chant about 100 times and I love it.

"Now I AM the voice. I will lead, not follow. I will believe, not doubt. I will create, not destroy. I AM a force for good. I AM a leader. Defy the odds! Set a new standard! Step up!"

I say it and feel it over and over again. The words saturate my subconscious mind.

Tony walks us through the Empowering Dickens (Christmas Past, Present, Future) Process. He takes us through our limiting beliefs and dismantles them. He makes me go into the future and look at my life— if I don't do anything different, if I continue to stay the same, what will happen? Who will I hurt? Who will I let down? I feel and hear the screams which feel like a purgatory to me. I feel the screams I hear leave a mark on my soul. The thousands of souls screaming looking at the future they will surely have if they don't change anything. I see my future. I see myself an old woman in my cube. Still unhappy. Unchanged. Unchallenged.

Tony asks us, "Is this who you are? Is this what you want?" We all shout back "NOOOOO." He tells us to make our move and snap out of it.

He makes us go to the future and look at our life the way we want it to be. Tony says to write down what we want to accomplish and what we would do to close the gap from where we are now to where we want to be.

As I allow my heart's voice to flow from me onto the page, I write, "I will have a happy, exciting, fulfilled life. I will be making millions of dollars by being a motivational speaker. I will speak in front of thousands of people and I will inspire millions of people to open their hearts. I will fall madly deeply in love with myself and be an example for all those who look at me. I exist in this world to benefit and refresh all that I touch with my energy."

Tony leads us through another visualization. He tells us Our subconscious mind cannot tell the difference between something vividly imagined and something actually happening. How do we look? What car do we drive? Where do we live? Who is in our life?

He leads us to the past. I go back to the most painful memories in my life and pull out all the darkness and replace it with sunshine and magic. I decide the past no longer gets to have my present and my future.

I decide life is a beautiful gift. I have chills, my heart is pounding and I'm shedding tears. Tony says, "Gratitude changes everything. It truly is the secret to all abundance and happiness. Place your hand over your heart. Take a deep breath. Feel your heartbeat, feel the love, feel the happiness, and step into a moment you can feel deeply grateful for. Take a deep breath into your heart and feel the power of your heart. You are right where you are guided to be."

I never knew I could create that amazing feeling. I never knew I could have that much joy just by closing my eyes, without leaving a room.

26

Tony's instructions melt and resolve any resistance in my heart. Tony helps me focus on what truly is important in my life and says something that makes my knees go weak: "It's never too late to have a happy childhood." I start crying and smiling. A stream of gorgeous thoughts come to me.

I AM amazing. I AM happy. I AM brilliant. I AM beautiful. I AM MAGIC. I AM.

Truly, LIFE WILL NEVER BE THE SAME AGAIN. So many happy tears shed, I didn't know tears like that existed until I met Tony Robbins. I am a soul in a body and I have a mission—to infuse the world with love, to infuse this world with compassion and joy, happiness and smiles. As Tony would say, what's wrong with our life is always available. And so is what's right. WE decide where we put our focus.

WE ARE ALL GIFTS

Tony continues to say things that spark a sizzle in my soul. He says, "Modeling will get you to your goal 50 percent faster. If you really want to be successful, you must have a mentor who has what you want." That clicked and seeped into my subconscious. I get chills. I know at this very moment that I am something incredible. That I am supposed to be on stage. I have a vision. I am on top of the world. I allow all my desires I have been holding back to shoot from my heart into the universe like a firework. I spread my wings and as I do I send a ripple like a stone into a pond. I am inspiring the world and everyone's hearts are glowing bright. I will have a ripple effect around the world. I feel my heart calling to me! Yes! I feel a surge of energy between my mind and my heart. A chord created that can never be cut. My heart shines and tears come, overflowing with compassion, love and gratitude for my life. I am connected with everyone and everything.

That night Tony Robbins gets out a water gun and has a water fight with 7,000 souls. I feel like I am finally in the space I should be. I look around with gratitude when I feel him looking at me intensely, and I feel like I knew Tony from the moment I saw him a few days ago. Like two kindred spirits.

He calls me over to the stage and he looks at me. I don't know what to do but instinctively I raise my right hand up to touch his. He doesn't say a word, he just grabs my hand and with his wide eyes staring straight into my soul, I feel loved. Not just by him but by myself for the first time in my life. He lifts my hand up and he kisses it. We look at each other for another three to five seconds but to me, it feels like hours. I mouth to him, "Thank you." He places his big hand on his heart and nods at me. I may as well be walking on liquid sunshine right now. Something has been opened within me. I can finally see the light after all these years in darkness.

Later that night I'm in my hotel crying tears of joy and gratitude. I get on my knees beside my bed and I thank the universe for every bad moment, for every dark moment because I realized today that I needed every dark moment to make my mountaintops feel better, taste better and *be* better. I am truly grateful for the first time in my life. I go over to the mirror and I send myself love. I am a gift. WE are all gifts. I feel the presence of God all around me.

Tonight before I close my eyes, I look up at the Dallas stars and I wish on them. I allow myself to dream again like a child. I decide I want to wish on one of the stars. I allow myself to step into the field of infinite possibility. "I wish I were a speaker inspiring millions of people all over the world to open their hearts opens and make their dreams come true."

LIFE WILL NEVER BE THE SAME

I wake up the next morning sad and happy at the same time. I'm sad because it's almost over. I am happy because life will never be the same. I don't feel like the same person. I feel different. I feel lighter. I feel better more alive. I walk in to find thousands of people dancing and shaking their asses with Joseph McClendon. I smile as I walk and dance up the aisle. I can't help but feel Joseph keeps looking directly at me. Connecting with me. He locks eyes and smiles a smile that hits my soul. He is enlightened. I'm going for it. I play full-out all day.

As the day progresses I learn about my health, body, food intake and energy levels. We do a visualization about drawing a line in the sand, crossing it and stepping into the person we want to be. I look at the time. Its 4:23 p.m. I have to leave. My flight takes off soon. I have 10 minutes to make something happen before I must walk out these doors. How? I'm in a room with 7,000 people—how am I going to make this happen? I shine, I tell myself. I am not like anyone else in this room and I'm here for a reason and a mission. I am not going to leave here without a mentor. I'm making one of these men, either Tony or Joseph, my mentor.

I quickly rip off some paper from my notebook and I write my number on it with a few words. "Ready...Set... Mentor ME."

Mustering up all my courage. I bang on my chest. I decide to take massive action! The security guards are looking at me as I walk up to them. You see, I would have charged Tony Robbins but he has seven bodyguards, and Joseph McClendon has only three. I cannot take on seven bodyguards, but by God, I am confident I can take on three.

I charge the three security guards and reach my hand up with the note, and start screaming at the top of my lungs. "Please Joseph Take it, take it, take it!" Almost in slow motion, he locks eyes with mine and then reaches his hand down and our fingers touch briefly and sparks fly. He takes my note and puts it in his pocket. He motions for the security guards to let me go. He goes back to teaching the seminar.

Hurrying to catch my flight, I grab my purse and float out of this amazing seminar. I hug my friends, the people who say they will help build my website, the Vi people. Everyone.

I have just shifted my reality, the course of my destiny. I walk out of there with my spirit beaming. I am happy. I don't even care if Joseph calls me. All I care about is that I have done it. I charged the stage with the cosmic force of the universe behind me. I get on the flight from Dallas to Philly, with only one difference:

I am a such a different person from the one I was four days ago.

Chapter 3
Reentry into the World

"Life will never be the same again."

—*Tony Robbins*

I had turned off my Facebook account months ago after my husband and I could not handle each other's messages to others and comments. We decided to just get off social media altogether. After the Tony Robbins event I went back on Facebook because so many people said they wanted to keep in touch.

Here is my first post back on Facebook, with a photo of Krissy Richard and me at the Tony Robbins Seminar in Dallas:

I am glowing. LIFE WILL NEVER BE THE SAME.

My husband is so mad at me he will not even pick me up at the airport. My friend Brit Lamb (she calls herself Brit Wolf, which I find fitting) comes to get me. However, when she comes, she can tell something has totally shifted. Something big.

I feel awkward for the first time around her. I tell her about everything. We grab a coffee at a diner. I tell her my dream and vision. She says, "Carolyn, if there is one person in this whole world that can do what you want to do, it's you." I can tell she meant that because she chooses her words carefully and she does not speak one word of fluff. She only gives compliments when she means them. Brit is probably one of my best friends in the world and I am so grateful for her and for the ride home. I arrive home Sunday at 10:30 p.m.

I feel energized and on fire even though it's so late. I walk into my home but nothing looks the same. Everything is different. It is nighttime but I hear the morning birds singing inside my soul.

I go upstairs and as I get ready for bed and brush my teeth, I look at myself in the mirror. I'm silencing the inner of voice doubt. "No more will you torture me."

I smile at myself in the mirror. The inner critic was still saying, "You think this will last, Carolyn. You will not make it."

I don't listen to the critic tonight. I am so grateful I have finally leaped into the dark. Quietly, I crawl into bed with my husband. I can make this work. He will come with me into the world of infinite possibilities and swirling, twirling love and light. I can make this work. I will tell him all about it in the morning. I wrap my arms around him and close my eyes and fall asleep into the darkness.

But this time, as I fall asleep, I see myself as a bright star in a dim universe lighting it up with my beautiful fucking energy. I fall asleep smiling within and without.

BACK TO REALITY

I wake up the next morning and feel like I am being jolted back into reality. Car horns beeping. I'm stuck in morning traffic on my way back to my job. I am still smiling and "shaking thine ass" in the car listening to the amazing UPW playlist someone posted in the group, but I can feel the slow pull back into old thought patterns. "Nothing has changed, Carolyn, you are still just a sales rep for Medical Alert. You are just a telemarketer. You are average. You are not a hero.

Stop kidding yourself," the inner critic taunts me. I pull into the lot. I take a deep breath.

I decide that I am done with Medical Alert. Just as I was done with the cigarettes, I am done with Medical Alert. Not another moment will I stay nailed to the bland gray walls of my cube. I walk into the office and place my stuff on the desk like I had a million times before, but this time I'm different. I am changed. I walk into my boss's office. "Keith, I am giving you my two weeks' notice."

Stacy and Keith, the directors, stare at me. "Hi, Carolyn. How are you? Us? We're good, too." He's teasing—I didn't even say hello.

I say, "Sorry, guys. I'm just scared that if I don't act now, I'll never act on this feeling in my heart."

Keith stares into me. "Are you sure? You just got back!" he says.

I say, "Absolutely not. I am fucking petrified but if I stay here I'm certain that I will continue to die. And the pain of staying here is greater than the pain of finding something new so I have to embrace the uncertainty."

I've been with these two souls for six years. I am so scared I'm almost crying. I had been the one who connected the one director, Stacy, here and got her a job. We have been friends a long time.

"Okay," Stacy says and she stands up and grabs a paper from the desk. "Write down that you are resigning and sign here." She hands me a pen. My hands are shaking.

"What am I doing?" the inner critic is asking. The doubt is slowly seeping into my pores. I sign in spite of my nerves.

As I walk out of their office, my mind is going crazy. The bad inner voice says, "What did you just do? Go back there and beg for your job back! Are you nuts?"

I sit in my cube the rest of the day scared as hell. Too much change is happening. I'm so fearful, at 2 p.m. I jump up from my desk. I run back into Keith's office. "I rescind my quitting!" I look at putting in my resignation like telling a vampire it can come into the house and then deciding to rescind my invitation to them!

After thinking this, I realize how absurd and crazy I must sound. Keith looks up from the computer and he says, "Okay. I will take care of it. Let me call corporate and tell them you changed your mind."

I feel so relieved. "Thank God." He calls them with me in the office and he looks stressed. I can tell he really wants to help me but corporate is saying something on the line.

He says, "I don't understand. She's going through a lot and we should..." his voice trails off, and I can tell he was just cut off by them.

"Okay I'll tell her." He hangs up "Carolyn, I'm so sorry. You already signed the papers. You have to resign," he says.

I manage to say, "Thank you for trying. I'll be okay."

As I walk from Keith's office back to my desk, I feel like this universe has big plans for me, whether I believe it or not. I feel so scared, though. What will my husband say? I just took out a $5,000 loan. We have bills to pay. What am I going to do about money?

At that exact moment, as if by divine intervention, I get a call on my cell phone. "Hey Carolyn, it's Jeff, Ken's son." Ken Gross, the owner of Medical Alert, has treated me like gold for the past six years. Jeff Gross, his son, owned Medical Guardian, a sister company to Medical Alert. Medical Guardian was a skyrise on Market Street in Philadelphia.

Jeff says, "Ken just called and said you are on the market. Why don't you come work for me while you are moving towards your goals and dreams? You are such a go-getter, Carolyn, and I would hate to see someone like you with your potential to be stuck."

I'm so excited I immediately say, "Yes!" Jeff explains everything over the phone and tells me to stop in tomorrow just to say hello and get all the paperwork signed. He said there was a $10K raise, too! I cannot believe all I had to do was take a leap of faith, embrace uncertainty and all this amazing stuff would begin happening to me so very quickly. I feel like I'm in a dream and I'm about to wake up.

I decide to share the good news with my UPW family in the secret Facebook group, that I quit my job and I'm embracing uncertainty. Within one hour I have more than 200 comments from people cheering me on! They say, "YES! Go for it! Follow your dreams!" I have never had this much support and feel like I have a thousand unseen hands guiding me. I start to grasp how important a powerful positive group of people in your life is. I have 200 people from around the world telling me how outstanding I am. I shed happy tears as I read all the comments.

One of the names stands out to me: Mike Peppler—kind of sounds like Pepper, I chuckle to myself. The name Mike seems to follow me. Everywhere I go, I meet Michaels. I believe it's because when I was a little girl my dad gave me a pin with the archangel Michael on it. I always thought that people named Mike or Michael were angels. I carry on.

A SUPPORTIVE ENVIRONMENT?

That night at home, at dinner with my husband and daughter, I talk feverishly about how UPW was the best four days of my life. I tell them how I walked over fire, charged the stage, and overcame my fear today and quit my job.

My husband looks at me. "Really? What about all the days we spent together on our honeymoon? Was the event better than Disney World? Your Tony Robbins event was better than the moments we shared as a family?" KK looks at me to see my response. I look at Mike, feeling small and shrinking my energy.

"I'm so sorry. I didn't mean to say that UPW was better than the days with you and KK-Bear. It was just different, that's all." I eat with my head in my food the rest of dinner and do not speak. I realize now why Tony and Joseph cautioned us not to talk excitedly about the event to others. I should have asked Mike and KK how their week was instead of telling them I just had the best four days of my life without them.

After dinner, my husband tells me we have to go to his mom's, down the street, to pick something up. I think it odd that I have to go with him, but I oblige. I walk into my mother-in-law's house and instantly the energy is being sucked out of me.

Normally, they are so welcoming and loving that this atmosphere is unfamiliar. I have been extremely sensitive to energy since the event, as if something within was turned on and now I'm ultra- sensitive to everyone's energy around me. I feel like I have tapped into something that opened a new sense for me. I have no idea I'm walking into a trap until I see Mike putting on the TV for KK.

There in the dining room sit Mike's mother and dad, aunt and uncle, his sister, her boyfriend and his grandparents. Mike joins them at the table. There are no seats left so I stand up.

His mom looks straight at me and says, "I heard you took out a $5,000 loan two weeks ago and today you quit your job. How are you going to pay the money back? $5,000 is a lot of money."

I try to deflect the comment. I say, "Did you all know I quit smoking?" I watch for people's responses.

His grandmother says, "I remember the first time I quit I started back after a week. It's a lot harder than you think. It was by far the hardest thing I ever did."

Mike's grandfather says, "Do you have any money saved?"

His mom, Lisa, says, "Why would you spend $5,000 on an event like that if you didn't have the funds?"

I say, "I have to be honest, I feel like I'm being attacked right now." I look at Mike for help, but he says nothing.

His grandfather asks, "So what's your plan now?"

"Well, I decided I'm going to be a motivational speaker," I say quietly. "I am going to go for it."

His grandfather says, "You can't just go for it. You need a Plan B. People who don't have a Plan B always fail." I put my head down. I start to shrink.

Aunt DeeDee says, "I'm leaving. Come on, leave her alone. She just got back and doesn't deserve this."

My face grows hot. I start to enter victim mode. They're not even congratulating me on quitting smoking or being brave enough to quit my job and just go for it. The tears coming as their comments, doubts and questions seep into my soul.

I feel myself shrinking and that's when I hear his voice. It's soft at first, like a whisper. "I AM THE VOICE. I WILL LEAD, NOT FOLLOW." At first the voice comes from in front of me. Then it comes beside me. "STEP UP!" It's not until I feel his voice directly behind me as it shouts, "RAISE YOUR STANDARDS" and I'm jolted awake.

I make my move. I take a deep breath in, inhaling this new person and feel the certainty in who I am and why I am here. I feel myself changing. I look around the room, seeing this place with new eyes.

Everyone in the room stops talking, as they can also feel something just shifted. I wipe the tears from my eyes. Shoulders back, in peak state, I hold my head high and say, "Pop-pop, I don't need a Plan B because it will distract from Plan A. Lisa, I will pay the bank and quite frankly, that's none of your business. I have unshakeable faith that my dreams are coming true. You have two options. You can either be beside me and enjoy my success or you can fall back!" I smile at them.

Wow! I cannot believe I have just said that. I feel like I am flying because I have finally stood up for my dreams, for myself, and for my destiny. I walk out of the room and out of the house and fresh air greets me on their wrap around porch. This reality is changing very quickly. Every time I tap into this place I get stronger and stronger. My heart smiles and speaks to me, "Sweet beautiful girl, follow me, let's dance in celebration of you."

I know I can do this and I don't care who doubts me because I have UNLEASHED THE POWER WITHIN. No one and no force can stand between my dream and me! No one can tell me what I can and can't do. I decide my limits and today, I am limitless! I have never felt so powerful or so strong in my life. Ready?! Everybody up! Jump up, jump up! Fists in the air! Make your move—SAY YES Baby!

I close my eyes and I am transported back to the UPW seminar with 7,000 beautiful souls making magic with Tony Robbins. I open my eyes. "I am *ready*" I say out loud to the universe.

"I AM *READY*"

I post in the secret UPW group about my struggles.

"Dear UPW, So it's day 10 of no cigarettes and the urge couldn't be stronger to want to smoke. I haven't had one urge or withdrawal symptom in the past 10 days, but tonight I was very stressed out. It doesn't matter what I was stressed out about. What matters is I don't give up. What matters is I say FUCK YOU to my cigarettes! They will not win, I will not fail, and I will succeed and climb that mountain of success!!"

I get more than 300 comments—"You can do this!" "You're outstanding!" "Keep going." The comments are so inspiring and I realize I cannot let these people down. I would make all these people my accountability partners and the thousand unseen hands are here, guiding me in every step I take. Helping me, guiding me and comforting me as I take massive huge leaps into the dark.

Later that night, I see I have a message on my phone, left at exactly 7:33 p.m. I keep seeing that number: 33. So weird, I didn't even hear my phone ring. I don't recognize the number on the caller ID. I listen to the voicemail. I know his voice after one word, he doesn't even have to say his name. "Carolyn, this is Joseph McClendon, from the Tony Robbins event. Ready... Set... I will mentor you under one condition. Call me back."

Ass-shaking Joseph McClendon III, Ph.D.! OMG, my heart starts racing and I am transported back to Dallas when I charged the stage to hand this man a little note. *WOW. WOW. WOW.* I did not expect him to call.

I listen to the message a few times to make sure I'm not dreaming—you'd think I'd just won the lottery! I'm jumping up and down like crazy. My husband is looking at me like I'm nuts! He keeps saying, "It's just a phone call. Who cares?"

But you see, I saw the value in having a mentor who has what I want. I saw the value in someone I could model who already has what I want! As Tony told us, using modeling can get you to your dreams 50 percent faster.

I had to take 10 minutes to breathe. I'm hyper-ventilating.

After calming myself down, I call Joseph ass-shaking McClendon back. "Hey Joseph, this is Carolyn Rim and I would love for you to help me in this journey towards my dreams. I would like to be a speaker, sir, and do what you and Tony do."

He pauses. He says, "I'm going to mentor under two conditions. One, you never call me sir again. Two, you must send the elevator back down when you get to the top and do for someone else what I'm going to do for you."

I think about that for three seconds before saying, "I will do you one better. I will keep my doors open and raise people to the top with me! And I will call you Rockstar! Does that work?"

He says, "Now, *that* was the correct answer… Let's get started." I get off the call and I'm high on life.

I think about the one person in the world who can share my excitement. "Marie," I say out loud. I call my sister's number. "Marie! Guess who just called me?"

I tell her the whole story, about charging the stage, and my giving him my number and how he just called me.

Marie, says, "Carolyn, don't let anyone tell you this isn't a big deal. I truly know the value of having him call you. Wow, kid—I just can't believe it. You know, you're going to make this happen. All you needed was some positive people in your life to help you go to the next level. I love you so much!"

I love *her* so much. Marie is such a beautiful and powerful soul. She is an extremely talented artist. I talk to her for a few more moments and then I get off the phone. Before I close my eyes to sleep that night, I thank God for this happening. I thank the universe. Thank you. Thank you. Thank you. I close my eyes with a smile on my face and in my heart.

THE SIGNS FROM MY ANGELS

I'm on the train on the way to work. I really like taking the train. I love working in the city. It's been about three weeks since I started working at Medical Guardian. However, I'm still in a box, except this one is made of glass and I can see the clouds in the sky. I'm grateful, I keep telling myself. I'm grateful even if I'm not where I want to be yet. I'm so grateful for all the beautiful blessings unfolding in my life. I am grateful for where I am and where I am going.

I participate in the secret Facebook group from UPW every day and the energy from the people is beaming back at me. My "friends" list skyrockets. I now have 2,000 friends who are total Tony Robbins rockstars.

I start removing the negative people from my FB feed. I choose who I surround myself with, I keep telling myself. I become who I hang out with.

I look at the people in my life and wonder, how am I serving them? How are they serving me? Do I want to become them?

I start writing "Dear UPW," whenever I make a post because I feel such a connection with this UPW group. I feel like I'm home. I feel like for the first time in my life, I have people who believe in my dream with me.

I decide to do some research on the numbers 333. According to Melanie Beckler, it means that the divine is working through me and with me on a number of levels to help me make my dreams come true. Beckler says to get clear on what I want, ask for help, follow the signs, and take action to co-create a beautiful life experience. I research more on her site, www.ask-angels.com.

It says, "The number three reminds us of oneness and the link between Mind, Body and Spirit. It's closely aligned with the energy of the Divine." It says to open my heart and watch for the signs everywhere that my angels are with me, because they are. Open my heart and align with the invisible energy all around me.

I watch for the signs everywhere. I start to see them all around me. I follow and listen to my heart. I'm so scared of all the uncertainty I'm facing but I try to remember that I'm guided. I feel fear, but instead of pretending like it's not there, I do what Tony Robbins told us to do at the UPW seminar: I align with my fear, grab that bitch and ask her dance.

> **"I leap into the unknown, into uncertainty with faith that what I desire deep within my core, in my soul, in my big heart, is not only just possible, it is a must and is inevitable."**
>
> **—Carolyn Rim**

I align with my fears and say to myself, "Yes, I'm scared but we are going to follow my heart and dreams anyway. I leap into the unknown, into uncertainty with faith that what I desire deep within my core, in my soul, in my big fucking heart, is not only just possible, it is a must and is inevitable."

Ever since the UPW event, I have these flashbacks. I flash to when I was four years old in my kindergarten concert singing the song, "I Don't Like You, But I Love You," when I realized that I loved performing for people. I loved making people smile. I loved people. I had always had the dream of wanting to be this rockstar on stage.

I keep fighting the voice of fear that tells me my dreams are not worth it. That they are not real. I continue to have an angel/devil conversation mentally. I'm starting to understand the famous quote, "All battles are either won or lost in the mind."

So far I had quit my job, quit smoking, got Joseph McClendon to be my mentor, and started to go after my dreams.

The next call I receive is from web designers Angie Alaniz and Tony Berkman, who I met at the UPW event. They tell me it's $125 for the website and then $25 a month. That's a lot for me right now, but I decide to do it!

Angie needs content to add to my website. I pause. "What the heck is content and why do I need it to make my dreams come true?" I ask.

She laughs. "Listen, sweetheart, you need content. You need a story. Why are people going to follow you? Why are people going to read your blogs?"

I stop to think about it. Why *would* people want to follow me? "Can I just like, you know, be me?" I say.

She laughs again. "Of course. That's the whole point. People will love you for you." We spend hours on the phone helping me create my first website. It takes three weeks to set everything up. I'm so grateful for them. I work long into the night on content.

"I didn't know what loving myself meant, but I knew following my heart was helping me love myself and was helping me set an example for others."

—Carolyn Rim

I still don't understand what the web designers mean by content. Okay, I say, I decide I will share my story. I start blogging. Just posting daily blogs about working out and loving self. Learning to love myself again and do nice things for me. I write that I didn't know what loving myself meant, but I knew following my heart was helping me love myself somehow and was helping me set an example for others. I start to shine my light on the world.

"YOU ARE A CHILD OF GOD"

Once in a while the voice of doubt creeps in to say, "Who do you think you are?"

I truly begin to understand what Marianne Williamson meant when she wrote, "Our deepest fear is not that we are inadequate. Our deepest fear is that we are powerful beyond measure. It is our light, not our darkness that most frightens us. We ask ourselves, Who am I to be brilliant, gorgeous, talented, fabulous?

Actually, who are you not to be? You are a child of God. Your playing small does not serve the world. There is nothing enlightened about shrinking so that other people won't feel insecure around you.

We are all meant to shine, as children do. We were born to make manifest the glory of God that is within us. It's not just in some of us; it's in everyone. And as we let our own light shine, we unconsciously give other people permission to do the same. As we are liberated from our own fear, our presence automatically liberates others."

That day, I listen to an emotional flood gratitude exercise by Tony Robbins and he advises that I need a "Why" to keep me going when I want to quit, I will need something that will help me carry on. He says most people quit because their Why is not strong enough.

I know what my Why is. My little girl. I see the whole universe in her eyes and smile. I want her to know that Mommy went for her dreams and that she could be, do, and have anything she wants in this world.

My Why is also for me. I start to believe in my worth slowly but surely each day I become more certain in my inherent worth and value as a person.

The following are posts from the UPW Dallas Facebook group and my Facebook page from November 2014:

NOVEMBER 12, 2014

Dear UPW,

This is such a positive feed! I love scrolling through UPW Page and seeing everyone's positive quotes, and stories of overcoming their fears. I have 17 days without a cigarette today!! My website is going live tomorrow. I'm so excited about everything that is happening. Even if I do get upset or fearful about my future, I picture Tony saying, How fast can you change your state? And then I snap my fingers. Lol I'm grateful for the people I have in my life, I'm grateful for my little girl and husband, (even if he doesn't like the motivational stuff). I will post my website

41

tomorrow after it goes live and I hope you all check it out!! I enjoy my life because I'm doing what I love. I decide today I'm going to love myself enough to follow my dreams. "She loved life, and it loved her right back." I love you all. You rock baby!

NOVEMBER 13, 2014

Dear UPW,

I walked over fire in Dallas, three weeks ago. It showed me that my limiting beliefs were holding me back. I let go and let God. I walked over fire without one scratch happening. Anything is possible when you unleash the power within. Don't let other people's fears bring you down! Say yes to your dreams and Make your move!

NOVEMBER 17, 2014

Dear UPW,

My website is finally live! Please check out and share **30daystolovemyself.com**! Make the decision to change your life today. Thirty days ago, I was looking up bridges to jump off of.

Today, I have 22 days off cigarettes, I quit my job and I am going after my dream of being a motivational speaker, life coach and helping others become lit up from within! Imagine and visualize your dreams daily!!

Go to 30daystolovemyself.com and start finding your inner superhero!! I am humbled and happy that after much hard work my website is finally live!! Please check it out!

Tony Robbins and the UPW Community changed my life and the encouragement I received through you all helped me!! YES I CAN!!

NOVEMBER 18, 2014

Dear UPW,

Find Your Inner Superhero

I'm silencing the little voice inside that says I can't, I won't or it will never happen. I can, I will and it's happening now. Visualize yourself succeeding! Get a clear picture in your head of what you want, why you want it, and feel the excitement you would feel of your dream coming true.

Visit it every day and every night. I pictured myself rising on an elevator and every time the elevator went up a floor, I imagined that I was getting closer to my goal, I was getting into a state of being grateful for my dreams coming true. Imagine the cape flying off your back!!

30daystolovemyself.com

November 20, 2014

Today I was feeling fear and I asked God to help to me to find a way through the pain. A few seconds later I looked up and saw this sign. I'm pretty sure He made it big enough. Ask and ye shall receive.

November 21, 2014

Don't stand in your own way! The only one that can stop you is you! Every single day we are making new decisions and creating new actions all fueled by our emotions. It is up to us to tell ourselves how we are going to feel and act! Tony Robbins says our brains are constantly doing three things. What to focus on? What meaning to give it? And how is that going to make me feel? Point the camera and zoom in on what's right. So many times we allow circumstances to control our lives when all we have to do is accept full responsibility for where we are and then decide where we want to go!

NOVEMBER 23, 2014

Find Your Passion! Check out 30daystolovemyself.com to get motivation and inspiration to find your passion! Stand like Superman for two minutes and find your inner superhero! Imagine a cape flying off your back! Standing like Superman raises your testosterone levels by 20 percent making you more likely to take risks and be up for a challenge! Just by standing like Superman you can lower cortisol level (stress hormone), which will help you deal with stressful situations better. What could you accomplish right now in this Superman state? Anything? YES! Stop looking at all the limitations in your life and start focusing on what small steps you can take daily towards your greatness! So next time you have a problem and don't know what to do, STAND LIKE SUPERMAN!

NOVEMBER 28, 2014

Dear UPW,

I am going to stop counting the days. It's been 31 days and I am a non-smoker. I picture my little girl and myself on a pack of cigarettes if I ever get the urge to smoke. I know if I smoke my face will be cut out of the picture but if I continue not to smoke, then I will be in the picture!!

Thanks again for all your support and I am truly grateful for all of you!!
YOU ALL FUCKING ROCK!!

NOVEMBER 30, 2014

I found an old picture at my mom's that said Coach Carolyn. I decided to recreate it since I had the same nail polish and shirt on when I found it. Signs are everywhere. It is never too late to recreate yourself.

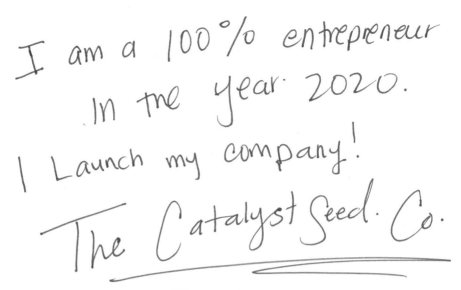

I am a 100% entrepreneur in the year 2020. I Launch my company! The Catalyst Seed. Co.

Chapter 4
A Date with Destiny

"A mentor empowers a person to see a possible future and believe it can be obtained."

—Shawn Hitchcock

I speak with Joseph every week. I research what a mentor is and how I should interact with him. According to Google, "Mentoring involves a relationship in which the mentor, usually a more experienced individual, works closely with the protégé for the purposes of teaching, guiding, supporting and facilitating the professional growth and development of a colleague."

A mentor should have what I want already. I look at Joseph's credentials and bio online to make sure he has what I want. This is what I found on Joseph's website, www.MakeYourFate.com:

"Joseph McClendon III is one of the most sought after Ultimate Performance Specialists in the industry. His unique brand of 'Tell, Show, Do' teaching and coaching creates rapid personal change that effectively moves people to take more consistent action and go 'Further Faster' with their personal and business achievements.

"He holds a doctorate in neuropsychology and several certifications in the neuro sciences arena. Joseph taught at the university of Southern California for seven years and is frequently called upon to lecture at other higher learning institutions like Harvard University and several Fortune

500 companies.

""Having performed hundreds of workshops, coaching sessions, seminars and training programs, one on one therapeutic interventions and has presented to well over 3 million people around the globe. His remarkable ability to go straight to the core of the challenge and effect rapid change makes him a unique commodity in Business, personal and health and wellness and personal improvement.

"In 1986, Joseph met and teamed up with best-selling author and speaker Anthony Robbins. After mastering the technology, he became extremely proficient in assisting people in overcoming the fears, phobias and emotional challenges that hindered their lives. Mr. McClendon has authored Several best-selling books including two with world famous Anthony Robbins and has shared the stage with him for two decades.

"He has also authored several other books as well as a line of human change technology products and services. He is a philanthropist whose most recent project is developing a program with Forest Whitaker and the United Nations to bring a psychology shift in the child soldiers and forgotten battle babies of war torn countries around the world. Joseph McClendon is frequently called upon to provide corporate training, keynote addresses, workshops, and seminars for many fortune 500 companies in the United States and across Europe and Australia.

"He is an expert in coaching sales business professionals in overcoming the behaviors and inner and outer obstacles, that may impede their results and effect their bottom line. Joseph McClendon provides them with the influence, skills and tools that give the professional the competitive advantage necessary to prosper in the market place of the new millennium."

Holy shit, that's one fucking impressive bio. OMG, so Joseph McClendon III is a total rockstar! Shake thine ass! I'm so totally grateful for having the courage to charge the stage. I pat myself on the back like Joseph says to do. He continues to tell me by text that repetition is the mother of all skills and praising yourself is the father. I say it to myself over and over.

I explain to him that I researched what a mentor is and how to get the most from one. One of the best ways is to spend time with your mentor so I can model him.

He tells me to come down to the Date With Destiny seminar, which is for people who want to have a total shift. It's five days of Tony Robbins. How am I going to make this happen?

I call my dad, the person who believes in me most. He always makes me feel better. "Hey, Babycakes. How are you?" my dad says in his usual cheerful tone.

"Daddy, do you believe in me?" I say.

He pauses. "Of course I believe in you. Talk to me."

I can't seem to control my emotions and I start to tear up. I say, "I want to go see my mentor in Florida but I have no money but I can't stop this feeling that I'm supposed to be in Florida right now."

My father. My dad. He's always been a superhero to me—the type of guy you could call at 2 a.m. and tell him to come pick you up because you just hit a truck while intoxicated. (Not that, you know, anything like that ever *happened*. LOL.) Yes, thinking about "those days," my years of alcohol and drug abuse, and my dad's assurance that everything is gonna be okay, no matter what. He makes people feel like they have an invisible net underneath them when they walk.

One of the greatest lessons I learned from him is about failure: "Always remember Carolyn, to make one life breathe a little easier because you existed. That is the definition of true success." His voice brought me back to the present moment.

"You still there, love?" he asks.

"So can you help with a room? I promise I will pay you back, Dad. *Please?* I believe I can make magic happen if I go down there," I say with complete certainty.

There is a 10-second pause.

"Yes. Goodbye. I love you!" He hangs up.

OMG. I was actually going to make this happen. I am going to Florida. Now I only had one other person to speak with. My husband, Mike.

I dial his number. I say, "Babe. Hey. So, you know how I have this unquenchable thirst to help others awaken within? Well, to do that I have to go see my mentor, Joseph, in Florida for a few days so I can model him. I need to go to Florida. It's very important. It's for my dreams." I try to sound not as excited as I really am.

"Whatever," he says and hangs up.

I hang up. Okay. It's okay. Everything is always going to be okay, I tell myself. Oh shit. I almost forgot, I have to ask my new boss... oh boy. Lots of hoops to jump through today.

I jump up from the desk and run into Gene's office. Gene is about five foot eight and has one of those personalities that you can just really get along with. "Gene? You got a second?"

"Hey Carolyn, yes what's up?" he says looking away from the two large computers on his desk.

"I need to go down to Florida and work with my mentor a bit. Do you mind if I take two days off?"

He looks at me and gives me a warm smile. "Kid, you got it. Let me know if there is anything else you need." He turns back to his computer and continues to evaluate grids of numbers.

As I'm taking the train home that evening, I think about all the incredible events taking place. I look in my journal on the train… OMG, I think. I wrote down one week ago, "I want to be on the beach in the sunshine." I had booked a hotel at the Boca Raton Beach Club, right on the ocean, the only room they had left and I got it for one night.

I pray Joseph will let me sleep on his couch the first night I am there. I will have faith, I say. I will have faith that everything is working as it should. As I look out the window of the train, I realize that I'm manifesting. I'm creating my destiny. Tony Robbins says, "Where focus goes, energy flows." I am that I am. I am that I am. I am that I am and I am a powerful creator. *Same as my daughters name.*

Later that night, Mike and I are in the kitchen after Kaylee is in bed and fast asleep. I'm standing in one of Mike's white tanks, which comes just below my butt and I'm making tea for us. I'm trying to make it up to him that I'm going away. He is staring at me. We had gone most of the night with minimal conversation. He finally speaks. "I feel like I don't matter to you anymore. I'm trying but I just don't get this motivational bullshit."

I stop making the tea to connect with him. I put my hands on the counter and slid myself onto the countertop. I just look at him, deeply into his blue eyes and pull him in between my legs. I say, "You matter to me more than all the tea in China." I wrap my legs around him.

He wraps his arms around me and pulls me into him. His eyes dilate. He starts kissing my neck softly and then more aggressively, just the way I like it. We have an intense love-making session. After, he keeps me on the countertop just holding me, his hands gently stroking my face. He looks deep into my eyes. "Was that good for you?" he asks.

"OMG, baby. You made me completely happy."

He smiles, his sweet side smile. "Good I am glad. Thank you, baby." I don't know why but every time after we had sex we would thank each other.

"Okay, you can go to Florida but then can I have my wife back, please, when you get back? I don't know who you are, but I just want the old you back. I don't understand this Tony Robbins stuff but I do know that's not who you are. You don't believe in that self-help stuff and neither do I."

I smile at him as I go back to our tea cups, not saying a word. I will do my best to make him feel better and make him feel like he is my number one.

All these racing thoughts. I feel like he is asking me to choose between this dream I have in my heart and him. True love would not do this. I believe with my whole heart that true love would only help you reach your dreams, not choose one or the other.

I lie awake in bed and can't seem to stop dreaming about this vision, this dream that was placed in my heart, my soul, this dream of saving the world and spreading love all around the world. I see thousands of people jumping up and down in front of me. I vividly visualize this in my heart, body, mind and soul. I close my eyes and fall asleep into the bright light in my dreams suffusing every cell in my body.

> *"You must understand that love never keeps a man from pursuing his destiny. If he abandons that pursuit, it's because it wasn't true love... the love that speaks the Language of the World."*
>
> **—Paulo Coelho, The Alchemist**

On the train ride to work the next day, I make a little checklist in my notebook. Mentor check. Visiting mentor, check. Speak with family and get sitter for Kaylee, check. Speak with job and ask for time off, check. Book room and flight, check. Here I come, Florida.

I leave for Boca Raton to hang out and train with legends, thanks to my mentor, Joseph McClendon III. I can't wait! My mind is racing. I'm excited to be around people who share my excitement and common interest in motivating others and helping others transform their lives! In the past 30 days, I have transformed my beliefs and my life completely! Having a mentor like Joseph is changing my life drastically. Just speaking with someone who is so sure of his worth and everyone else's—he is so daring, courageous and bold.

I walk through Philadelphia with my new white roller jet-setter suitcase. I have a smile so big that it vibrates. I feel everyone is looking at me. I keep connecting with people passing by and looking into their eyes and smiling at them. Almost everyone smiles back today! I have to go to work but I can think about almost nothing else but Florida. At 4:30 p.m. exactly. I roll myself down to the train station to Philadelphia International Airport.

I fly into Florida wearing a large winter jacket, so in the bathroom at the airport, I quickly change into shorts and tank top because it's so hot. I step outside into sunshine and palm trees. I met two gentlemen on the plane who say they can give me a ride to my hotel. I was grateful because I have only $100 for two days and I was not sure how much a taxi from the airport to the hotel would be. They pull up at the beautiful Boca Raton hotel and I see the biggest Christmas tree I have ever seen, with Christmas balls, pink ribbons and bows, large and small packages all wrapped up under the tree. This is so magical. I quickly open the door and as I get out, they wish me luck on my dreams. As I think about what I just did, I thank God that they were not murderers.

I smile and wave to them and say, "I have the belief that all people are good." My old beliefs were that people were bad. My mom was so cautious. She was constantly saying, "Be careful not to fall, Carolyn." I'm learning only now she should have been saying, "You can do it Carolyn! Go for it!" I realize sometimes I say this Kaylee. I need to inspire her to take the leaps she wants to take and not be afraid. I love my mother dearly and she has done so much for me; in fact, she has my little girl right now! My thoughts are taken to a different place as I walk into the Boca Raton hotel.

Something big is going on here. The energy is different. People are buzzing around like crazy at Date With Destiny. I text Joseph about sleeping on his couch tonight and he says I can stay with him. I meet him at the hotel's front desk, as he's escorted by security. He smiles big and hugs me and says, "Ready to eat?" I can't hold back my excitement. People keep coming up to him and asking for pictures but finally we're able to get away.

We talk at the restaurant until almost midnight. I ask him so many questions and he answers every one. We get back to his room. I laugh about how I would be sleeping outside the hotel tonight if he didn't let me sleep on his couch. He laughs. He shows me videos of him and his son. I feel as if we have become friends.

As we are about to go sleep, I don't feel uncomfortable or awkward. I feel like I'm home. I feel like I have known him forever. If you had told me at UPW Dallas I would be on Joseph McClendon's couch a month later, I would have said you were nuts. However, here I am, just a few steps from his bedroom, happy as hell that I have Joseph McClendon in the room next to me. I close my eyes and I'm out like a light.

I Am *Supposed* to Be Here

At 4 a.m., I'm wide awake. I want to see the sunrise on the beach. I gently sneak out of the room. I go to the desk and ask for an early check-in if possible. The guy at the desk looks at me—my hair's a hot mess, but there's a big fresh smile on my face.

He says, "I'm not really supposed to let you in this early to your room. Can you keep a secret?"

I looked at him with a wink and a nod, "What secret? I'm not even sure what you are referring to."

He smiles and says, "Very good. Follow me."

He shows me to my room. It's right on the water. I'm literally 10 steps from the beach. I am so grateful. I sit in the sand and look up at the clouds floating by. I once read that looking at the clouds float by is a form of meditation. I watch as the sun shines through the clouds one inch at a time and as it rises, I feel this incredible feeling of gratitude. The sunrise changes the colors of the sky and the ocean waves glide over my feet. I speak to the ocean. "Hello, old friend, I have missed you."

I believe in the energy of the sun. The energy of the clouds. The energy of the ocean. The trees. I believe I can pull in their energy into me and harness it to help make my dreams come true. I used to talk to the moon, the sun and stars when I was a little girl. One day I stopped, but ever since UPW I feel like my inner child has also been unleashed!

I go back into my hotel room and Joseph texts me, "Let's grab breakfast. Meet on the balcony." The balcony overlooks the beautiful water. After we eat, Joseph says he has to stop at the event. I ask him if I can come with him. He says, "Yes." I'm thrilled! I know I will be here only a few hours but it will be worth it.

I try walking into the event room first but the man standing at the door stops me and says, "Sorry, where is your necklace?"

Joseph steps in and says, "Hey, this one is with me."

The man looks a little embarrassed for having stopped me and gives a big smile and says, "So sorry, Joseph—please come on in, Rockstars!"

I could twirl around again and again in the energy I feel in this room. The magical Tony Robbins event Date With Destiny. I'm supposed to be here, I say to myself. I feel so much love and energy, I'm overwhelmed to tears with gratitude. I lock eyes with Tony as soon as I get in the room. He stares just long enough to let me know he sees me and I go up to the stage and say hello to a few people.

Then, I walk back to the end of the room and grab a seat. The lights flicker. A clip of the ending of Mr. Holland's Opus comes on. It really gets to me. It is about a man who takes a job just to pay the bills as a teacher as he works on creating his masterpiece. Little does he realize how little free time there will be as a teacher. Initially, he is frustrated at his inability to get through to his students but over time, he becomes quite competent at his profession and in fact has a number of successes. When, after 30 years of teaching, the music program at his school is canceled he wonders what, if anything, he has really accomplished in his life. Friends and students, past and present, show him just what he has meant to them. They all gather and allow him to lead them in a symphony. Even the mayor speaks to the crowd about how he has affected her life. I cry at this. The movie stops and the lights stay down and beautiful music starts to play.

Tony guides everyone through a process, asking them to write down if they want their life to be a romance novel, a comedy—"What's the story of their life? My friends, make your life a masterpiece. You are writing the script here."

The energy in this room makes my heart sing. I want to hug everyone. Something magical is happening here. God is here. I mean, I believe God is everyone and everywhere, but this energy is something I have never experienced before. I am at a new level of consciousness when I step into this room. I can't explain why I feel so strongly about this. I stay for only a few hours and then Joseph comes back for me. "Come on, Rockstar, let's go," he says.

At dinner, I tell him sometimes I'm so doubtful and scared about everything at times and other times I'm beaming! I feel like I'm two different people, like a good voice and a bad voice. One voice is certain I can achieve my dreams and the other doubts my every move and makes me question everything.

He says, "You need to read *Think and Grow Rich*."

I give a knowing look, brushing off what he says, and reply, "Oh yeah, I've already read that and it didn't do anything for me."

Joseph says, "Then read it again. And then again. And then again. And then again. And then once more." I laugh at this ridiculous request and then see Joseph is dead serious. "*Think and Grow Rich* changed my life. I had to reprogram myself to be the person you see before you. I had to create this Joseph McClendon person. You will have to create this person that you want to become."

"Okay, I promise I will read it again and again until it saturates my mind and I feel the same way about it," I say with conviction.

I model my mentor's gestures and demeanor. He shares his stories with

54

me. He anchors me. He tells me I can be, do and have anything I want in this world. He tells me about his mentors, Jim Rohn and Deepak Chopra. He tells me to write down what I want.

I write, "Dear Rockstar Special Energy Souls, I'm ready. Come find me and let's light up the world." He tells me to affirm what I want out loud every day. He tells me "I AM" are the two most powerful words in the universe and I must use them wisely.

THE CONFIDENCE—AND CERTAINTY—OF A ROCKSTAR

After dinner, I sit on the beach, dig my feet in the sand and breathe in the beautiful sunset. I relax and just go with the flow. Joseph anchors my doubts and shows me how just by squeezing my fist a few times and thinking about powerful confident moments, I'm creating another state. A rockstar confident state.

He tells me about his life and how he met Tony Robbins. "I was standing in the back of the room at this seminar 28 years ago. I had just spent my last few hundred on a ticket. There were a lot of people in the room and we were waiting for this Tony guy to come on stage. I was debating whether I should get a refund and just leave. I was leaning on the back wall with my arms crossed. I was broke, and just didn't know where to go with my life.

"Then this man comes up to me, staring at me funny. Then he asks me, 'How you doing?'

"I think to myself, 'Oh great. Now to top it all off, I have a big gay guy hitting on me here.' I say, 'I'm debating getting a refund.'

"'What's your name?' he asks me. "'Joseph.'

"Then he smiles big at me and says, 'Well, I'm glad you are here.' He pats me on the back says, 'I hope you stay. I have to go on stage now, but if you stay, I would love to talk afterward. By the way, my name is Tony Robbins.'"

OMG, Joseph is so awesome! I'm so interested to hear all about him. I am in the presence of a true Rockstar. I make the most of the 43 hours I'm there.

Before I know it, I'm on my way back to Philadelphia. This time, though, I have a different energy about me, more than just confidence.

Confidence will take you only so far. Joseph explained if I want to be a famous motivational speaker, one who inspires others to take massive action, I need *certainty*. He explained it even further: For instance, I could say, "I'm confident I can fly a plane," but confident and certain are two totally different things. He is absolutely 1,000 percent amazing. I'm certain of it.

As soon as I step back into Philadelphia, I'm going to plan my first seminar. I'm just going to begin. I don't know where to start since I'm not an event planner and in fact I have only a high school diploma but I am determined to make it work. Several memories come to mind.

What am I saying? I know who I am. I know what I am doing. My whole life I have been on stage and holding events.

When I was eight years old, I had all the kids from my neighborhood perform a play in my garage. I wrote the script about a fortune teller, a prince and an evil queen. Of course, as the director, the writer, and the casting director, I cast myself as the lead in the play. What's even funnier, I didn't let my neighbors' parents in until they paid to come in to my mom and dad's garage for the show! I had all my friends go sell tickets to their friends and family. We ended up having more than 20 people there. I even made flyers selling tickets!

I made $55 from that little play that was 12 minutes long. We even had a curtain call. I came out on the stage and bowed to them as the kids and the parents clapped for me. I pretended like I was in front of millions of people. I bought the whole cast and crew pizza after the play—not by my choice. My sister, Mary Beth Rim (who is two years younger than Marie), who helped co-direct the show, made me. I wanted to keep the money and invest in props and the next show, but she overruled me.

I have been doing this all my life and I love it. When I was nine, I opened a store in my dad's office where he worked. And in ninth grade I tried out for the school play *Annie* and during my audition, I saw everyone there was bored with the same old script. So I decided to shake things up and started dancing and singing like a rockstar on stage. The casting director quickly got on the mic and said, "That will be enough, Ms. Rim. This is a *singing* audition, not a *rock concert.*"

I said into the mic, "Then I'll go direct and write my *own* play!" Mic drop. Everyone in the room started cheering for me as I walked out of the auditorium.

> **"My energy pulsates inside me constantly. I will put a dent in the universe and it will never be the same again because I walked this way. I'm going to electrify people with my energy, enthusiasm and joy. I will wake them up one by one with my musical Rockstar roar. Come follow me into the jungle and roar with me."**
>
> **—Carolyn Rim**

56

Back to the present moment. I have to begin. So, I begin. This is my chance, my chance to rewrite my story. I look at the calendar. I have no idea where I will have my event, but I don't want to lose this courage I have after meeting with Joseph and I decide to follow the signs. I decide to listen to my heart and my gut. I pick a day, a city, and I have total faith that a space will open and people will come. I don't want a lack of resources to be a reason I to lose my dream.

I believe truly that it is never a lack of resources; it's only a lack of resourcefulness. *100% agreed.*

I post this to the UPW Dallas group about my upcoming NLP seminar. (NLP is defined as a method of influencing brain behavior through language and other types of communication to enable a person to "recode" the way the brain responds to stimuli and manifest new and better behaviors. NLP often uses hypnosis and self-hypnosis to help achieve the desired change.)

"Planning my first NLP seminar for February 21, 2015. I have a mentor, and I have taken the first step towards being the reality architect I am and building the life of my dreams. More details coming soon on where you can buy a ticket."

"I have anchored myself that when I feel doubt, I go into a state that makes me excited, happy and ready to achieve my goals. I think about the voices chanting 'Yes, Yes...' I think about right before I walked over the fire. I see myself smiling and jumping up and down and then I jump into myself and open my eyes and scream YES!! It's such a gift that I get to relive that moment, when I went from impossible to possible, in less than just a few seconds. That's what the anchors are for, Joseph says.

"Everywhere I go I start connecting with the right people. I'm feeling them with my heart. I feel their sadness, their love, their joy. I feel compassion for others instead of judgment. I start being so grateful for every breath. Even in all the swirling, twirling uncertainty I'm facing, and all the fear that comes up, I keep putting one foot in front of the other and embrace uncertainty like the gift that it truly is.

"My heart is smiling and expanding. I feel magnetized to my destiny and my dreams. I'm awake and I know why I was born. I'm here to spread love and compassion around the world. I'm here to help people remember that we are all connected and we are all one."

Every day, on the way to work, I have a 30-minute train ride. I get to be with Tony and my other mentors in my mind. I ask them questions and ask them to help guide me. I close my eyes and imagine that I have a mastermind with the greats and I am the leader of this Rockstar mastermind. Deepak, Oprah, Tony Robbins, Les Brown—we are talking about how to spread massive change of compassion and love around the world. I take five minutes to visualize my dreams coming true.

> ### *"Imagination is everything. It's a preview to life's coming attractions."*
>
> ### *—Albert Einstein*

I listen to emotional music when I visualize, bringing on strong feelings. Have you ever listened to a song and it brought back happiness, or sadness? Or how about a song that made you want to stand up and dance? I listen to "Take Me to Church" and it makes me feel, alive, vibrant and sexy.

The songs you listen to bring forth certain emotions, so start. Music is the only thing that uses every part of your brain. Interesting, isn't it? My soul is dancing in my body. I'm swirling and spiraling towards my destiny. I visualize every day: If I can see it in my mind, in my heart, in my soul, then it can be done.

I write blog posts for others to overcome their fears and make the impossible possible, even though I still hear that voice of fear, that voice that says, "You are a joke. Everyone looks at you like a big old joke. Look at the past, Carolyn. You are not the hero."

I just keep going. I continue to take leaps into the dark even though I'm scared. I face every day with the faith that I'm guided, protected and loved by the universe. I decide the universe wants me to be happy, just like Joseph told me.

I still hear his voice: "Dare to make your life magnificent, Carolyn, because fortune favors the bold!"

The following are Facebook posts from UPW group, personal FB page and Instagram.

DECEMBER 15, 2014

Where will your path lead you? In Boca Raton incredibly grateful to be on my path.

DECEMBER 16, 2014

Hanging out with my mentor. He is an incredible person. Grateful to be spending time with my mentor.

Do *you* have a mentor?? Yes? No? You need a mentor who already has what you want! Then model their behavior and ask the right questions!

The Top Three Reasons You Need A Mentor

Mentors are critical to your success in all areas of life. Some people prefer the title of counselor, consultant, coach, or guide, but all share the commonality of being experienced and trusted advisors. We start life depending on the guidance of parents and caregivers, which then evolves to teachers and coaches. Those individuals prepare us for life, and yet at some point many of us feel like we no longer need guidance. Maybe we think we have learned all there is to know and now we are supposed to be strong and independent. Maybe it is because all those mentors along the way were put into our lives and we don't know how to seek them out. Maybe we expect the leaders within our company to fill that role. How we came to believe any or all these ideas is less important than the awakening that the truly great seek out mentors and constant improvement.

A simple example is that CEOs do not have just one mentor, they generally create entire board of directors to help steer their and the company's success. All Olympic athletes have coaches. At a reported net worth of $480 million, self-help guru Tony Robbins surrounds himself with mentors and coaches to hone and improve continuously.

1. A Mentor holds you ACCOUNTABLE and keeps you on track

I'm sure we've all been there, that overwhelmed feeling, knowing exactly what we want to accomplish but no idea how to get there. When you find the right mentor, who has achieved your desired goal, they have the experience to keep you on track with the work that will truly move the needle. A good mentor will help you outline the path to what you define as success, and knowing someone will check on your progress helps you get it done!

2. A Mentor will ELEVATE YOUR GOALS

We all start in different places, but the personal relationship with a mentor will help them understand where you are and how to push you to the next level. Mentors can draw out the potential inside of you and, like a mirror, reflect it back.

I remember going through a difficult time and I start to compare myself with others. I kept telling my mentors I want to be where you are now and I was getting very frustrated. I will never forget what my mentor, Joseph McClendon said to me "Stop comparing my chapter 20 to your chapter 3." Comparing does not serve your evolution. The only person you should compare yourself with is the person that stares back at you in the mirror every day. Now I enjoy the journey :) I am not in a rush to get to chapter 20. I am enjoying my chapter 3 and I don't want to be anything other than the best version of me.

60

3. A mentor's sole purpose is to SUPPORT YOU without pre-judgment, baggage, bias

I believe this is one of the most under-discussed benefits of a working with a mentor. They want you to be successful, but what they don't tend to do is bring their own baggage to the table. Have you ever gone home to your family or coworkers with a new goal or idea, only to have them shoot it down or remind you of all your other failed attempts? That feeling of being so small creeps in. Like nothing you do is enough. Like all your passion and knowledge in the world is worthless.

A mentor's reaction will likely be to encourage you to craft that idea—tell you to see it all the way through in brainstorming, have you prove or disprove it. They will test your passion and competency for the idea, but they should never just dismiss it. A trusted mentor with the insight to keep you on track for your goals, who cares enough to hold you accountable, and challenges you to be even better all without bringing negative bias to the interaction is invaluable.

Mentors are by far one of the reasons I succeeded. Tony Robbins himself says you will reach your goal 60 percent faster with a mentor!

Don't have one yet? Start looking! Who do you want to be your mentor and why? JUST GO FOR IT! NO MATTER WHO IT IS! NO MATTER HOW BIG YOU THINK THEY ARE… ASK FOR WHAT YOU WANT MY FRIENDS!

DECEMBER 17, 2014

Why do you wake up in the morning? A lot of people don't have a clue why they wake up in the morning. They unconsciously go about their day and complain about everything and everyone that has ever wronged them. They put others down in attempt to make themselves feel better because the old saying holds true: HURT PEOPLE, HURT PEOPLE.

"LIFE ISN'T HAPPENING *TO* YOU, IT'S HAPPENING *FOR* YOU."

Mark Twain once said that the two most important days in your life will be the day you are born and the day you find out why you were born. I have found my purpose and it's hard to stop someone once they know where they are going. I believe with my whole body, mind, and spirit that I was born to help others turn weaknesses into strengths, fears into faiths, wounds and scars, hate into love, lies into truth, deafness into sound, blindness into sight, and darkness into light. I was born to spread massive change to the end of the world and to the corners of the universe.

I have peace of mind knowing that every day I will selflessly pour my soul, my strength, my truth and my heart into helping others make their dreams come true. I want to help others open their eyes to the gift that's inside. I want to help others turn on the light within them.

Some people say they don't believe in self-help at all. Understandably, there is a lot of skepticism out there about the self- help industry but I believe the problem is in our expectations of self- help programs and specifically our misunderstanding of what it means to really help ourselves. You have to take full responsibility and that's super fucking scary. I get it. I know. But no one is promised tomorrow, so we should do what we love now. Life isn't happening to you, it's happening for you, as Tony Robbins would say.

DECEMBER 31, 2014

I picture myself at this moment with a big S on my chest and a cape flying off my back. I picture myself helping and saving thousands of people from their self-imposed purgatory and from the cruel voices saying they don't deserve wealth, they are not good enough and they will always be a failure. I help others love themselves. I inspire others by being a passionate example of the absolute joy we have available to us at every moment. I'm ready to fly.

"Nothing is impossible. The word itself says,
'I'm possible!'"

—Audrey Hepburn

JANUARY 1, 2015 ADDED A LIFE EVENT ON FACEBOOK

Carolyn Rim: Rockstar Transformation Expert

It's time to take action and become the reality architect I was born to be. I will build the life of my dreams.

I, Carolyn Rim, declare here and now. I'm a motivational speaker and a Rockstar transformation expert. I will be the number one motivational speaker in the world, helping transform millions of lives live a dream come true.

NO ONE SETS THE LIMITS OF WHAT YOU ARE CAPABLE OF BUT YOU! Act as if your success is guaranteed and start expecting great things to happen!! Yes!! You can!! Greatness begins inside of you and expands outwardly.

January 9, 2015

ORDER YOUR TICKETS TODAY FOR THE LIVE EVENT LIVE WITH PASSION NOW WITH CAROLYN RIM IN PHILADELPHIA PA! YES YOU CAN!

www.30daystolovemyself.com

January 10, 2015

Good Morning, you amazing gifts to the universe!! Are you ready to have the best day ever? I read an inspiring blog or positive story every morning before I start my day. The story I read today was about a man called Walt Disney. He had to go to 302 banks before they gave him his YES. That means he heard the word NO 302 times and banks would tell him his vision of a theme park with a character named Mickey Mouse was a ridiculous idea. Walt Disney had to continue on believing in his vision and seeing it even though no one else could. That it was possible and that he was going to follow his dreams and he was certain he would find someone to believe in his dreams and visions and give him a yes. Finally after 302 no's, he found someone to say YES. Success leaves a trail and today I'm modeling excellence and success. When I hear the word no, I know I'm one step closer to my YES! Now, get excited and invest in yourself!! I dare you to get to know yourself and your passions, visions and goals!! Yes you can!! You must continue to visualize someone saying YES even if you have no all around you.

"No matter what's happened in your past or how many times you've tried or failed, none of that matters because each moment is a fresh new opportunity."

—Tony Robbins

JANUARY 13, 2015

I believe that seeing it in your mind's eye and believing in your heart, mind and gut that it will happen with unwavering certainty is the key to turning any dream into a reality. In the past three months, I quit my job (and had a new one paying double within a week), quit smoking after 15 years of smoking habit, and have started going after my dreams with my heart, body and soul. I believe! I believe! I believe! I AM BECOMING WHO I WAS ALWAYS MEANT TO BE AND MY SOUL IS SET FREE!! What this is about is not changing yourself, but rather about becoming yourself, becoming who you were truly meant to be.

I want each and every one of us to fall in love with ourselves. You know when you get chills or a tingly feeling when you think about the person you love the most? What if we could create that kind of love for ourselves? The more you know who you are, what you love, what you don't love, what makes you tingle and excites you, and what drives you, the easier it will be for you to achieve what you want and to be fulfilled.

The most important relationship you have is the one with yourself.

I truly believe deep down inside each of us is an inner thirst for something more, something deeper, richer, and lasting. Each one of us has an inner certainty that, no matter how great our lives already are, there is yet another level—one of compassion, gratitude, connection, bliss, and success and we can continue to climb. After all, the climb is what makes you happy. If you were dropped off at the top of the mountain, would you feel like achieved it? Earned it?! Nope! It's the climb that makes you happy.

You are either growing or dying, my friends, and it's just that simple. Climbing or sliding. Just by being yourself, your true beautiful authentic self, you are contributing to the world. That is truth. The universe applauds us when we figure out what we want. And once you take that first step into action towards your goal, however small or big, the universe will support you with a thousand unseen hands. All you need is to take the first step and then, there is no stopping the force of energy this big.

JANUARY 14, 2015

Surround yourself with the things you love. Swinging on the hammock in the sunroom with my sunshines. My lil' girl and two nieces.

JANUARY 15, 2015

I am an "I will" person. I believe even if you have everything you have ever wanted in life you can always take it to the next level and everything counts. Even the smallest decision you make counts and the decisions you made thus far are the reason you are standing right where you are. Accept responsibility for where you are and take your power back. You can start making better decisions now. You can become accountable and get around the right people to move you towards making your dreams come true.

"There are three types of people in the world playing three very different games. The 'I wills,' 'I won'ts' and the 'I can'ts.' The 'I wills' play to win and accomplish much. The 'I won'ts' play it safe and accomplish little. The 'I can'ts' play to lose and they don't accomplish anything. Which one are you?"

—Gary Ryan Blair

Chapter 5
A Thank You That Manifests

"To live in gratitude, to experience the magic
in your life, Thank You must become the two
words you deliberately say and feel more than
any other words. They need to become your
identity.
Thank You is the bridge from where you are
now, to the life of your dreams."

—*Rhonda Byrne*

I'm nervous. I stare at my computer screen. I still don't have a place for my event that's in 12 days, even though I'm advertising it like crazy everywhere. I knew how risky it was to advertise just a city and state without a venue but I was not willing to let a lack of resources prevent my dreams coming true. Who cares if I didn't actually have a venue yet? I have faith that I will find a place. I already had a few tickets sold, too.

It was so exciting to think about. All these people supporting me, believing me and I would be on stage sharing valuable information with my heart. Ohhh, I'm so excited and scared! I have never felt so alive. I feel like for the first time I am creating and I have no guidebook or rulebook to follow like I normally do. I have always worked for someone else to help *them* achieve *their* dreams. Now, I was finally working towards *my* dreams and could create *my own* magic.

On my way to work that day on the train I think about my first seminar, what it will be like to just unleash and be me. As I take in the skyline of Philadelphia, I pray. I pray to God. I pray to the universe. I say "Please. I don't know why I want this so badly. I have never wanted anything so much in my whole life. I ask for help to manifest a place to have my first seminar." I then send out gratitude as if I already have the place. I thank the universe before I even have what I want.

After getting off the train, within five minutes, I get a text message from Ajay Gupta. I had spotted him in Dallas from a mile away. He had what looked like an expensive suit on and leather shoes. He was not a participant but he sat in the Diamond Premier section with a notebook and a pen, paying attention to Tony, listening intently to every word. On purpose, I sat next to him.

Within a few seconds, he looked up from his notebook at me and smiled. "I like your energy," he said.

I said, "Thank you. Nice shoes."

He chuckled and said, "Thank you." I had no idea he worked for Tony at the time, but I knew he was someone who was not a participant, just like Taylor Weiss, and a few others. These guys were total Rockstars and I loved their energy level. We had all grabbed a bite together in Dallas. Funny, out of the thousands of people at the event, I end up with Tony Robbins' sales team. Ajay and I ended up exchanging numbers. We wanted to stay friends.

I now stare at the text message from Ajay. "Hey girl! What's up? I'm coming to Philly tonight to speak. You should totally come." I cannot believe this. He'll be speaking less than one block away from my work. The chances of this happening are slim to none. "Yes, Ajay! Can't wait to see you! I can't believe you are going to be a street away from where I work. See you tonight."

Later that night, I'm on my way to the event and since it's so nearby, I decide to walk. The cold night air hits my cheeks and I breathe it in. Feels good to outside in the fresh air after a day in the cube. I'm still in disbelief that I'm about to see Ajay. I get a text from him at that moment, "Ask for Danny B. at the front desk."

I walk up to the front of the Murano, a gorgeous, massive building. After I ask for Danny B, the security guard escorts me the seventh floor for the seminar. I walk in and I love the space. It has glass windows looking out to a beautiful city full of lights. It has a rooftop and it has big TV screens. I see Ajay in the front and beeline for him. I almost tackle him.

"HI!! Did you miss me?" We both start laughing and I realize I interrupted the conversation he was having with someone. I turn and lock eyes with this man. He is blonde, blue-eyed, athletic and I feel almost like I already know him. He looks at me and I can tell he is feeling the same way.

"Do I know you?" he says.

"I'm Carolyn Rim and now you know me," I say and instead of a handshake I raise my fist for a pound and wonder if he will know what to do. He fist-bumps me and we both start laughing. We sit down next to each other. I realize he never told me who he was or his name. "What's your name?" I say.

"Oh, right," he says with a bright smile. "My name is Danny Benenfeld, or as Ajay told everyone, Danny B."

I look around. There are 30-plus people in the room and Ajay stands on a chair to start the seminar off right. He talks about patterns and beliefs and actions and tells us about Tony Robbins. He talks about how incredible it was when he first walked over fire at only nine years old.

Then, he tells everyone about the Unleash the Power Within event in New Jersey. I have no idea how I'm going to get there but I'm *going* to get there. It's $2,700 for Diamond Premier and $895 for VIP. When Ajay is finished I go up to him. I say, "Ajay, I cannot afford a ticket but I have unshakeable faith that I'm going to manifest a ticket to UPW NJ!"

He looks at me with a weird look and then says, "You know what? If anyone can do it, it's you. You are incredible. You can do anything you put your heart into, Carolyn. Remember that."

Danny B. and I are talking and I tell him about my upcoming seminar on February 21 and my dilemma about not having a place to have it. "Carolyn, have it here for free! You can do it in this room!" My breath is taken away.

"Really? Really?" I ask in disbelief. Too many synchronicities are all around—the signs all leading me to my beautiful destiny.

I say, "Thank you Danny B. You have just helped me save the world, you know. Every step counts, no matter how small." I hug him and we exchange numbers. I hug Ajay and tell him what just happened. He is smiling just looking at me. He has that energy where you just know everything is going to be okay no matter what.

"See you in New York," he says. "Text me if you end up with a ticket. Let's meet up." I walk out of there and I feel like I could fly.

I hold it together until I get to the elevator. I thank the universe and jump up and down! "FUCK YES!" I scream just as the elevator doors open.

An old man and his little dog are looking at me with alarm. I smile, "Oh, sorry!"

I'm walking out of the building and the glorious cold wind hits me in the face again as I start my three-block journey towards the train station. Thank you. Thank you. Thank you.

Everything seems like it's coming together. All the signs keep pointing me in the right direction and I have never felt more on fire and grateful. I finally for the first time in my life feel as if I'm moving in the right direction., like I'm on the right path. I realize a valuable lesson that day.

If you follow your heart, and have the faith in yourself and your dreams then every moment following your dreams is like an encounter with God. When you send out the gratitude for something that you want as if you already have received it, that's where the magic will happen. Signs will appear everywhere to point you towards your destiny.

"Everyone believes the world's greatest lie."
says the mysterious old man. "What is the
world's greatest lie?" the little boy asks. The
old man replies, "It's this: That at a certain
point in our lives, we lose control of what's
happening to us, and our lives become
controlled by fate.
That's the world's greatest lie."
—Paulo Coelho

Chapter 6
The Power in Vulnerability

"Owning our story can be hard but not nearly as difficult as spending our lives running from it. Embracing our vulnerabilities is risky but not nearly as dangerous as giving up on love and belonging and joy—the experiences that make us the most vulnerable. Only when we are brave enough to explore the darkness will we discover the infinite power of our light."

—Brené Brown

Ever since UPW Dallas, I have been on fire for my dreams. I have decided to become a motivational speaker. I have set up my first PowerPoint. I have been thinking about all the amazing things I am going to say at my first seminar. All the tools I've learned about negative self-talk vs. positive self-talk, and how we have to fall in love with ourselves first before anyone else. How the most important relationship we will ever have is with ourselves and if we truly want to change the world, the change has to start within.

I am on fire with passion for helping others. In less than 48 hours, I have to do a live talk over the phone for an online group for more than 20 people. So I'm doing both. Planning my talk, "Picture Yourself like Superman," and my first seminar.

At home, my husband is behind me, lying in bed scrolling through his phone. He says, "Do you want to take a little quiz?" He starts asking me these silly ridiculous questions.

I answer him a bit annoyed, "Yes I like that," "No not that," and so forth. At the end of the questions, he reads my personality type to me. "Wow that's great babe," I say, trying to sound enthusiastic but desperately wanting to finish creating the talk I'm doing at 7 a.m. I think, doesn't he see I'm working here? I'm still facing my computer when I see him come around from the side of the bed. He starts getting dressed silently.

Then he says, "I'm leaving. I'm not happy."

My chest tightens. I stand up and turn towards him. "What are you saying?" I say, unable to really respond without hyperventilating.

"I don't know who you are, but I want my old wife back. My real wife never got off the plane from Dallas—the one who goes to work, comes home and chills in bed with me at night. You constantly work on this motivational shit. I don't want any part of this. It's all bullshit. I don't believe in the self-help stuff you do," Mike says.

He goes to the closet and pulls out the duffle bag. A million thoughts race through my mind. I need him. The fear of being alone is too great to bear. The fear of not being good enough. The fear of not being loved. Of being a single mom in a big scary world. The fear of losing everything. The fear of having to face the world without anyone having my back. I start to hysterically sob. I can't even control it.

He looks at me, "Jesus. Please don't."

I grab him and I push him up against the wall. I'm staring at him, with tears streaming down my face. "I want five minutes with you. Just sit down," I say.

He sits on the bed. He puts his hands over his face. "I can't look at you," he says.

"Why?" I say.

"Because then I will stay and I don't love you. We're not meant for each other. I've felt this for a while," he says and he starts to cry also.

"Please," I beg. I had officially lost it. I manage to get these words out in between sobs. "I can change," I say. "I can go back to the girl you want me to be. Please don't leave me. I'm so scared of being alone in this

72

world without you, Mike. Don't leave me and KK."

He says, "You don't appreciate me and I deserve a wife who does. And you deserve someone who actually is interested in all this motivational shit."

Mike takes his hands away from his face and he pushes me off of him. "I'm moving out," he says. "I don't believe in what you're doing. You'll find someone who loves what you do. I know you will." I follow him as he grabs his stuff and puts it into his army- style duffel bag. I follow him down the stairs, and watch him in silence as he walks out the back door.

I stare at the door as Mike starts his car and pulls away. I slowly back into the wall, because I need something to support me. I just lost my best friend. My love. I feel like someone just shattered my heart into 10 million tiny pieces. I slowly slide down the wall and sink my head into my hands. I pull my knees into my chest. I'm crying so hard, I feel like I'm going to be sick. He promised he would never leave me. I'm sick as I think about all the good times and memories of Disney World and our wedding and trips and I can feel my stomach churn. I say a prayer to God: "Please help me. Please help me. Please help me."

I close my eyes and go back to my 30th birthday just six months ago. Mike is standing on his mom's lawn with a dozen roses, with about 60 of my friends and family behind him. I'm pulling up with my sisters. They told me they were just taking me to lunch but when we pull up, I see the love of my life. He is standing with his arms spread open, "Surprise! Happy 30th Birthday!" he, along with everyone behind him, yells! I jump out of the car and run to Mike. He grabs my face with both hands, "I love you, baby."

How could I let this happen? I start beating myself up emotionally. How? How could it have gotten to this point? Were we not okay? I feel like I'm having an out-of-body experience, for God's sake. This is so sudden. I feel like I have just been hit by a Mack truck.

> *"True love will never keep you from going after your dreams. If it is meant to be then it will be and if it is not, then it was never true love to begin with."*
>
> **—Paulo Coelho, The Alchemist**

So many memories are flooding in it's as if our whole 10 years is flashing before me. I remember Mike having dinner ready every night when I walked in from work. My laundry done and folded on my bed. I see him cleaning the whole house. He is so thoughtful. I think about every morning before he went to work he would kiss me goodbye and I start to wonder how many kisses over the past 10 years I have received from him. Every day. The card he got me on our anniversary about growing old together and being on the porch with our rocking chairs, holding hands and covered in blankets. He loves me fiercely. He loves me, I love him.

What's happening? I'm having a panic attack? Like someone is sitting on my chest. I think about how much we have gone through together. I think about being a single woman. The room is spinning and I can't breathe. The ups and the downs. All these memories start to make me incredibly sick. I can't be alone. I can't do this by myself. My body is curling up in a little ball on the floor. I'm staring at the wooden baseboard in my basement. The floor is cold. It hurts my skin it is so cold. I spin into another memory.

I'm remembering back when Mike and I were living together but before we were married, back when Kaylee was only one year old. Mike and I were in the car with her. He looked at me out of nowhere and said, "I just don't think we can see each other anymore."

My heart shattered. "What?"

"I don't want to be with you," replied Mike.

That night I cried in our bed, while he slept on the couch. It was hell for three days while he told me he didn't want to be with me. I was on my knees in the apartment crying.

Then all of sudden, he came through the door with a dozen roses. "Babe." He was crying, saying he was fucked up in his head, and that he loved me. He got down on his knees, and asked, "Will you marry me? I love you. Can we be together and grow old together? I'm so sorry I hurt you, Carolyn and I promise, I will never leave you again."

He pulled me into him and I wrapped my arms around him as I watched his tears fall and I said, "Yes."

Have you ever felt like that? Like you want this one person so badly within your soul, but they do not want you and then all of sudden, they want to be with you. My Catholic beliefs told me that I had to marry the man I had my baby with, so I was unable to see any other way it was going to work.

I come back to reality. That day was eight years ago and here I am on the basement floor going through the same emotional turmoil. I'm sick and tired of being sick and tired. But there is a voice in my head that says, "You think you do this by yourself? You need him. You better beg him for your forgiveness. You need to beg for it! Make him be with you. You cannot be happy alone. What is everyone going to say now?" This voice torments me. I can hear the judging now by others. Maybe it's just me, I think.

I manage to stand up and get to my phone upstairs. I message Katonna Snooks, my accountability partner. "My husband just left me. He says his real wife never came home from Dallas."

Instantly she replies, "Share it in the UPW group and I promise something amazing will happen. You will get all the support you need! I posted something a week ago and was able to let go of my ex too! I promise God has your back, the Tony Robbins community has your back and so do I! Post it!"

I tell her I will sleep on it. Posting that my husband just left me is *way* too outside my comfort zone. It's so real and raw. So vulnerable. I thought being vulnerable was a weakness. Why would I share that with everyone? What would they think of me? I was just used goods probably. I am awake most of the night with my face hot and swollen from all the crying.

I sleep for only a few hours. I awake to Kaylee telling me, "Mommy, it's time to take me to school." I jump up.

"Okay, my love." I quickly dress and I take her to school. She can tell something is different or off.

"Mommy, are you okay?" she says before she gets out of the car.

"Oh, yes, baby! I'm great! Just so you know, Daddy went to Mom- Mom Lisa's last night. He may be there for a while. I just..." I stop talking and my voice trails off as I stare into those beautiful brown eyes. I can see she is a little scared too.

Shit. Great. I just scared my little girl. I put on big smile and say, "Baby, Mommy and Daddy love you more than all the stars in the sky. We just have some of our own issues to work out so he may stay at Mom-Mom Lisa's for a little while. Is that okay with you?"

"Okay Mommy—I love you, bye."

I blow her a big kiss and yell at the window like I do every morning. "You rock, baby!"

I park my car in the lot across the street from her school and get the train to work. The fear starts to well up and I begin to break down again. I probably just scared Kaylee. I start to beat myself up for this. I wipe tears away with my white gloves, getting my black mascara everywhere. I get to my office and get right to work without making eye contact with anyone.

I try to focus all my energy on taking calls but I have to stop all of sudden and breathe. It is funny. For something we do 20,000 thousand times a day, we rarely bring attention to our breath. I take a deep long inhale and exhale through my nose. I need help.

I text Katonna, "I feel like I'm crumbling. Like I have just shattered into a million little pieces. I'm not strong enough to be alone."

She tells me again, "Promise me you will post in the group today."

"Okay," I reply. But what will they think of me? How will people see me now? They will think I'm nothing, useless loser. Just some dumb woman whose husband left her. They will not understand. I'm *so* afraid of what they will think of me.

This would be my first experience with getting vulnerable and allowing it to be my strength. I post in the Secret UPW Facebook Group:

JANUARY 19, 2015

Dear UPW Family,

My husband left me last night. He said his wife never got off the plane from Dallas. I'm gripped with fear. We have a seven-year-old little girl. Somehow even though I know this is the right move to make, I'm still gripped with fear of the unknown. I need your support more than ever since Dallas. I'm crumbling."

That day, within less than one hour of posting, I received more than 300 comments telling me I am loved and that I am right where I should be. One of those comments was from Tony Robbins himself. Out of all the hundreds of posts, he sees mine.

Here's a snapshot of the comment he posted on January 19.

Tony Robbins
I'm sorry to hear of the pain you're going through. Even though things look so dark right now what's next is always better! If it's important to come back to the UPW in New York in March or in Chicago in July come as my guest. Just reach out to your personal account representative copy to this text. Sending you love and blessings on this journey.♡

Unlike · 👍63 · More · Jan 19

Did Tony Robbins really just tell me to be his special guest? This is crazy.

I'm so grateful that I jump up from my desk at work. "OMG, Tony Robbins just commented on my post!" The people around me just stare at me like I am totally nuts—of course they cannot understand how much this means to me. I am pretty nuts, if I think about it.

I get a text from Ajay five minutes later:

"Hey Carolyn, I'm so sorry to hear about what happened between you and your husband. I saw that Tony gave you a ticket! You manifested just like you said you would. See you at UPW NJ. You are amazing. And even though this will be hard to read, I know everything that is happening to you right now is for a reason and a purpose and it serves you."

This was another comment from someone in the UPW FB Group:

"Hi, Carolyn... Go on a little visual with me here... You come back from Dallas a bigger, more expansive person. You see possibilities you didn't see before and life holds a lot of new promise. The world looks easier and more in your control. Imagine yourself 10 stories tall because of this new knowledge. Your husband stands before you a mere one-foot tall, surrounded by his small dreams and limitations. He's yelling at you to stop this nonsense that you've learned and come back and be small again like himself, or he's leaving. How would you feel if you had to shrink back down to that tiny, dark size, now that you've seen the world for what it can truly be? Could you honestly be happy going back to that size—in that limited life? See him as small—and you've been given the opportunity to grow, and you DID. You've invited him to rise up and see what you see as this giant person and he's not interested. That is his choice and it's his right to live as he wishes, but not to pull you down to his level. Embrace and be thankful for what you've had together and acknowledge that you've changed (for the better) and need to be able to embrace your life with his beautiful, freed spirit. There are no mistakes, and your spirit was desiring this—so here you are—although very difficult at the time—very necessary to allow your spirit to soar. You need to follow your gut feeling here and respect your spirit's tugging."

Another comment that truly stuck out to me:

"Carolyn, you are like a skyscraper and your husband is like a little house screaming at you to get back down here with your big dreams. 'Shrink! Shrink!! Shrink!!'"

I never want to shrink for anyone. That does not make my heart happy. I didn't want to hide anymore in the dark. I had stayed in the darkness alone and unhappy too long just to shrink back down to the box I was told I should fit into.

I had also reached out to my mentor:

"Joseph, my husband left me and I'm scared and feeling totally uncertain. I know you are busy doing an event in Asia or something, but I would be grateful for a response." He replied within 10 minutes to my text. He was unconsciously teaching me how to be a good coach and mentor:

"Hey C. So sorry to hear you're going through difficulties. Yes I went through it as well and what I will say is that although I had lots of advice from my coaches and mentors and friends, including Tony as he went through it, too, one of the best things I can tell you now is to continue to remind yourself that this too shall pass. And as clichéd as it may sound, it's always darkest before the dawn. And your reasons why or what will keep you going. For me it was my little boy and his happiness and to see that he grows up in the midst of me being happy. Set your focus on what your future will be. And turn it into a vision versus a dream, which means visit it and experience it every single day with excitement. And of course, Keep shaking... well, you know."

VULNERABILITY IS MAGIC

Having both Joseph and Tony's support along with the more than 300 comments, hundreds of private messages from people from the UPW group and people all over the world mean so much to me and I am so grateful for the special ticket. But my heart hurts still and I still feel broken. My vulnerability is the reason I have a ticket to UPW NJ as Tony's special guest and I focus on being grateful for that.

I'm going to be authentically *me* through it all. Through the pain I feel. Through everything. I am me. I am enough. I am worthy. I am going to own this. I am going to accept where I am at this very moment and decide where I take myself. I will continue to plan my seminar that is less than a month away. I will continue to grow and tell my story.

> *"We are sick and tired of being sick and tired. Definition of courage: Tell your story with all your heart. You are imperfect and you are wired for struggle; but you are worthy of love and belonging. Vulnerability is our most accurate measurement of courage. I now see how owning our story and loving ourselves through that process is the bravest thing that we will ever do."*
>
> *—Brené Brown*

The following are the actual posts from UPW group, Facebook, and Instagram.

JANUARY 22, 2015

Today, I feel like a legend in the making. The voices in my head fight all the time. They battle back and forth, the good voice and the bad voice. I want to be a fucking legend but there is a personal battle going on in my mind and that's okay. I'm still learning to fall in love with myself and listen to the good. I always post positive things into the world. Even if I'm going through something painful, I find a way to look at it positively. I hang out with Rockstars who see solutions not problems. I only focus on my past successes, not my past failures. I never use common sense because that will only lead me to common results. I use my mind, heart and gut to guide me and have a belief that a thousand unseen hands guide me on my journey. I use my heart and wear it on my sleeve daily.

I am unique. I am special and I am worth it. I am a child of God and I deserve to be happy. I'm naturally a joyful person. I am legendary and the whole universe is cued up to give me everything I am wanting and more. I am a giver. I empower and help those around me. I am also grateful for all the support I have in my life. Angels are everywhere. Spread your own wings today and make it amazing!

JANUARY 23, 2015

90 days no cigarettes: 90 days pursuing my dreams, goals and passions. 90 days of being kind to myself and my body... Unleashing the power within... Priceless!

> *"Beauty is when you can appreciate yourself.*
> *When you love yourself, that's when you're*
> *most beautiful."*
>
> **—Zoe Kravitz**

JANUARY 23, 2015

I feel like I have found the secret and I want to share it with you. It's self-love and self-acceptance.

This is how you go from being ordinary to extraordinary. Put down the bat you use to beat yourself up with and just be who you are. When you end the resistance to being yourself, exactly as you are right now, in this moment, then you will start to experience the shifts all along.

When you see that you embody all the same gifts, talents and abilities as the divine, then you will know the truth. You are limitless potential; there is nothing to heal and nothing to fix. When you apply the qualities of love and trust to the experience of yourself, then you will know your soul's innate unbreakability.

Life is not a journey of overcoming obstacles. Your life is a state of being to be celebrated and enjoyed. Major life events such as becoming a parent, getting divorced or managing a financial loss are not being done to you. They are a chance for your greatest evolution and growth. I know it may not always feel like this, but it is these very events that help you into a greater state of harmony with yourself.

I believe this is how one shines brighter than the others. It's only when you give up the conflict with just being yourself, that you be your true self.

> *"Follow your inner moonlight; don't hide the*
> *madness."*
>
> **—Allen Ginsberg**

JANUARY 25, 2015

What if I told you that the average person has 60,000 thoughts a day and that these thoughts were controlling your reality?

The subconscious mind is 90 percent more powerful than your conscious mind. See, your beliefs, values and opinions are shaping your reality. Do you believe you deserve the best life has to offer? Do you believe you deserve a loving, supportive, trusting relationship? Do you believe that it's possible to make $300,000 this month using your God-given talents? Do you believe you contribute to the world just by being yourself and doing what you love? Do you believe that every step is guided by infinite intelligence?

See: These are all beliefs. I had to change my beliefs and fall in love with myself. I'm a leader, an entrepreneur and I will put a dent in the universe with my love. I will inspire millions to change their lives and fall in love with themselves.

This is the way I talk to myself most of the time. When the world is going crazy and everyone is saying, "Oh no! What do we do??" I'm on the sidelines ready, willing, and able to step in and say, "I will handle it." *You* set the tone of how others treat and respect you.

Today, your mission is to create new truths about yourself. Now, I don't want you to look at this as if you are changing yourself. I want you to look at it as you were finally willing to BE YOURSELF. Because you are beautiful.

Did you read that right? YES! YOU ARE BEAUTIFUL.

There will be a moment in your life when you are going to realize the way you talk to yourself internally matters. The thoughts that you think about yourself matter. What if every thought was tattooed on our body? I bet you would have nicer thoughts about yourself!

Can you fake until you make it? YES! Our vibration and our nonverbal cues govern how people think about us and how they treat us. So our thoughts create our reality.

What thoughts are you telling yourself? I used to be mean to myself and I used to say some pretty mean things inside my head. Everyone around me would treat me badly, too. It was only when I started treating myself with respect and I started being kind to myself that magic started happening and people started to treat me like a ROCKSTAR!

Your beliefs create your reality, so create new beliefs to create a new reality. Thoughts and feelings create your reality. Therefore: Change your thoughts and change your life.

> **"A man is but a product of his thoughts;**
> **what he thinks, he becomes."**
>
> **—Mahatma Gandhi**

January 26, 2015

Just for the moment, be still. Breathe. Smile. Feel safe, listen to your higher self, the one with all the answers.

January 25, 2015

Did you know that your mind cannot tell the difference between something vividly imagined and something that actually happens?!

Isn't that amazing? The science and application of creative visualization is more than just a method to alter your own reality. So you have to visualize what you want in your life. Feel the bliss of your dreams coming true. Breathe it in. Taste how it would taste.

You must see it, sleep it, eat it, and feel it deep down with every fiber of your soul!

You will manifest your dreams faster than ever before. You are so powerful! I believe with every ounce of my soul that I will be the top motivational speaker in the world. I see it. I feel it. I taste it. I breathe it. Every damn day. Every damn day. I don't give one speck of mental energy to *how*. I just focus on the final outcome, the vision, the dream. Then my brain can't tell the difference and it automatically comes up with things to help me achieve it. Try visualizing today!

January 28, 2015

SHE HAD ME FROM HELLO. SHE IS MY WHY.

JANUARY 29, 2015

Tickets are on sale!! If you keep thinking and doing the same thing, you will get the same results. Don't you think it's time to turn autopilot off and direct the course of your life to the destination you desire? Invest in yourself! Stop telling yourself it's not possible to have the life of your dreams—and start living your dreams now!

JANUARY 30, 2015

WORK WITH ME ONE ON ONE! HAVING A COACH WILL CHANGE YOUR LIFE!

30daystolovemyself.com

FEBRUARY 1, 2015

"Be your own superhero and never give up your dreams—no matter how out of reach they seem. When you start reaching for your goals, passions and dreams, the universe starts working in your favor and you will be filled up with love and abundance.

Check out 30daystolovemyself.com. Tiny shifts in our thinking create mammoth shifts in our reality. Get rid of the self-limiting beliefs you hold and spread your wings to fly. I will put a dent in the universe. I will not slap my creator in the face by playing a small game so I don't frazzle those around me. Come hungry, and prepare to be inspired. I will spread my wings and fly despite my fear. All of my fears are dissolved by the light of my courage. My story and energy will wake up and shake the world." —Carolyn Rim

Dear UPW,

I couldn't help but share this. My ex-husband told me yesterday he doesn't believe in my message, my dreams or what I'm trying to teach others about loving themselves. He told me to stop being so selfish and ridiculous and come back down to reality. He told me I'm brainwashed by Tony and wasn't going to help or inspire anyone and to stop chasing my dreams.

For about 10 seconds I felt like punching him in the throat...then something happened. A shift in my pattern. I thanked him. I said the more he tried to tear me down with words, the more I would love myself, love him and others.

I'm a fucking wolf and I will be damned if I stop howling at the moon because someone tells me not to. I will not stop chasing my dreams. It feels too good to climb. To grow. That's what success is about: The climb. It is not actually about getting the goal itself. It is about who you become in the process. To pursue every passion, dream and goal with intensity, persistence, drive and courage. I'm acting with complete faith like my success is guaranteed.

I may stumble, I may fall down but I will climb inch by inch out of this life and into the life I create. I will keep getting up and I will keep giving myself second chances! I WILL NEVER QUIT. My life will never be the same again because I shined this way. I finally found the light switch within myself and there is no going back to the darkness! I have a support group with the UPW and the morning calls. Hell, I feel as if I have 6,000 people from all over the country cheering me on. All of us deserve the best life has to offer. Thanks for letting me share and Shine Brighter! Breathing in the magic of NOW.

"Imagine right now that you are a reality architect and that you are going to build the life of your dreams. Build a wall around your dream and let no person come in and burn your dreams to dust. Those are your dreams. Protect them."

—Carolyn Rim

"What a difference what you say to yourself daily has on your self-esteem! Joy is my natural state of being! The average person has 60,000 thoughts a day. What you say to yourself matters!! Write a love letter to yourself and fall in love with you one word at a time."

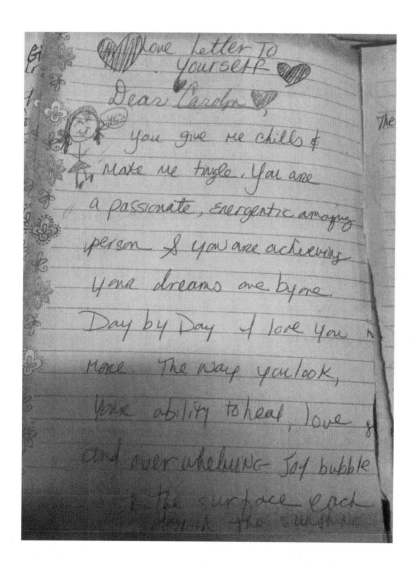

Chapter 7
Dancing With Fear

"Life is found in the dance between your deepest desire and your greatest fear."

—Tony Robbins

Day before of my first motivational speaking event. I am running around at my dad's. My mom is watching my little girl while I'm working. I yell out, "Pam, I need help!" Pam is my dad's secretary but she is so much more than that. She cleans, she cooks, she helps take care of my dad and she also helps me as well, thank God. Especially when I'm running around like a crazy person the day before my event.

I'm so excited to share my message. I have sold only three tickets to the event but I have 15 people scheduled to come. It's supposed to snow like crazy tomorrow but I'm going ahead with it anyway! I have John Beinlich and his girlfriend, Caitie, coming to help with speakers and sounds and, of course, to be supportive. John told me today I would be great and if I'm serious about what I'm going for, it's going to be like a roller coaster ride, so just smile and enjoy the ride. He is such an awesome support and friend. I'm so grateful for him.

My sister Marybeth and her husband, Brad Thomas, are coming to film this and they are so supportive. Brad even went out and bought me a clicker so I could click through the slides. I even ordered us shirts but they will not be done in time.

I'm typing up my first outline and I'm getting so nervous I could scream! So I breathe in and out and realize that I'm on a path towards my destiny. I realize as I type my first program and outline for the Live with Passion Now event that I feel that God is speaking through me. I feel like every time I listen to my heart and follow my dreams that I'm having an encounter with God. It's this incredible explosion of bliss and joy in my soul.

I'm so grateful for my life, and so scared and excited about tomorrow. I breathe in the magic of this present moment and take in all its gloriousness. Tiny shifts are now making mammoth shifts in my reality.

Before I sleep, I pray, and I thank God for every valley I've had. I thank God for all the bad times, because I know I needed every low valley to make my mountaintops better. I needed every lesson and heartbreak because it made me who I am today. All the good and bad moments led me to right now so I am grateful for both. I'm ready to shine. Ready to stand out and share myself with the world. All my flaws, all my gifts, all my love.

> *"Love is the force that transforms and improves the Soul of the World.... It is we who nourish the Soul of the World, and the world we live in will be either better or worse, depending on whether we become better or worse."*
>
> *—Paulo Coelho*

I wake up smiling. I was up well into the night making sure everything was perfected. I am alive and energized. I almost feel as if I can feel my vibration rising. It is strong and my frequency clear.

ON THE RIGHT PATH, LIVING WITH PASSION

When I arrive to the Murano and walk into the room for my event, I notice 15 chairs are set up, all lined up perfectly. John, Katie and I move some things around. People start to show up. Danielle Cline, Rebecca Poultney, Paul Barris and several others come in and take their seats. I am so ready. I am so nervous.

I start out the seminar by saying, "Ready... Set... LIVE WITH PASSION NOW! Let's Go!" I have everyone jump up and down. I share the benefits of rebounding! With the Superman theme song playing, I have everyone get into a peak emotional state. I have everyone shout, "Yes!" We are on fire. I notice a man come in with a hat and scarf that say "Platinum Partner" with Tony Robbins' name on it. The man grabs a seat in the back and smiles at me.

Two hours later, I am getting to the end of the seminar with everyone visualizing their desired outcome. I want everyone to visualize and see in their mind's eye dreams coming true. I tell them about the subconscious mind and how it cannot tell the difference between something real and something imagined! I'm so nervous during the seminar that I forget and do a visualization for speakers. Let us hope all these beautiful people want to be speakers. I gently walk them off the stage and to the place they feel safe after I realize what I did.

Before I know it, it's time to close the seminar. As everyone is leaving, but I see the man with the Tony Robbins hat in the back. I walk over to him and before I can introduce myself, he says, "So, my name is William Pasquale. I want to be the first person with a Carolyn Rim autograph," as he hands me a pen and paper. I stare at him for a moment because I can tell this person really believes in me.

"Okay," I say. "Absolutely." I sign it. My first autograph. I feel special.

I can tell William does that to people. He has a way of making others feel really special. Like they matter. I hug him and he walks me out to my car. He tells me he drove in the snow an hour and a half to get to me. He said, "Your post made an impact on me, Carolyn. I believe your story has the power to change the world. I have no doubt you will achieve whatever you put your heart into."

As I watched this soul drive away, I realized that sometimes God sends us angels to let us know we are on the right path. I inhale and stick out my tongue to catch some of the snowflakes falling from the sky. Thank you, God, thank you.

The following are actual posts from the UPW Facebook group, Facebook, and Instagram.

FEBRUARY 21, 2015

Danced with my fear today, and had my first motivational speaking event! I FEEL like I AM flying. It was amazing, and I've never felt more alive in my whole entire life. I finally found my dream! Say yes, and make your move! Thank you to all who came! Especially to William Pasquale, who drove an hour and a half in the snow to see me.

FEBRUARY 28, 2015

I can't believe in just a few short days I get to be Tony Robbins' Special Guest!! Super-duper excited!! OWOOOOOOOOOO! I am howling like a wolf! Got my superhero shirt on and I'm ready to rock! Hurry up UPW New Jersey! I can't wait!

Just finished an amazing seminar and one of the girls, Danielle Cline, messaged me and said she started her own blog after my seminar. She said she had never been so inspired by someone. I cried when I got her message.

So many beautiful things to be grateful for. I believe that changing your self-limiting belief patterns and creating new empowering beliefs changes people for forever. My mindset is no longer held down by doubt and fear. I believe that the reason I have had so much success in the past 100 days is because I changed my beliefs and imprinted new ones into my subconscious mind.

I developed a crystal-clear picture of what my dreams looked like. I had the ultimate end in mind and did not worry about the "how to" get there. I just focused all my energy on my dreams and that it was possible. I stopped hanging around people who thought it wasn't possible or told me I was weird for following my dream. I started hanging around peers that were on the same enlightened path as I was.

I got a mentor who already has what I want and follow the steps he took towards success. Joseph McClendon has helped me so much already on my journey.

I don't compare my Chapter 1 to his Chapter 20. Someone once told me once that comparing can only do one of two things. It can make you feel better than and the ego will inflate. Or it can make you feel less than and you feel deflated.

I stay in the present moment and believe with all my heart and soul that there are a thousand unseen hands supporting my journey and guiding me. Step into your moment and follow your dreams. Even if you only take one small step every day towards your dreams, even the smallest steps amount to great distances.

Chapter 8
Bumps in the Road

"Maybe this is a sign to see if I will give up at every little bump in the road. Maybe it's a sign to see if I really want it."

—Carolyn Rim

March 4 already! I'm so excited—in less than 24 hours I will be in Tony Robbins' special friends and family section. I am preparing to leave for UPW in the morning, and watching the news. I am three hours away from Secaucus, N.J.

"Worst Blizzard in March ever in Philadelphia history..." and I grab the remote and turn it off before I hear another word. I am *not* going to miss the Tony Robbins event. I am not supposed to leave until tomorrow but I decide I must leave, *right now.*

I grab my suitcase. I have this ridiculous grin plastered on my face. I don't even have my room until tomorrow but I feel like I am being pushed out my door to leave now. Think, Carolyn, think. If you go now, you will not have a room to sleep in. I am tapping into my intuition and listening to my heart. My heart, gut, intuition, whatever you want to call it is pushing me out the door. Leave now, it says, and so I listen.

I wonder what it is going to be like there as Tony Robbins' special guest. I wonder what he will do and say. Will I get to meet him? I know I will get to see my mentor Joseph McClendon but Tony is different story. I take a deep breath. I am so very grateful.

I put my black leather jacket on and look in the mirror for a moment. As I stare at myself in the mirror, the voice of my ex comes to mind. "You think going to these Tony Robbins seminars are going to save you? Get real. No one cares about that positive self-talk bullshit."

I think about him. He is the whole reason I am invited to this event. I let go of the feeling of fear and instead picture Mike smiling at me. I say thank you to him in my mind because he is part of this. The other reason is because I decided to get vulnerable and open up on the UPW Dallas page that my husband had left me. I got this ticket because I was vulnerable. All of these thoughts seem to come at me at once. And then again I feel a strong urge to leave right now.

I'm ready. I smile and wink at myself in the mirror. "You freaking rock, girl." I open my door to the freezing cold. Suitcase, hat, gloves, and the whole kit and caboodle beside me. I go outside and it is already icy and slippery on the ground. It has started to snow. I watch my breath in the cold night air.

Tonight is the night that something magical happens. I look up at the snow falling and I put my bags down on the ground, and I reach my arms out wide like I'm an angel and I see crystal white snowflakes falling. I love the snow. It's the kind of snow that you dream about—thick white snowflakes. I stick my tongue out and catch snowflakes. I'm twirling now and smiling. I can't believe I'm going to be Tony Robbins' guest! I said thank you to the universe again for making this happen. Thank you to God!

I don't know where I will stay since I cannot check in my hotel until tomorrow morning. However, I had one thing and that was faith that everything I need will continue to speed its way towards me. I let go of how it happens. A thousand unseen hands guide me every step I take— I am guided and I am on a mission for good. I feel as if I am surrounded by this quite magical force or energy, in every fiber of my being, in my heart, in every cell of my body.

You see my whole life, I always knew there was something watching me. Something guiding me, a gift of energy and light. I used to be afraid of it. In fact, just six months ago, I would tell this force not to come towards me because I was so scared of it. I did not accept this gift until the Tony Robbins seminar in Dallas.

I pick up my bags with enthusiasm and a skip in my step. I get in my car with determination, with certainty, with confidence and start out towards my destiny. With current traffic I am about three hours and 12 minutes away. I pull away from my rowhome and watch it disappear behind me. I am jamming out to one of the UPW playlist songs, Follow Me Into Jungle, when I feel a jolt of energy to the right side of the car.

POP! My car has hit the biggest pothole known to man. I feel the jolt now in my body as I almost swerve into another car but manage to pull my car over. My heart is racing. My eyes are wide. Wow. That was scary as hell. Okay. Breathing. I'm okay. I put the car in park. I get out and look at my completely flat tire. "Shit," I say out loud.

Mike said he was staying in this weekend with his mom and dad, snowed in, and he won't need his car, so I call him. "Hey! I'm on State Road and I have a flat tire. Can I borrow your car until Sunday, please? You all will be snowed in anyway," I say in the sweetest tone I possibly can.

I'm literally right down the street from his mom's. I wait. There is a long pause. "Are you kidding me? No. This is a sign, Carolyn. It's a sign that you shouldn't go to this stupid fucking seminar," Mike says.

I swallow back the rising anger and allow my higher self to take over. "You know," my voice cracks, "maybe it's a sign to see if I will give up at every little bump in the road. Maybe it's a sign to see if I really want it."

Mike laughs and says, "Well then, let's see how bad you really want it. Find a way to get there without me." CLICK. Mike hangs up on me.

My sister Marybeth has never let me down. She has my little girl and the whole family over at her house. I call her. "Marybeth, I just got a flat tire and I need help. Can I borrow your mini-van for the weekend please?"

She pauses, and puts me on hold, and I can hear her shout "Brad! Can my sister take the mini-van to New Jersey?" Pause. Before she can respond I tell her I'm getting towed to her place. I hang up and call the tow company. I sit and wait in my car.

I want to share this energy, this love, this determination with all the new people I will meet in UPW New Jersey. I take a picture of my flat tire and I tell them what's going on, how Mike says it's a sign to give up, and how I say it's a sign not to give up at every little bump in the road. Plus, I tell them, I do not even have a room either, but I AM A FIRE-WALKING ROCKSTAR and it will take a hell of a lot more than a little flat tire to stop me! Come hell or high water, here I come UPW NJ! I click POST.

Within 30 seconds, I hear a ping and see a message in my FB inbox from Michael Savage. I don't know him but I click on his message. "Hi, Carolyn, I saw your post in the UPW FB group about the snow, and driving up early. I also saw the picture of the flat tire in the UPW group.

95

I work for Mr. Tony Robbins. I want to offer you a place to stay for the night. Oh, and don't worry, I'm happily married so the only intention I have for you is that I provide you warm couch and a hot breakfast in the morning."

I somehow trust him and my intuition. I click on his picture to check out his profile and he really does work for Tony Robbins. I see a lot of pictures of him at events with Tony and even on stage. "Michael, I will accept the gift of a warm place to stay. That would be amazing. I will not be arriving tonight until after 2 a.m. with the snow and just leaving now. Will that be all right?" I press send.

Within seconds... Ping "YES. Please message when you arrive."

The tow truck arrives behind my car. Forty-five minutes later we pull up to my sister's, who is standing at the doorway holding the keys to the mini-van with a big grin on her face. My little girl is at the door to, and I grab her and give her a big hug and kiss! I give Marybeth a huge hug as well and then jump in the mini-van. I'm finally on my way again. I take a deep breath and thank God for a moment.

I put on my UPW playlist music. The song playing makes me smile and move: Halo by Beyoncé. I carefully drive in the blizzard, in the dark of night, to continue on this incredible adventure.

I drive and I drive and I drive. It seems like hours and hours pass. For a while the music is off and I just think about my life. I think about all the coincidences. I believe. I believe. I say it over and over again. I am ready for the gift.

I AM the belief. I say it in my mind a thousand times. I believe in the invisible. I have faith! I believe. I say it and I mean it! I know that I AM are the two most powerful words in the universe and whatever I put after them, I will become.

I finally pull up to the Hilton at the Meadowlands Expo Center. I park and message Michael Savage. He's waiting for me outside in the cold. Its freezing but he stands there with a smile. "Hello," he says.

"Hi! I am so grateful for this! I looked at your profile pics just to make sure you were not a serial killer or anything," I said. We both started laughing as he grabbed up my bag from me.

"Yes, I'm glad I saw your post. Let's go inside," he says.

"Thank you so much," I say. "I don't know what I would have done if you didn't message me tonight. I would have had to sleep in the car."

He says, "I normally don't do this, to be quite honest, but something about your post about not giving up at every little bump in the road struck me. I figured you might need help."

96

I like this guy right away. He has one of those souls that you immediately just trust. We get into his room and I sit down on the sofa. He makes me tea and tells me about his journey with Tony Robbins and how incredible it has been. He shows me pictures of his wife and little girl. At 2:30 a.m., I finally decide I should sleep. He can tell. He hands me a pink ticket.

"This ticket will get you free hot breakfast downstairs tomorrow. You can use the shower and anything else you need. I'm glad you made it, kid. Good night." He walks in the other room.

I lie down and close my eyes. I whisper to myself, "I made it God. Thank you. Thank you, universe. I'm so grateful. Please keep the blessings and miracles coming." I fall asleep with a huge smile and gratitude filling in my heart for Michael Savage and this warm room. I must have been exhausted, because I don't remember anything after that except sweet sugar plums in my dreams.

UPW NEW JERSEY

The next morning, I awake to the smell of brewed coffee. It's 7:30 a.m. I'm so excited I can barely take it. I literally jump up off the couch with a big smile on my face. There's a note: "Carolyn— Enjoy your morning, feel free to use the shower and please let me know if you need anything at all. Here is my cell number. See you later, Rockstar. —Michael"

I take a shower and quickly dress. I get downstairs, I have waffles and eggs. I seem to light up people everywhere I go. People are staring at me more than usual though. Maybe it's because of the smile on my face that hasn't left since I know I'm going to be Tony Robbins' special guest today!!

After breakfast, I make my way to the Diamond Premier lounge. I take a deep breath in. I walk in, walk up to the counter and say, "Hi! I'm here to be Tony Robbins Special guest!"

Before the woman behind the table can respond, another crew member in the room grabs my hand. "OMG, It's Carolyn Rim!" she shouts. The woman is someone who follows me on Facebook in the UPW Dallas FB group. She gives me the biggest hug ever. She grabs her phone and says, "Can I get a pic? You touched me so deeply with your vulnerability in the UPW FB group."

"Yes, of course," I say, surprised someone wants a picture with me just for sharing my heart. I hug her and connect with her for a moment. I then turn back to the woman who is clearly waiting behind the table for me to continue.

"We have a problem Carolyn. I do not have you down as Tony Robbins' guest."

"Oh, but you must. Let me look for the text on my phone that Tony Robbins sent me."

The woman is clearly busy. She is sending some strong vibes to hurry up. I find the picture of Tony Robbins saying to come as his special guest to this event. I show it to her with a big smile. "See. He invited me. I'm here to sit in front with him." She gets this look on her face and puts on her glasses. She stares at the text on my phone.

She shakes her head and says, "I'm sorry but this is not going to work. You see, the Tony Robbins Special Friend and Family section is only for celebrities, Tony's friends and family and, you know, like, important people."

The smile that had been plastered on my face for two months straight since Tony sent me that message literally just crumbled to the floor. I fought back the tears. I could feel my face getting hot. "Oh," I say. "I guess that wouldn't be me then."

She says, "I would go to the main front desk and see what they can do to help you."

I walk out of the Diamond Premier lounge feeling like a loser. I was such an idiot to think Tony would ever invite me to be his guest. I message Joseph right away and tell them what's going on to see if he can help. His response, "Hi Doll. I fly in tonight. I'm not sure what I can do. I will talk to them once I get there tomorrow." I even try to call Michael Savage's cell to see if he can help me. Nothing.

I go to the main customer service table and I tell the woman there the whole story and show her the text. She says the exact same thing the other woman said. "Here's what I can do. I can put you in Power Pavilion 2. Come with me. I have a spot for you," she says.

I see Scott Chamberlain on my way to Power Pavilion 2. I run up to him and give him a huge hug, "Hey Carolyn! How are you? Still not smoking, right?"

"Yes! OMG it's so good to see your face, Scott!" The woman looks at me, like who the hell is this woman, and says, "Okay, Carolyn, come on, follow me." Scott gives me one more hug and says to come say hi later.

I walk into a room with no more than 30 people in it. Screens are everywhere. I look around at the people in the room and quickly notice everyone has headphones on. "Why does everyone have on headphones?" I ask.

"Because we have to translate to them. They don't speak a lick of English."

My heart sinks once again. I have gone from thinking I was in the front row as Tony Robbins' guest to being in a room where Tony isn't even there and no one speaks any English. The hits just keep on coming. I feel the tears. The lump in my throat. Stay grateful, I say to myself.

The necklace saying Power Pavilion 2 hurts to wear. I'm so upset. I try to breathe. I say okay, I can make this work. I'm still grateful to be here. Through the resistance, I say, Thank You, Universe! In the meantime I go out to walk around the tables, and everywhere I go, someone wants to take a picture with me. I smile. I am still grateful. I accept the situation and let go of all resistance.

FROM A FLAT TIRE TO A FULL HEART

Five minutes later Tony Robbins comes onstage. I see him on the screen. I see the room with 7,000 people in it on the screen. I wish I was in there, I say to myself. I belong up there in the front with Tony but I accept this, I say to myself. The 30 people in Power Pavilion 2 are cheering and I'm trying to get into it but it's not working. I sit here and try to remain grateful for the gift. Then, Tony Robbins starts to speak. These are the first words out his mouth: "There is a woman in this audience who knows how to make things a must in her life. She got into an accident last night and got a flat tire."

I think, "Oh, how funny, there must be another girl here who got a flat tire."

Tony continues, "She called someone for help. This person said it's a sign you shouldn't go. It's a sign you should give up and not go to this stupid seminar. This woman decided to look at this differently, though. She said, maybe it's a sign to see if I will give up at every little bump in the road!"

Then something flashes on the screen—my name! My post. My picture. My flat tire. Tony Robbins says, "I'm not sure if she made it here yet but I want everyone here to stand up and give Carolyn Rim a round of applause!"

I'm staring at the screen in a trance. Did this really just happen? Someone says, in broken English, "Oh my God, that is you!" He points at me as everyone in the room realizes I'm the woman on the screen. I smile. I take a deep breath. I belong in the front. I stand up. I take this as a sign from the universe. I take off my Power Pavilion 2 necklace.

I walk into main room where Tony is. I think, I'm going to walk up to the front row with so much certainty that the security guards are not going to say a damn thing to me. I'm going to walk up there like I own this place. I make my move and tap on my heart. I can bend these walls with my mind, I say to myself. I spot Rohan Williams on my walk up to the stage and he hugs me.

"Rohan, I need your help. Walk with me to the front." He can tell I'm determined but a little bit scared and he can tell my heart is racing.

"For you, and only you, I will." We walk up to the front and he hugs me and tells me, "You belong up front, Carolyn."

I watch Rohan walk away and then I lock eyes with Tony Robbins. He is looking down at me. I turn around, maybe he is staring at someone else. I point a finger to my chest and mouth, "Me?" He smiles the sweetest smile I have ever received. He places his hand on his heart as he looks at me. He nods and motions for me to sit down in the Family and Friends section.

I place my hand on my heart and send gratitude. He continues the seminar. During times when we have to answer questions, he comes up to stage directly in front of me. Even people in the section were asking me how I know Tony. I look around and see that Hugh Jackman is actually sitting in my section. His name tag says Mike Smith. I'm blown away right now!

I grab my notebook out of my bag to start answering the questions Tony wants us to answer. I turn to the last open page of my notebook and I see I had written this down: "GET TO THE FRONT AND GET TO TONY AT UPW NJ." I knew I was supposed to be in the front because I saw it in my mind thousands of times before this day.

I wonder what would happen if everyone realized that they had this power. Of course, it was not all me. My angels were next to me the whole time.

The lesson I learned that day is not to give up at every little bump in the road. I learned that sometimes we hit bumps but we must continue to move forward no matter what. Sometimes those bumps in the road are leading us beyond our wildest dreams. We must believe that everything is happening for our highest good. Even in the moments when it doesn't look good, we need to have faith that everything is leading to something better.

That night, Joseph McClendon messages me, "I have a seat for you, doll. Come right up to the front, come backstage and we will give you your blue necklace and you are sitting in CSI front row. By the way—keep shaking that... well you know."

I smile when I see his text. I thank God. I thank God for all the magic of right now. I thank God for all these experiences I'm having. I thank God for the flat tire. I'm so grateful. I feel these overwhelming feelings of pure connection and bliss to my creator.

A VIP TREATMENT

The next morning when I walk in, I see Joseph McClendon on stage. He motions for me to go backstage. He points to me and says, "That's her, Rocky." Rocky is a beautiful redhead who is always on stage right running the show, and she leads me backstage.

Backstage was gray and curtained almost like in the Wizard of Oz. Then, Rocky moved the curtain back, I saw it looked almost like a home. There was a bathroom, a sink, and even a beautiful fish tank. "Wait here," Rocky says, smiling.

On stage, Joseph says, "Here's Tony!" and then I hear his footsteps as I wait in this magnificent place backstage. Rocky pulls the curtain back for him and says, "I found your girl."

I'm amazed at how calm Joseph is. He asks me right away how my divorce is going and how I'm handling it. I'm struggling with it. He says, "I understand. Have you picked a song to celebrate it yet?"

This confuses me. No one has mentioned anything about celebrating my divorce. All I have ever heard is horrible divorce stories.

He looks at me like a mentor and says, "Kid, you got to start to shake that ass and celebrate your divorce. It's over! You do not have to worry anymore. You don't have to fight, or be confused whether it will work or not. It's over. Now shake that ass and celebrate your victory!"

I feel like Wendy when Peter Pan came in the room, sprinkled pixie dust on her and said, "Follow me into Neverland!" Wow! Wow! Amazing Amazing Amazing. What a concept. To celebrate my break-up. I agree, "Okay I will start to celebrate, Joseph."

Rocky says through the curtain, "Two minutes, Joseph."

"They work me like a field whore here," he says. We both laugh at the reference. Joseph always knows how to make me smile and laugh. I silently say thank you to the universe, I give Joseph the biggest hug ever and tell him, "Thank you so much—you are helping me help many others."

"Remember doll, the best way to help others is to help yourself first and serve from your overflow, not from your cup." As Joseph pulls the curtain back, Rocky is holding my blue necklace and puts it on me. She gives me a sweet smile. I walk out of there so grateful for my blue necklace. I walk into CSI and I smile at all the beautiful people around me.

I look around and I feel the energy in the room. I love it. This space that

101

Tony Robbins creates is a space like no other; it is magically amazing and I love it. I will play full-out every day, every moment, all the time, I will give it my all this weekend!

I'm so grateful for this weekend. I met so many incredible people. One person in fact I will never forget—Sun Mary. I first saw her when we were dancing in CSI. She was dancing on her knees. She had no legs. I decided I would never be ungrateful or go into victim mode again. She has no legs and she is dancing on her knees celebrating life! I have never known a woman like that. Heck, I have never met any disabled person who celebrated life like she did. How dare I be ungrateful when this woman is dancing on her knees. I connect deeply with this woman. Gratitude, love and greatness all around us.

The event is over before I know it. Time flies when you are at a Tony event. I get home from this UPW NJ event. I feel so alive! I'm on fire and ready to light up the whole world.

"So many people will tell you 'no,' and you need to find something you believe in so hard that you just smile and tell them 'watch me.' Learn to take rejection as motivation to prove people wrong. Be unstoppable. Refuse to give up, no matter what. It's the best skill you can ever learn."

—Charlotte Eriksson

The following are posts from UPW groups, Facebook page, and Instagram.

POST BY BYRON INGRAHAM ON MARCH 5, 2015

Look who I ran into here at UPW New Jersey.

With Carolyn Rim. North Bergen, N.J.

This picture was on the screen at Tony Robbins Unleash The Power Within Event. The bumps in the road are not there to stop you, they are there to keep the people who do not want it bad enough out.

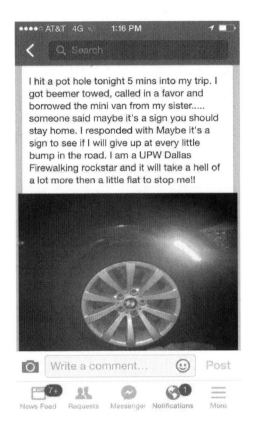

104

Spark Your inner Rockstar! Following that dream. At the Tony Robbins event in NJ. Excited. Life is too short not to Believe in yourself and Believe in your dreams. Give yourself permission to dream big and allow all the beautiful blessings into your life. Walked over fire last night with certainty!! Yes! It's amazing what you can achieve in your life once you realize that you have the choice to live your life however you please!! I decided to be a Rockstar and follow my dreams! So: What have you decided?

MARCH 7, 2015

My new belief is that a thousand unseen hands support me on my journey and I deserve the best life as to offer because I AM OUTSTANDING! Speaking of outstanding, Sage Robbins touched my heart today without saying one word. She and Tony kissed on stage and I could feel the love between them. They were beaming. Thank you both for showing me love like that exists, is real and it's possible. Tonight, I was able to show myself the same love I normally only show another. I loved myself with the same tingling chills you normally can only love another with. Now that I love myself fully, I can finally give and receive love and be impactful on the world!! The secret is self love!! I am a rockstar and so are you!! OWOOOOOOO!! Yes!

> *"I can finally give and receive love and be impactful on the world! The secret is self-love first."*
>
> **—Carolyn Rim**

MARCH 8, 2015

Definition of a Rockstar: A person who follows their dream and makes it become their reality. My next speaking event! Spark Your Rockstar!! My dream is to be a female Tony Robbins and transform the world with my energy!! LIFE WILL NEVER BE THE SAME!

MARCH 9, 2015

Dear UPW,

UPW NY gave me the courage to share this with you all. Hi. My name is Carolyn and I'm an addict. That is how I classified myself since 2006. I went to NA meetings where we talk about our problems and overcome our addiction. However, the meetings started to become something of a chore. I stopped going because I didn't like the environment I was in. Anytime I tried being my real shining self, I had to dwarf back down so they would understand what I was saying. I felt so judged.

Maybe it was because at the time I was judging myself. I'm not saying all meetings are bad because nine years ago these same meetings saved my life. I have also met some amazing people in these NA meetings, but I believe it's important to find people that are on the same mission as myself.

Then, I went to a Tony Robbins seminar and it all changed. I found people who were speaking my language like a rockstar. I found people who were climbing towards their dreams and people climbing to be the best versions of themselves. Four months ago after UPW Dallas, I decided I would not classify myself as an addict anymore but as a rockstar. It happened when I was on the phone with 20 bright shining Tony Robbins fans on the morning calls. I was about to share and whenever you share at an NA meeting—you say who you are and what you are. So when it was my turn to share on the call, I said, "Hi. My name is Carolyn Rim and I am a Rockstar! OWOOOO!" I howled like a wolf! Everyone on the call started cheering and clapping!

Since that day, I have started my own business, became a coach and built two websites. *I am*. Two very powerful words. Use them wisely.

My name is Carolyn Rim and I am a Rockstar. Thanks for letting me share.

> *"Trust yourself! Most important, dig deep down and ask yourself, who do you want to be? Not what, but who you want to be. I'm not talking about what your teachers, parents or peers tell you to be. I'm talking about figuring out for yourself what makes you happy no matter how crazy it might sound to other people. It is impossible to be a maverick or true original if you're too well behaved and don't want to break the rules. What is the point of being on this earth if you just want to be liked by everyone and avoid trouble?! Be bold and stand out! Be happy!"*
>
> —*Arnold Schwarzenegger*

MARCH 29, 2015

Dear UPW,

Close your eyes and think of three things you are grateful for every day. Studies show that those who take a few minutes every night to practice gratitude sleep better and how well you sleep determines the energy level the following day. It improves your mood and motivates you to keep going. If you want abundance in any area of your life, whether it be business/finance, spirituality/faith, or relationships, you have to start getting into the alignment with abundance.

Once you are in alignment, you will find yourself embracing avalanches of abundance and joy. You must practice gratitude daily for it to have the amazing effect it does. Today I'm grateful for you all and this UPW support. Thank you all for being unique. Thank you all for shining & being your own kind of beautiful. Good night.

APRIL 1, 2015

Dear UPW,

I show up every day with the intention of living my greatness. FEAR is a signal that I need to step forward and expand myself. I have so much support here and I believe that each and every one of us has greatness within us that is worth bringing out. Tony Robbins and Joseph helped me unleash the power within.

I believe in asking for help and support because, as my mentor would say, "Ask and you shall receive."

Like a stone being thrown into a pond, I want to have a ripple effect around the world. After a UPW event, ripples of love all over the world happen. Little acts of kindness bring sunshine into the world and make the big difference. I want to create that but make it my own.

I know having the goal of being the next Tony Robbins but female may sound crazy, ridiculous or silly to some. But to me, it sounds beautiful and vibrates through my being because my passion points to where I can contribute most in this world. The vibration of energy that courses through my body when I focus on inviting divinity's love in brings me to my knees thanking the universe for everything.

APRIL 7, 2015

Dear UPW,

I'm a motivational speaker and my next event is May 1, 2015. You can check out my website at www.SparkYourRockstar.com. The people who went to my first event have had amazing results already. One built a website and built a blog, another overcame procrastination and the other decided to follow their dream of owning their own business and quit their job! One person can make a difference! You're worth it! Invest in yourself and take the time to come to this event and you will get crystal clear on what you want in life in all areas! Whether it's business/financial, personal relationship, spirituality, health/wellness, you will get clarity. Stop the confusion and start celebrating life!

> *"When was the last time you did something for the first time? Spark your Rockstar and ignite a dream come true!"*
>
> —*Carolyn Rim*

Dear UPW,

I wanted to share one of my visions with you all. My whole life, I have always tried to make myself fit into someone else's mold of what I was supposed to be. I no longer try to be anything but myself. I no longer try to fit into a mold or idea of what someone else thinks of me.

I feel like I'm pulled toward my visions. I imagine myself taking a big bite out of this world and it tastes as sweet and juicy as a ripe peach!! I see the final outcome of what I want. The first one who has to see and believe it is me. I have to visualize it from every angle, design the house I want, the car I want, the emotions I want to feel consistently and daily. In descriptive detail I imagine my dreams coming true.

This is my vision about motivational speaking: I vividly visualize the final outcome, because my subconscious mind can't tell the difference between something vividly visualized and something that actually happened.

I walk onto the stage ... I feel my feet on the ground, and the vibration in between each step and the floor, even though it feels like I'm flying. I breathe in the energy and enthusiasm of the 5,000 people. All that lies between the crowd and me is the curtain, and my senses heighten as it starts to rise up and the crowd starts to cheer! They are shouting, "YES!" And they are dancing, singing and clapping. I feel my fists closing tight and I'm making my move, smiling, waving, and in turn they make a move as well.

I put my fist in the air and yell "ROCKSTARS! ARE YOU READY??!" The 5,000 souls chant "YES!" back at me! The words vibrate and reach the very core of my soul. I clearly hear the excitement in their voices for the seminar to begin. I start jumping up and down and the cells in my body ignite. The crowd starts jumping as well and we are shaking the building. I'm shouting into the mic and I say, "Double and triple the intensity—no matter what it takes! Jump higher, high five each other because you all are unstoppable, unbeatable and unbreakable! Yessssss!"

I imagine telling my stories and testimony and one by one the crowd awakens their hearts within to the gift they really are. I take them on a journey to bring out the best part of themselves. I transfer belief to them that anything is possible. The words vibrate and reach the very core of their souls.

I start dancing on stage and 12 gorgeous back-up dancers join me on stage and the cells in my body ignite. I have always loved to dance, and today I dance for love. I dance for God and I dance for them and they dance, too. Some of the people in the audience have not danced in years.

Then I say into the mic, "Ladies and Gentlemen, boys and girls, rockstars of all shapes, sizes and colors, "LET'S MAKE MAGIC! MY ROCKSTARS! ARE YOU READY TO DANCE ON STARDUST WITH ME? We go into this journey with angels surrounding us! Breathe in the magic, my friends, and feel every cell igniting like a beautiful firework in your soul! Out-do each other's energy! Yes! YES! YES!"

I imagine telling my stories and testimony and one by one the crowd wakes up to a higher consciousness. I take them on a journey to bring out the best part of themselves. I transfer belief to them that anything is possible. I help them ignite their light and spark the flame within.

> *"I have always loved to dance, and today I dance for love. I dance for God."*
>
> **—Carolyn Rim**

APRIL 10, 2015

I love to smile and laugh too loud. I love to dance, sing and write and share from my soul. I believe there is magic in kindness. I believe a thousand unseen hands guide me on my journey. I'm a coach, a motivational speaker, a mother, a friend, and I'm damn proud of who I am.

What if I stopped living my dreams because others told me it was impossible to travel the world to inspire and help people? No. I won't let that happen. I'm following my dreams and making me smile. I'm loving every passion and pursuing every dream and just being who I am feels amazing!! I realized I was stuck in a restrictive thought pattern so I decided to do what I always do. I meditated, visualized and remembered that I have the power of choice and by God, I get to choose who is in my reality!

I surround myself daily with superheroes, rockstars, firewalkers, champions and warriors. They say you become like the top five people you hang around. I'm so grateful right now that I'm surrounded by people like you. Keep being the protectors of the universe. Keep defending and protecting your dreams. Keep sharing your light even on the darkest days and nights. Ordinary people and an ordinary life does not interest me. Remember who WE are. We are the 2 percent. I stand before you motivated, inspired and on fire.

I pray you can feel my soul and beautiful energy from the words I use. I'm infused with infinite intelligence and have never felt stronger in my whole life.

"Today, celebrate you and who you are. You are one with extraordinary abilities and you make a difference in the world."

—*Carolyn Rim*

Chapter 9
The First-Ever Spark Your Rockstar Event

"It is the cave you fear to enter that holds the treasure that you seek."

—Joseph Campbell

I call my web designers and as much as I love them, their blogging site is not for me anymore. That's when I decide I would ask how much a site would cost. To build a site from scratch is $4,000. I do not want a lack of resources to be the reason I don't get my dreams. So I research and decide to teach myself how to code websites. Within two weeks, I have built my own website. Then I decide to launch my next event on May 1, 2015.

MY OWN SPARK YOUR ROCKSTAR EVENT

Who plans an event and posts its city and state without a place? ME! I again post the date and city of my next speaking event and put the $99 tickets on sale! Twelve people buy tickets and keep asking where the event is and I kept letting them know, no worries, I will get that information to them. I never doubt I will manifest a place. I cannot afford a place right now; however, I have faith and I send out gratitude as if I already have the place, just as I did before with my last event space I manifested.

I get to work and start contacting people I know in Media, Pa. I reach out to my old boss and ask if he owns any vacant buildings in Media, and if I can use it for that day and time. He emails back immediately and tells me he has the perfect place and I can have it and he won't charge me a dime. He believes in me and what I am doing. He says if anyone can make it against all odds, it's me. I then contact my friend Wes Mahon, who is in charge of video marketing for Medical Guardian. I ask if he will help me make a video about the fighting voices in my head—the good voice and the bad voice—for a very cheap price. He smiles and he says yes. Three days later, I have a marketing video to sell the Spark Your Rockstar event. Within 48 hours of posting my video, I have 40,000 views. People are going crazy over it and I all of a sudden have more than 600 shares of it.

And if that isn't enough, my friend Pam Dortone calls me and tells me her son will DJ my event for free. My sister calls and says she is getting tee shirts made and she and her friends will crew for me. She asks what the tee-shirts should say. I ponder for a moment.

I tell her:

"I didn't let_____get in the way of my dreams."

Fill in the blank and go after your dreams. Don't let anyone or anything stand in the way of your dreams! Send them to the universe and she will respond! Break the rules and be your own maverick. The whole universe is cued up and ready to give you anything you believe you deserve and believe is possible. Give yourself permission to dream big today. Know that your dreams deserve to come true.

THE DAY BEFORE THE EVENT

I'm awake all night working on the outline. I have worked on the PowerPoint for months but I wanted to work more on the worksheets that I handed out. I'm prepared and ready for today. I'm a little bit scared but so excited! It's 8 a.m. and I check my messages.

From Matt Smith: "Carolyn, I have no doubt that today will be a phenomenal event, because it has your name on it and your presence always offers phenomenal experiences, whether in person or on the phone. Many of us coming today know that you are a star at heart. Not only because of what you have done for others already by sharing your story, but most important the shining soul you have become and are

114

becoming. See you at 1 p.m. Keep giving the world the gift of just being you."

From Ana Conlin: "Hey Rock Star! Excited to meet you tomorrow. Carmel is riding with me. I connected with Carmel so we are making it a fun road trip with Tony Robbins CD's and UPW music the whole ride, smile. You ROCK!! If you like I can also do some video testimonials on my camera that you can then share later too. I love your energy and your passion. Keep shining—a year from today you will be on that Time magazine. If not that one Carolyn, then we will create one for Rock Stars only with you on the cover!! In my book you are a super star!! You will be great today."

From Carmel D'Arienzo: "Thank you for bringing out the rockstar in all of us. Your story touched me. I'm grateful and blessed I will meet you today!"

From Elizabeth Taylor: "I have decided to drive the 10 hours to come see you. Today is the day and you own this shit! Your vision is lighting up the eastern seaboard. YOU WILL SHINE TODAY! YOU ARE A ROCK STAR!"

I stare at the messages. I have 100 in my inbox and so many people are messaging me and telling me, "Dreams do come true." "You got this."

I'm so nervous but so grateful and excited. All of this love I'm receiving, I'm so grateful for, and I embrace it. I pack the rest of my things for my event and I'm ready to rock and roll.

I get to the event. I sit in the car for a while. I'm staring at the clouds in the sky. I'm overcome with worry for some reason, even after all the love. I'm so scared. What will they think of me? What if I'm not good enough? I close my eyes.

I hear a whisper from my heart. "When you be who you truly are and do what you truly love, the universe will applaud." I see myself in front of the 50 plus people I knew would be here today. I see myself succeeding. I see them clapping. I see us celebrating.

Then, I hear a bing from my phone. Ana Conlin and Carmel messaged me. They were on the way and sent me a picture of them in red clown noses. It instantly was a state-changer. I smile, and I send out gratitude for both of them. I get out of the car! I'm ready! I go into the back room and read some more of the many messages people were sending me. Jacob Thompson messaged me and said I was a superhero in his eyes and I would be great because I lead with my energy and my heart. My friend Heather MacDonald said that if we looked down in Philly today from space there would be an extra bright light shining. My sister, Brad, Pam, and Tye (my DJ) and everyone else sit there and rock out with me

115

as I'm getting ready in the back room.

When it is time to go on stage, my sister introduces me and I see my dad, my family, my friends, my clients, my supporters. I see magic in the room. I see Ryan Liberty and Martin Ponce, who actually surprised me by being there! I see Michelle Rader Taormina and Linda Lammie. I see so many incredible people in the audience! My mastermind (from a group of people who are my accountability partners) at the time is messaging me like crazy sending me love and encouraging me. I feel like everything is lining up just the way it should. My friend Mike Devito comes in before the show and is pumping me up. Sifu Terryann DeAngeles comes in and looks like a total rockstar. Everyone is there. My Aunt Sharon and Uncle Randy come. My friend Danielle Cline, Gabrielle Finch, Joe Malriat and Cherie are in the front row. Brian Fulginiti is there. Danny Benenfield is in the crowd, and has brought a friend. I see a man named Sanjay and his wife. Everyone is here to see me, and I run around the room high fiving people because if not I will cry, I'm so grateful.

All of these people are there to support me. They believe in me, I think. I believe in me. I am a rockstar. I breathe in the energy with all my being and decide to give it all I have today!

I ROCK it. I shine. I love every minute of it. We jump up and down. We shout. We affirm our goals. We visualize and meditate. We connect deeply and share dreams and write down new beliefs! We dance. We connect deeply. I unleash on stage. During one of the priming sessions, in which we breathe into our hearts and we move from our heads to our hearts, I see tears on my aunt Sharon's face as she feels the gratitude in her heart. That made me happy.

Before I know it, the final song is being played. I thank my family: Marybeth, Brad, my dad, my mom at the house with the girls, Grace and Kaylee, giving a day of sunshine up for me to make my dreams come true. I thank everyone for coming and we all celebrate!

Ana gets testimonies and we all connect deeply. I hug Elizabeth Taylor, who drove 10 hours to come to a four-hour event, and will drive ten hours home. I hug Carmel. I hug Ryan Liberty and Martin Ponce. I hug everyone. My dreams are coming true right before my eyes because of the love I'm opening up to receiving.

We all go to dinner to celebrate and I tell them my next event will be on August 7, 2016. They all agree to be there, too! I'm so grateful for this day.

After celebrating my successful event with these incredible souls I connect so deeply with, I go outside alone and look at the moon and the stars. I silently say thank you 100 times. I send gratitude and love into the universe for everything that has happened to me so far and for what I know is on its way to me.

I shed tears of happiness. I have never in my whole life been filled with such desire to live, to love, to give. I am truly inspired by the people who decided to invest in themselves! These are the people I have in my life. I could not help but think it only takes one bright star to light up a whole universe of darkness.

One of the lessons I have learned is belief in yourself is more important and valuable than all the skills in the world. If you believe in yourself and you believe in your vision, then you don't have to be pushed; your vision pulls you and you get results 100x's faster.

I learned that practicing humility and gratitude makes those around you feel incredible. I learned just how worth it I really am and I realized what you can make happen when you get around like- minded people. A ripple effect, just like a stone you throw into the pond, the people who attend my events will find peace among turmoil, start or continue the exciting adventure into self-discovery, and be a shining light onto others in need.

After awakening my heart, it will send ripples of love all over the world because the quickest way to change the world is changing yourself.

I'm thanking the universe for every prayer answered and unanswered. It has all been leading me to this moment.

"Belief in yourself is more important and valuable than all the skills in the world."

—Carolyn Rim

The following are posts from Facebook, my personal page and Instagram.

APRIL 10, 2015

Stand out. Push yourself to be the best possible version of you! The only thing stopping you from living the life of your dreams is the bullshit stories you keep telling yourself! If your life were a novel, you would be the star of it. If things are not going your way, know that you are the author, you are holding the pen and it's never too late to rewrite the story. Write it the way you want it to be, rather than the way it is. Every moment is a fresh new moment to step up and take a bite out of this world like the sweet ripe juicy peach it is! Lift off towards your dreams! Yes!! You can!!

> *"What lies behind us and what lies ahead of us are tiny matters compared to what lies within us."*
>
> **—Ralph Waldo Emerson**

APRIL 12, 2015

Ready... Set.... Spark Your Rockstar Event! Buy your tickets today! Check out SparkYourRockstar.com to buy your ticket today! It's never too late to start writing a new story. You are the author.... Tell the story of you winning.

APRIL 14, 2015

I'm understanding the difference between unsuccessful people and successful people. Belief in myself and in others is crucial to my success. My life has taken on new meaning since I made a move towards my dreams. I'm grateful I gave myself permission to dream big and spark my inner rockstar. Grateful to the amazing people I have around me that only lift me higher towards my goals. To me, the definition of a rockstar is a person who follows their dream and makes that dream a reality. A rockstar is someone who gives themselves permission to dream big. I can. I will. I did! I'm fulfilling my destiny! To constantly grow, approve, achieve, contribute and love. I'm the light in the dark, and I will continue to shine because it only takes one bright star to light up a whole universe of darkness. Shine on.

"Definition of a Rockstar: A person who follows their dream and makes that dream a reality."

—*Carolyn Rim*

APRIL 15, 2015

Dear UPW Dallas,

What vibes do you bleed into the world? Remember, whatever vibes you put out will come back to you, so make sure you are conscious of the energy and vibes you are putting out to the world. Vibes truly do speak louder than words, so be your true self, be authentic, be grateful and be a passionate example of the absolute joy that is available to us at any given moment.

APRIL 16, 2015

Dear UPW Dallas,

THESE ARE MY RESULTS FOR MY NEW WEBSITE! More than 8,300 people went to my website!

Yes! It's possible! Behind every fear is the person you want to be. I truly believe that the things that excite us and make us happy are not random. They are connected to our purpose. Follow them and be your true gorgeous, talented and fabulous self! You were put on this earth to shine and create your own wild, open hearted, custom- made path of happy. SOME THINGS ARE MEANT TO BE TAMED... YOU ARE NOT ONE OF THEM! FOLLOW ME INTO THE JUNGLE AND ROAR WITH ME! Shine on!

APRIL 17, 2015

Dear UPW Dallas,

I was feeling fear today. I closed my eyes on the train to work. I asked God to show me a sign that I would be okay no matter what. I open my eyes and saw this. I believe this sign was big enough. When you face your fears-the impossible becomes the possible. Step up, stand out and shine bright. Open your eyes. Behind every fear is the person you want to be. Fear is self-imposed meaning it doesn't exist. You create it, you can destroy it. You face your fears and you become the person you want to be. You run from your fears and you are not living. You are alive, but you are not dug in the freedom. You are not running the day; the day is running you. We all fall down in life. The question is who gets back up.

Overcoming negativity may mean breaking years-long habits of negative thinking, DOUBT, depression and stress. Start today down the right road to turning negativity around, and you may discover a beautiful world right in front of you. Don't let *you* talk *you* out of taking the first step. See the video at http://facebook.com/story.php?story_fbid+7838837411706954&id=1 000002560071023.

"Today will be the day you face your fears—not tomorrow, not next week, but right now, right here.
Never give up climbing to be the best possible version of yourself because ultimately it is the small steps that climb mountains."

—Unknown

APRIL 22, 2015

Dear UPW,

Tony Robbins inspired me change my life. Six months ago after I went to UPW Dallas. I quit my job, quit smoking, quit a toxic relationship, built and designed my own website, held my first motivational speaking event, am planning a second motivational speaking event coming up in two weeks, built my own coaching and speaking business...

Watch out world! Wait until I actually get the funds!! I did this without the funds, without the resources, all I had was a vision and a passion that was awakened inside me at UPW.

It's because of the people in the UPW Facebook groups that I didn't give up. They kept cheering me on and saw my worth, even if—at times—I doubted myself and my own worth as a being. No one can measure what is in someone's heart, and I'm going after my dreams with every ounce of my soul!! I believe 1,000 unseen hands guide me in every step I take towards my dreams. The more I share my soul the more the universe applauds. Now: These are beliefs I can get down with!

APRIL 22, 2015

I'm so grateful for these two. I'm so grateful for my family. Nothing would be possible without them. The shirts came in for the people I have crewing the event and they just look awesome!!

*"There is no greater gift you can give or receive
than to honor your calling. It's why you were
born. And how you become most truly alive."*

—Oprah Winfrey

APRIL 26, 2015

Dear UPW Dallas,

I'm sending love and gratitude to you all. This group changed my life. All because I went to UPW and realized I could make a positive difference in the world. So much has happened. My journey began with you all and continues with you all. I'm excited about my upcoming event in two weeks. Yes!

Wow! Just had to share this! Yesterday—someone asked how much my rates were to come and do a 30-minute talk to their sales team and organization! This is what it's all about!! I will be speaking on body language and how studies show that 80 percent of all communication is body language, and only 20 percent is actual words! I will also be talking about how you can "Fake it until you make it." Studies show that even just standing like Superman for two minutes actually raises your testosterone levels by 20 percent and lowers your stress hormone cortisol! Wow! I love what I do!! So excited!

APRIL 27, 2015

Dear UPW,

I did the math. One month. One month and I can quit my job and live my passion full-time. I celebrated by taking my little girl out to dinner and told her, "Guess what, baby? I achieved my goal."

Her eyes widened and she said, "You mean I don't have to go to aftercare anymore? I can ride the bus home with my friends at 3:15?"

"Yup." That was my Why. I wanted to spend more time with my little girl.

She cried in the beginning of the school year saying, "I don't understand why some moms work and others don't."

Well, tonight, my friends, I celebrated.

APRIL 28, 2015

Check out my new group, please—SPARK ENERGY! at

https://www.facebook.com/groups/SparkEnergy

The reason I created it is because I want to bridge the gap between regular people and self-development people. About 70 of my closest friends and family are on it. I figured that they could really use some support like I have, but I can't do it alone. I need your help.

I need rockstars like you all to be on it that are leading the way. It's all about promoting and supporting each other. I have never heard of anyone going broke by giving. In fact, in the past six months, I have tried to be as giving as possible, and I have received back love, wealth, and passion to go towards my dreams. I'm truly living my dreams, walking my talk, and just enjoying this wondrous life.

I believe there is magic in kindness. Spread some magic today.

APRIL 29, 2015

"I don't understand why some moms work and others don't," Kaylee said. She didn't understand why some kids get picked up at 3:15, and she has to stay until 6 p.m. I made a decision six months ago that I was going to be able to pick my little girl up at the bus stop at 3:15 like the other moms. I didn't care what it would take— I made the decision. She was and still is my Why.

Just wanted to say thank you to UPW, Tony Robbins, Joseph, and everyone else who has helped me in my journey. That was one of my goals. Well, last night, my friends, I celebrated. Excited to see what other blessings come into my life! Sending gratitude to all of you outstanding souls!

MAY 1, 2015

My event Spark Your Rockstar is tomorrow. I have never felt so ready for something in my whole life. Writing this post I have goosebumps, I feel the magic.

I have doubted myself, I have been beaten and broken only to realize I was the one holding the bat. I believe every human being has greatness within them that is worth bringing out. I have never been more excited or terrified in my whole life. I believe that is how you know you are making the right decision because what is found in between our deepest desire and our greatest fear is the true dance of life.

Sending gratitude for you all supporting me. And especially, for believing in me even if at times I didn't believe in myself. Ironically, my little girl's teacher asked me to come read a book to the class today. I chose a book about how important it is to believe in yourself. I picked my favorite book since I was a little girl, *The Value of Believing in Yourself! The Story of Louis Pasteur*. I read to the kids and had them stand like Superman. Priceless. Life is such a gift. The teacher grabbed some pictures that I'm forever grateful for. The look on their beautiful faces as they stood like Superman was magic.

MAY 2, 2015

Just spent time in meditation thinking about how many people I will have at the next Spark Your Rockstar event. Seeing 300 people in front of me and zip-lining!! It will be a full day event from 8 a.m. until midnight. Immersion, baby.

That's what it's all about. My dreams are coming true right before my eyes. My next event is in three months from now... Mark your calendars if you are ready to step it up to a new level of intensity and spark your rock star!! The excitement I feel!! I have already the name for it! SPARK ENERGY!

MAY 4, 2015

So many people have reached out to ask how the SPARK YOUR ROCKSTAR EVENT went, that I wanted to let you all know here that it was amazing. I must say the people who came were truly inspiring to me.

About 50 amazing people came. Ten of them drove five hours to the event, one woman drove 10 hours each way, showing not only love & belief in themselves, but also love & belief in me. All of them played full-out and rocked at a whole new level of intensity! What I learned from this event & from those who came is that belief in yourself is more powerful than all the skills you have.

My events will be exciting and unlike anything you have ever experienced. If you are ready to invest in yourself and see the greater return in your future, not only with wealth, but avalanches of abundance in all areas of your life, then you must come to the next one!!

My *next* event will have 300 people, teams, and zip-lining and will be all weekend long!! Tickets go on sale May 10 and MARK YOUR CALENDARS for the next seminar AUGUST 8, 2015! Come hungry and prepare to be inspired and unleash your inner ROCKSTAR WARRIOR!!

MAY 8, 2015

Just a normal Friday night. Sure it is. A normal Friday night, when I'm about to walk on fire with around 15 amazing people. I'm going through some major changes, some genuine breakthroughs, being honest with myself for perhaps the first time ever—all due to the amazing people who now fill my life. Surround yourself with those you want to become like and you will become that. Thank you, Michael Agugliaro and his beautiful wife and family!

MAY 12, 2015

For some reason, when I made this picture the voice in my head started laughing at me. "You will never be on the cover of TIME. You are nothing." I don't know how the voice starts. Maybe as kids it's all the critiques or people who told us we could *not*.

But then the good voice came in and said, "Why *not?* Why *can't* you be on the cover of TIME? Why *can't* you see yourself achieving your dreams and goals?" It's amazing what you can achieve when you truly believe in yourself. Belief in yourself conquers all things and you are halfway towards your dream when you believe it."

The good voice wins every time now, because I'm banishing the voice of doubt. Because ultimately it comes down to two things: Do I choose love or fear? People make decisions and they act from either love or fear.

Today I choose love for myself and others! I will be on the cover of TIME. I will shine so others may consciously let their light shine as well. Break through limiting belief patterns that keep you stuck in old behaviors! Once you break through it, your mind can never go back to its old dimensions!

"I'm going to show you how great I am."

—Muhammad Ali

MAY 13, 2015

Dear UPW,

Caught in the grips of an old limiting belief. Most of you know who I am and what I stand for. I wear my heart on my sleeve and shine bright like the sunshine. However, one belief I still cannot shake. I have this belief, due to growing up Catholic, that if you marry someone, you stay married to them, no matter what. Through thick and thin. Through storms, gray skies, blue skies and rainbows.

But, what if every day was a struggle? What if every day you were spiritually killing yourself by not listening to your heart? It reminds me of the story Tony Robbins told about making $600 million in one day, but going home that night and his wife at the time telling him he is too loud. He was miserable in his relationship. He decided he didn't want a life like that.

My husband left me shortly after I came home from UPW Dallas. He moved in with his mom and dad. He said his real wife never came home from Dallas, because I was forever changed by the bright light of UPW. In the past few weeks, he had tried to come home, saying he loves me. He said his mom and dad told him he could not stay there anymore and he just walked in and said he was moving back in, whether I was ready or not. However, I refuse to drown in his sadness anymore. He was telling me how shitty the cards were that God dealt him and how awful his life was because he could not be a body-builder anymore because of a heart condition he has. I tried to be compassionate for his dreams being crushed, but I just cannot stay in his space.

Meanwhile, back in my bat cave, I have never been more grateful!! I told him about my friend Sun Mary, a woman at UPW I connected deeply with, dancing on her knees.

I tried to explain to Mike about Sun Mary, about gratitude and how there is love and greatness all around us. I told him we get to choose where we put our focus, and what's wrong is always available and so is what's right. I truly feel in my heart that we are not meant to be unhappy.

He mocks me often for wanting to help people. He said, "Go pretend to help people! You better block me on Facebook before I tell people who you really are."

I asked, "Who am I really?"

He said, "You are a fraud. You can't even save your own marriage, but you think you can save the world? You think you will make a difference?"

I'm not saying he is a bad person because he is not, but I'm not the woman for him. He is an incredible soul inside and I understand that hurt people, hurt people.

He told me I was not allowed to go to Tony Robbins events anymore if I wanted to be with him, that I would give up Tony Robbins and the events if I really loved him. I begged him to go to a UPW with me, but he said he would not waste four vacation days on a Tony Robbins event in a million years.

I just can't fight this fight anymore. I feel so frustrated and just feel like crying. It's literally killing me. I'm stronger than this! I called my sister tonight and asked if my little girl and I could stay there until I could afford a place on my own. She said yes right away. So—I have to make this decision. He doesn't have anywhere to go, so it's either live with him or move to my sister's.

MAY 14, 2015

Dear UPW,

So, yesterday I felt a little sad. I have to make a big decision in the next few weeks that will change my life and also affect those around me. My sister saw that I was sad and not my normal, happy, shining self. I have to decide whether to move into my sister's or not. Mike's mom will not let him stay there anymore. Marybeth said, "I wonder what you would look like if you just followed your heart and trusted what your gut told you."

I got the biggest smile on my face, and I said, "Come outside, and I will show you what that looks like." Here we are at a fancy restaurant, Harry's Savoy Grill, and I started smiling and jumping up and down. I was thinking about trusting my heart—finally, listening to that voice that keeps speaking to me and letting me know to make the jump and to take the leap of faith! My sister changed my state, and she didn't even realize it!

After she took this picture, she showed it to me and said, "You've already made your decision. You just have to take action on it."

This reminds me of what Tony Robbins says: "How fast can you change your state?"

Snapping my fingers at this moment, saying, "Just like that!"

Dear UPW,

I have more support than a girl could wish for and tonight I decided to be fucking brave and break the pattern. I'm breaking the "rinse and repeat" pattern that I have been stuck in for 10 years. I left home tonight and came to my sister's. I packed what seemed like eight suitcases. I do not know what's coming next, and to be honest that excites me and scares the shit out of me. I'm definitely not interested in finding another man to fill the void. I want to take six months to a year and just enjoy my life's beauty and truly focus on my daughter and me.

> *"It is in the moments of our decisions that our destiny is shaped."*
>
> *—Tony Robbins*

Chapter 10
Moving into the Basement

"Mommy, let's create love."

—Kaylee Donnelly

I have a huge red suitcase and I am standing on my sister Marybeth's porch. I knock on the door with my daughter by my side. KK opens the door, and runs in to go play with little Gracie and Rosie, my two nieces. As soon as Kaylee is inside and out of sight, Marybeth quickly comes to the door. She can tell by the expression on my face, I am about to crumble. I fall to my knees. I am so hurt by this crippling love and I am so hurt that I allowed him to kick me out of my own house.

"Why does love have to hurt so much?" I ask, crying. I feel so overwhelmed with all these emotions I had never had before.

Marybeth picks me up and hugs me. I'm so grateful for this woman. I don't know what I would do without her. She has been my sister, my protector, my mom, my love, my heart. Marybeth is like an angel and you immediately feel safe in her presence. It's not just me— anyone she meets, she just right away makes them feel at home. I am holding on to her shoulders tightly as I continued to just sob. I have just allowed someone to kick me out of my own home. I am so mad at myself. Then KK comes running out on the porch and sees me crying and my sweet little girl, who starts crying, too, says, "Mommy, I want to go home."

I grab her and pull her into the love hug and we cry. Marybeth holds us both. Marybeth is strong and sturdy, and as I am crumbling within, she is the rock I need. Then Brad, my wonderful brother-in-law, comes on the porch and makes a joke and comes running towards us and embraces us all in a hug. Then Rosie and Gracie come in for a hug, too. We are all hugging and this crying session turns to little bursts of laughter at how funny we must look out here on the porch hugging. We all start laughing. Then, I wipe away my tears and we carry the bags in and I start unpacking in the basement.

As I'm unpacking things, I think about how *done* I am with my marriage, with this ridiculous rinse and repeat cycle.

My inner voice starts saying vicious things to me. "Well, well, well. You just let him kick you right out of your house. You better go back home and beg for him to stay with you. You will never be able to be alone, Carolyn. You are such a joke. You think you'll save the world? You can't even save your own marriage!"

I don't know how to find the off button to this inner voice that taunts me constantly. Why am I so scared to be alone? As sick and tired as I feel, somewhere I still love him. Or do I just love the *thought* of him? Being without him is so confusing. I feel my heart telling me he is not the one, but my mind keeps going over all the moments that were good in our life and none of the moments that caused pain.

I now begin to focus on everything I will miss about him. I stop focusing on all the reasons why I'm here unpacking suitcases in my sister's basement. I start thinking about the way he makes me laugh, the way he makes fun in this sweet way. The way he tries so hard to love me. He would do anything for me. I think about how much he loves me!

I stop unpacking as I see a picture that I had put in my suitcase. It's a picture of the whole family, Mike, KK and me at Disney World with Cinderella. I start crying softly at first and then I just start to sob but I don't want anyone else to hear me. I lie down on the bed and I shove my head in the pillow and scream into the pillow so others cannot hear my frustration, my anger with myself and my life. I'm stuck! I feel like I can't be alone. Why do I feel so scared? I'm so mad that I let him kick me out of my own house. How could I let this happen?

I think about all the things I need to get from the house still. All the things I bought that are mine! I'm so frustrated. I must stop thinking like this. I jump up but I don't feel as though I have control over my body. I run up the steps and tell my sister that I need to run to Mike's to grab more of my stuff. She says she will watch KK for me.

I get in the car. What am I doing? What is fueling my body right now? Anger. Frustration. I need nothing from the house, really, but somehow I'm pulled back there. Maybe I want to pick a fight with him. Maybe I need to tell him how mad I am at myself and him right now. I need a release maybe.

As I pull up to the house, I don't remember how I got here. I am so wrapped up in my mind and in my thoughts that I cannot even remember how I got here. What's wrong with me? Why am I acting this way? I was just crying into the pillow and now 40 minutes later I'm outside my old home. I stare at the next-door neighbor's kids playing in the yard. Kaylee should be playing with them.

What the hell is wrong with me? My anger is starting to build and is spiraling into something I cannot control. I can feel it. Nothing will stop the energy streaming through me. I cannot control my legs that seem like they are moving in slow motion again. Am I having another panic attack?

I walk into the house like I still own it. Mike is watching TV. I'm so upset right now I can barely take it. I stand directly in front of the TV. I demand he speak with me. "Hey, I'm *really* upset right now. We need to talk." He stares at me with kind of a side smile like he is enjoying seeing me so angry and fuming. He looks at me with those deep blue eyes and I know instantly it was a mistake to come here. Oh no, I say to myself.

He stands up and starts walking towards me. I say, with a much softer, more feminine voice, "I'm just going to grab my stuff I need." I turn and start to run up the stairs. It was just Mike and me in the house, which if you ask me was a totally dangerous combination. We were emotionally unstable and both a mess. I needed a release, though. *That's* why I was here.

How could I be so careless and stupid? I was feeling so low, I just wanted to feel the release of being close to him again for a moment. In the middle of all the anger, I was needing to be wanted. I was needing to feel like I was enough and loved. Plus there was a sexual synergy between Mike and me that kept me with him for 10 years, after all. It was like I was high when I thought about him sometimes.

He was my drug. He knew exactly what I wanted, when I wanted it and where I wanted it.

Why am I thinking like this? I'm spiraling again. I can hardly breathe. I feel like someone is sitting on my chest again.

As I walk into my bedroom and look around, I need nothing, I had already packed, so why am I here? I hear his footsteps coming upstairs. My heart starts beating really fast, and warmth spreads in my entire body.

What is happening? I allow this inner lustful energy or person to take over me. I allow this dark energy to take over my entire body. This is so wrong but it feels so right. He walks into the bedroom. I stare at him. He is looking at me up and down slowly. We lock eyes and I swear I can see his eyes dilate. I read somewhere that a person's eyes dilate when they look at someone who they find very attractive. I lick my lips, so ready for his.

He doesn't say anything. He slowly stalks toward me like a hungry wolf and I his willing victim. I often told him in our marriage I love the way he just takes me. It turns me on. He moves right in front of me. He wraps his arm around my waist and hoists me up onto him with one arm. I wrap my legs around him and my arms around his neck. We put our foreheads together breathing each other in. We know we can't resist each other at this moment. We know we don't work together. But we are like sexually charged magnets and connect instantly. I stare at him and he presses his lips against mine slowly and soft and then like he needs me. For the next 15 minutes the rest of the world seems to fade away while I jump down that rabbit hole of desire and lust and insanity. I love and hate every second.

When we are done, I am out of breath. Moving into my regular emotional home of sanity, I stare silently at the ceiling wondering how the hell I ended up here. We both quickly dress and get up. No cuddling or touching.

I think, shit, what's wrong with me? The mental verbal beating has already begun. Mike says he has to go to a friend's house and that I should take all the time I need to pack up whatever I need to take to my sister's. He leaves.

I'm sitting silently on my bed, which I bought him as a Christmas present and he now owns it. What the hell just happened? I text him and tell him we can't have sex anymore. He agrees it messes with our emotions too much. I'm a mess. I'm shaking.

I lean on the bed, and drop to my knees as if praying. I feel like I may throw up. I say I'm sorry over and over and over again to myself. Why do I keep doing this to my heart? I know he's not the one but I torture myself like this. I take deep breaths and slide onto the floor. I still feel like someone has ripped my heart out of my chest and I lay there immobile once again, like I have just been run over by a truck or something.

I pray. I close my eyes and ask my angels to come help me. Please help me resist the urges I feel inside my body for Mike. I close my eyes. Just for a few moments, I need to rest. I allow myself to fall into the dark abyss and swirling in a pool of shame and guilt.

I awaken 20 minutes later to my cell phone ringing. I'm jolted and sit up. I grab my phone. "Hello?" I say. "Hey, girl. When you coming back? KK misses you," says my sister.

"I will be there in an hour. Love you, bye."

I have to fake it. I must fake being okay. I decide to focus all my energy on my dreams and being the best mom I can possibly be. I will fake it until I make it.

In the bathroom, I look in the mirror and turn on the water. I just stare at myself for a long time and allow the sound of the water to lull me for a moment. Then I cup my hands and feel the cold water hit my skin as I splash it on my face a few times. I'm washing away the energy that does not serve me. Slowly my thoughts start shifting from beating myself up to loving thoughts. I vividly imagine that each time I splash the water I'm shedding skin like a snake does. I'm shedding the skin that no longer fits me. I feel better already.

I think about what Tony Robbins and Joseph McClendon taught me. If I can't, then I must; and if I must, then I can. I can. I must. I will. I can and I must, I tell myself. That was the last time, I decide. I'm raising my standards. No more. No more. No more would I disrespect myself like this. I will not let uncontrolled sexual urges be the reason I fail and don't get my dreams. Sex energy is the most powerful of all the stimuli that move people into action. Because it is so powerful, it must be controlled through transmutation and converted into other channels.

> **"If I can't, then I must; and if I must, then I can. I can. I must. I will. I can and I must.... I am raising my standards."**
>
> **—Tony Robbins**

I don't want to numb the raw pain that I feel; I want to transfer this raging raw energy into something productive. I know in my heart and soul if I continue to think about Mike, sleep with Mike, fantasize about Mike, then I will repeat the past and I do not want that. I have come full circle and it's time to let him go.

I drive back to my sister's, having stopped obsessing about myself and focusing instead on KK and my family. That is what's going to lead me out of suffering right now and into a beautiful state of mind.

I'm going to put all my energy into being a good mom and making my dreams come true. I'm in the present. Colors are looking more vivid. I feel more present with myself.

When I get back to my sister's, I pull KK downstairs and ask her if she was a little nervous about the move. She said, "Yes." I then explain to her that we can create the most amazing space, whatever we want, right here. It's our energy. My sister and I are planning to paint the next day and we have some paint brushes and white paint in the basement. As we stand there, just my little girl and I, I witness magic take place. My little girl looks down at the paint brushes and the paint cans. She picks up the paintbrush and bucket of white paint. She goes over to the wall. She dips the brush in the white paint and she starts drawing a heart on the wall. She says, "Mommy, let's create love."

My little girl has the answer. Love is the answer. Love for her, love for myself and love for the world. Love is so healing. It's the most powerful force in the whole universe, I think. Love always wins. Watching her draw the heart on the wall, I place my hand on my heart and breathe in the magic of this present moment. Something very special is happening right now. I feel my heart and I feel guided. I feel loved and protected. So loved. She smiles and comes over and hugs me. "I love you, Mommy." I hug her tightly and I say, "Aw, baby. I love *you* so much."

I feel like I'm not just hugging my little girl. I feel like I'm hugging myself.

I have learned by embracing the present moment and becoming one with it, merging with it, I began to experience a fire, a glow, a sparkle, a spark in my heart. I learned by contributing to others and being present and there for them, I can heal myself, too. I can share my heart with others, and even if it feels broken, only by letting others in will my heart mend.

> *"By contributing to others and being present and there for them, I can heal myself. I can share my heart, and even if it feels broken, only by letting others in will my heart mend."*
>
> *—Carolyn Rim*

So my little girl and I are getting our new home ready at my sister's and she was a little nervous with being in the new place. I explain to her that we can create the most amazing space, whatever we want, right here. It's our energy. My little girl looks at the paint brushes and paint cans. She goes over to the wall. She dips the brush in the white paint and she starts drawing a heart on the wall. She says, "Mommy, let's create love."

Chapter 11
Becoming a Full-time Rockstar

"Sometimes the universe will grant your wish
sooner rather than later and you must be ready
to embrace it."

—Carolyn Rim

I stare at the screen at work. I have three clients booked that day. I am getting so many messages on Facebook from people I'm coaching that I am having to schedule some appointments during my workday. I put my headset on and sneak under my desk so others won't hear my conversation with my personal coaching clients.

I am 30 minutes into my session with one of my clients when I hear a knocking on top of my desk. I peek out, muting the call. Gene smiles at me, shaking his head at me. No one has really said anything to me about my calls. Gene says, "Carolyn, come to my office when you are done that call." I say I'll be right in, in 20 minutes.

I continue with my client. "Please continue, Nicola, what were you saying?" I am on the phone with someone who doesn't know how to reach her dreams, her craving. My job has become helping people love the life they have now, while building the bridge to the life they want. I have become so good at seeing how people are getting their needs met on lower lying levels and helping them break out of the old belief patterns. I use simple visualizations, meditations, and NLP to help others break their patterns with others and I show them how to change their state instantly.

I also show people kindness and love. I tell them they needed to fall in love with themselves. They need to show themselves compassion and love, especially when they mess up. Instead of beating themselves up, they need to forgive themselves and learn the lesson.

A great mentor once told me, if you are not making mistakes than you are not trying hard enough. So I share all of this gold with my clients and they are loving it! Most understand and love the language I use. The ones who don't still join the rapidly growing Facebook community I am building. I am growing so quickly and am getting so many messages that I am helping others just by being me and doing what I love.

Twenty minutes later I get off the call. I walk into where Gene is standing in the Superman pose. I cannot believe what I see. Jeff, the owner of my firm, is standing like Superman, too. I smile because I stand that way with training groups here. Gene has had me go into every meeting and training session to get the energy up in the room! They even started calling me Spark Plug because they said everything I touched would light it up. They make me feel so good about me.

As I watch both the owner and the boss stand like Superman, I ask with a smile, "What's going on?"

Gene starts, "Carolyn, we have seen you grow here. You know we think there is no better sales person when you are focused and on, but in the past few months, it's clear to see your heart is somewhere else. We are going to give you a choice to leave, because we feel your dreams deserve your full heart."

I have been expecting this, but not until much later. True, I haven't been getting as many sales. "But I'm scared," I say.

Gene pulls the numbers. "Kid, listen, we will pay you unemployment. This is your heart. This is your dream. We wouldn't do this for just anyone." I hug them both.

In the human resources office I sign the necessary papers. This seems so sudden but I know this is all just a path leading me to what I really want. Magic is happening all around me.

I get outside on Market Street in Philadelphia and walk as slowly as I can, savoring in the last walk home. I look at the homeless people and give them money, like I normally do. But everything seems to be moving in slow motion. I wonder if Superman sometimes saw things in slow motion. I stare at the trains streaming by me. I get on the train home to Media.

That night I share with my family at the dinner table what happened. They are also stunned by everything that seems to be taking place as if by magic. That night I thank God for all the blessings in my life and for all the blessings coming into my life.

The lesson I have learned is sometimes the universe will grant your wish sooner rather than later and you must be ready to embrace it with all your heart.

The following are posts from this time.

MAY 20, 2015

So I took a picture with Santa at work in December and I just received this message from him. Listen: SHARE YOUR STORY! You never know who will be inspired by your posts and your passions. This is why I do what I do! Santa doing the Superman pose? That rocks!! He asked me not to use his real name... Because, after all, he is Santa!

May 20, 2015, 10:50 AM

Good Morning Carolyn!!! I meet so many people during the holidays as Santa Claus. Most, I never get to learn their story. You just never know how one picture tag could change your outlook on life and the future. I wake up daily now looking forward to your posts, videos, etc. They inspire me, they motivate me, I'm doing the friggen superman pose for goodness sakes! 😊 I just wanted to say thank you. Thank you for getting your picture with me, thank you for allowing me to follow you on social media, and thank you for being you and inspiring SO many people! Have a great day!!!

MAY 21, 2015

GUESS WHAT?!?! I get to pick my little girl at the bus stop now!! Yesssss!

Today something magical happened. So for the past eight months, I have been working on my dreams during my job and after my job. I was

143

scheduling coaching calls under my desk at work. I was constantly working on the site and giving only half of my energy at Medical Guardian. My bosses called me into the office today. They were both standing like Superman when I walked in. They said, "Carolyn, we love you and if you want to stay and work here you can, but we can tell your heart is somewhere else. We think you should leave to be a ROCKSTAR full time. Don't worry, we will still pay you unemployment until you can be on your own." I started to cry. They did the Superman pose with me one last time before I left.

Yes!! Anything is possible if you believe it is!! Seven months ago, my little girl was mad she couldn't ride the bus home with her friends. I made it a must that I would be able to spend more time with my little girl and work less! Now, seven months later, two events and 23 coaching clients later, working harder than I have ever worked before, and I'm able to leave my job and do what I love full time!!

Most people don't know what they want, so that's why they end up in someone else's visions. Just decide! Decide who you want to be and take action!! Check out my website for more tips on how to create permanent change in your life!!

http://www.sparkyourrockstar.com

MAY 25, 2015

I cleaned out my desk at work, since Thursday was my last day. I was unloading the box today and I found this paper. I stared at it in disbelief. OMG, I thought... It works. I'm now a full-time life coach and motivational speaker. I'm able to spend so much more time with my little girl. And, I'm helping people from all over the world! I have one of my clients in New Zealand and one in London and several all across America! I'm planning my next successful event!

I mean, come on, let's be honest here. Someone tells you to write down something on a piece of paper and it will come true, and at the time you think, "No way—impossible."

But, I did it anyway because what did I have to lose, right? And, of course it's so much more than just writing it down, but that was the first step—writing down what I wanted my life to be like.

When's the last time you allowed yourself to just write down what you wanted?

I used to say to myself, "Well, I can't go after what I want because I didn't have the money." BS! I have created my coaching practice and events with practically nothing! Don't allow a lack of resources to be the reason you didn't go after your dreams. I used to say, "Well, I have no free time at all to pursue my dreams." Lie! Wake up an hour or two earlier or go to bed later! All you need to do is take one small step towards your dreams every day because ultimately, it's the small steps that climb mountains.

Stop dreaming about living the life you desire and start living it! Today is the day. You are the author and you write your own pages. I'm so happy and grateful now that....

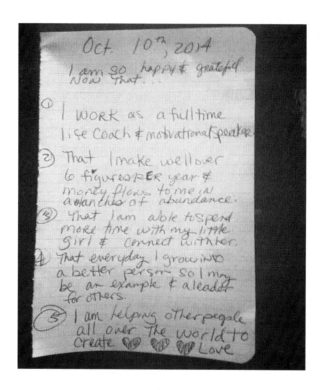

"Don't allow a lack of resources to be the reason you didn't go after your dreams."

—Carolyn Rim

Since moving in with my sister, we have joined the Riddlewood pool. Kaylee and I are there, and she runs over to me and says, "Mommy, I want to jump off the high diving board but I can't until I take the test. I'm ready to take the swim test. I know I can do it."

I say, "Baby, that's something you do in the beginning of the day, not the end. We have been here three hours and you're tired—there is no way you can do it now."

I look at my little girl's face and realize I just told her she couldn't do something—me, her mother, the one who preaches to people all day long that anything is possible. My little girl looks up at me and says, "You told me I could do anything if I believe I can, and I believe I can."

I get tears in my eyes because my little girl teaches me lessons daily, but this one strikes a chord in my soul. I say, "Kaylee, I believe in you too, and I know you can. Let's do it."

I watch my little girl jump in the pool and put on her goggles. She looks up at me through the goggles. I point to my heart and then point to her and tell her today is her day. I can see by her nervous smile that she needs a boost.

I say, "Kaylee, I got you, baby. Just promise me you will give me your best."

She says, "I promise, Mom," as she points to her little heart, "to give it my whole heart." The lifeguard comes over to do the swim test. She has to swim two laps and then tread water before taking a break.

The whistle blows. I see my little girl start swimming and she is slow but she is steady, doing freestyle. I am walking along the pool clapping. "Come on, baby!" I say. "You look great! You're almost there!"

About a lap and a half in, she looks at me through tired eyes and shakes her little head and starts swimming towards the wall to give up. I have been cheering her on and running alongside her this whole time, and I am not about to let her give up on herself so easily.

I say, "Kaylee, I will not allow you to give up because I *know* you can do this! Now, you have a half a lap to go! Now, kick those little legs and get to the other side!! You can and *will* finish this! I BELIEVE, BABY."

The two lifeguards are stunned. My little one gives me a huge smile and somehow she finds the strength to keep moving. Her little legs kick faster and faster until her hand finally touches the wall. The lifeguard looks at me and smiles. A small crowd has formed at my loud cheering and as Kaylee gets out of the pool, they clap for her. She has the biggest smile. She's tired, but smiling. We give each other the biggest high five ever.

146

Then I point to the diving board and say, "Your trophy awaits you, little champion." She starts running over to the diving board and stops. She looks back at me and comes running back to give me a squeeze and then runs back over to jump off the diving board.

As I watch her jump off, I realize opportunities to make a difference are all around us, usually in the little things. Everyday tasks may seem meaningless but they are the core moments of our life that can be the difference between believing in ourselves or not. Everything we say and do matters. I will never again doubt my little girl when she tells me she is ready for something. My rockstar warrior heart goes BADA BOOM for my little girl.

"Opportunities to make a difference are all around us and usually they are found in the little things. Everyday tasks may seem meaningless but they are the core moments of our life that can be the difference in believing in ourselves or not."

—*Carolyn Rim*

Chapter 12
The $30,000 Lesson

*"Once you make a decision,
the universe conspires to make it happen."*
—Ralph Waldo Emerson

I have become part of a Facebook group that inspires me to grow, and teaches me a lot. On May 28, 2015 I receive an intriguing message from a stranger. "You should have Jairek Robbins speak at your next event. I can connect you with him. Let me know if you are interested. He can really help you get to the next level with your events."

Events and virtual worlds come sliding together in my mind like a magical, beautiful firework. Jairek was doing a 90-day challenge at the time and I was a part of it. We had calls once a week. We loved the lessons and all the calls. And—wait a second—that's a great idea, because now we can make a live event!

"Okay, connect me!" I say.

I speak with Jairek. He explains, "Carolyn, it's a lot of money to hire me—are you sure you can handle it?" I go over the numbers with him. If I sell 300 people at $99 per person I will make $30,000 so I will have plenty of money to pay him and make a nice profit. I am a total rockstar when it comes to this!

Cut to 33 days after that message and call. The exact date as I stare at the calendar makes me sick to my stomach. It's July 1, 2015. The spiral of bad decisions that leads me to right now makes me cringe. I have one month to come up with $30,000. I don't know how I have done this to myself. This has been by far one of the most awful summers ever. I had to leave my home, move with my little girl into my sister's basement. And to top it all off? I was working all the time. I have gone from on top of the mountain to the low valley so quickly. What were the exact steps I took to get here?

1.   Hiring Jairek Robbins when I didn't have the funds. He did his best to help me, went above and beyond and was a Fort Knox of information, but I had no skills as a marketer or event coordinator and I was in a unresourceful state so there was no way I could pull it off, I thought. I was not taking action the way I should have. No matter who is working with you, no matter what teacher or coach, it comes down to your taking action.

2.   I didn't do any research on the event space. I chose the first one that gave me the first price. The Franklin Institute was $10,000 and they gave some to charity so I right away thought that was great. Another $10K in the hole.

3.   For the event dinner, I was required to use the vendor the institute used and the bill would be $6,000. What the hell was I thinking? Without any tickets sold, I was more than $25,000 in debt.

My friend Tom Vincent DeVietro is worried and comes to see me, asking, "Carolyn, how long have you been in your sister's basement by yourself?"

"Three days. I feel like I have spiraled into a dark hole. I have to focus on the event, so I don't go outside. I work all the time," I say.

"Isolation is deadly," says Tom. "Come with me." We go to his gym and work out. I feel better already. Just getting outside and getting some sunshine feels so nice.

I go home to my sister's and have dinner with the family and then I spend some time with Kaylee. I tell her how sorry I am about not spending time with her. I explain to her when I first start my own company, I thought owning my own business would be easy and I thought it would be less work. I had quit my 9-to-5 only to start a business that would consume my every waking moment. I tell her I will plan a trip where we can go swimming with dolphins together. So I start going on and on about swimming with dolphins and how amazing it is going to be.

She says, "Mom, that sounds good, but why don't we just color together?" I look at my little girl. She has all the wisdom right inside of her. She is living in the present moment and that is exactly where I want to be.

After a day out of isolation, I start taking action like crazy. I had hired a guy to help with marketing, advertising, and my event. Let's call him Bill Johnson. He was very mean to me. He said I was not resourceful, and that I was a failure. He would constantly yell at me. I paid him $1,000, and he helped me set up my webinar and did help with a plan of action but it was too much all at once. With no marketing skills at the time I was shark bait. One day while Bill was yelling at me, he said, "You know what, sorry but this event is going to bury you. You are so un-resourceful and you really fouled up this event. I will not stay on this sinking ship." Then he got on to his Facebook group and disparaged me, my programs, my events, and my whole brand. I had spiraled even deeper into a depression and then I just snapped.

I decide: In spite of this, my event is *going* to happen. I don't care what it takes.

I put this event before my family, before myself, before everything. But when you want to make something happen, you *have to* become obsessed. It's not something that comes easy and this event comes with great sacrifices. The obstacles are not there to stop you; they're there to stop the people who don't want it bad enough. And right before you succeed, you may feel incredibly defeated and not sure you can go one more step.

AN INTERVIEW WITH MY MENTOR

I call my mentor Joseph and tell him I don't know if I can pull this event off. He says, "Kid, you can either get up off your sister's basement floor and go make it happen or you can stay stuck in a web of your own bullshit."

I start laughing when he says that. He always makes me laugh. He agrees to do a video with me. Now I am again excited!

I interview Joseph and his interview has been watched by more than 4,000 people. It has helped many, many people, since it has many gems in it. Here is a transcript, edited for clarity:

Carolyn: You are such an inspiration to not only myself but to so many other people out there. I want to talk about not giving up. A lot of people get to a certain point and they just give up and they go back to settling. If someone you know is on the fence and they want to give up, what tips or tools would you give them?

Joseph: Well as fundamental as this is, I am going to start at the basics. Number one, know where you are going or know your outcome; look where you want to go or focus on your outcome. Even in what we are doing right now, it's important to always go back to that: What do I want? What am I after? What is my goal?

Our entire nervous system is designed to go where we are looking at, with our eyes open or our eyes closed. Your body can't tell the difference between what's real and what's not when you vividly imagine. So that's always number one.

Carolyn: What would you say has been the biggest motivator for you?

Joseph: Well, obviously the goal is a great motivator. However, it's a short-term motivator. In other words, if you always remain focused on what you want you are going to feel better in that moment but that doesn't keep you going. Then you always have to keep going back and reminding yourself. But what keeps our drive, or our *pull*, is our reason or reasons Why.

Figure out ahead of time what you're doing because that's what pulls you. It's not how, it's not even the goal itself—say you have a really strong goal or a really strong reason to go to the gym, to lose weight. Or you want to make more money or get up early or stay up late. When you think about it, you are all excited about doing it but when it comes down to doing it, we all make excuses and we rationalize ....

But, what comes from the internal are the reasons to have a better life for your children or because you want to buy your mum a house or whatever it is, your reasons why are your reasons Why. But if you focus on those secondly—this is what I want and this is why I want to do it— and you do the work to put that why inside, then you are driven. Then you are pulled into the future.

I always say, would you rather be dragged kicking and screaming into your future or gently pulled by something that makes you feel good? Obviously the second is the preferred.

Carolyn: I love that analogy of being pulled, it's almost like you are being placed in a sling shot into your future but the Why is so important. As soon as you said Why, my little girl came to mind, because she is my Why and has motivated me to keep going with my events even though it's been hard, to keep going with my separation, with everything that's come about in my life just to keep going.

And I am so excited that you took time to speak with us. I love it with the basics on just focusing on what you want and why you want it and really get that Why inside. And because the brain can tell the difference and it will push you. So I wanted to see is there anything else that you

152

wanted to say to viewers?

Joseph: Yes, there are a few. The first is you have got to *do* something. In other words, you know people say, 'Well, you have got to take action.' I agree. Remember action is only temporary, action is doing something once or twice and getting a little result but I say you have got to have activity. Activity is action repeated until you surpass your goal. In order to do that, once you know what you want, then you have to get a plan and then you have to *do* it.

And then once you do it, the fourth step is notice what you are getting and then praise yourself as well. If you go to the hard stuff and you get to the end and you go and 'Oh, that was hard,' then your nervous system goes 'Boy, that was hard and I don't want to do that again.'

But if you get to that place and you go "Boy, that was hard and I did it, I am unbelievable," then pat yourself on the back and slap yourself on the ass or whatever, then your nervous system says 'Hey, I got rewarded for the hard work.' and then starts what I call a cybernetic loop. You call that your reason, your number one, your reasons why, then you take more activity and you keep on going.

And then the last step: always praise yourself. So steps are: know what you want and focus on it; know your reason why and focus on it; have activity; notice what you are getting; and praise yourself. If you do those things, then it's certainly not guaranteed that you only have to do it once, it's like anything else. It's the rehearsal it's the practice over and over that makes it all work.

Carolyn: Well, repetition is the mother of all skills so I am sure the more you do it, the more you are programming.

Joseph: What's the father? It's a great thing and everybody knows that, what's the father?

Carolyn: I don't know, you tell me.

Joseph: The answer, my friend, is the catalyst to all human perpetuated growth. The answer is praise, the father is praise. Repetition will get you where you want and that will build a habit.

I am determined to show him and everyone else that I can do this. I start to notice what my daily habits are and my self-talk. What am I saying to myself? Well I am saying things like, "This is impossible. No one is going to buy tickets. How am I going to sell 300 tickets? I am worthless." I decide to make a video to help myself and at the same time help others understand how important self-talk is.

I research for hours the best three tips to improve inner self-talk. I then grab my camera and make a video. I know the more visible I become, the better.

Here we go, I say and I go live on camera.

"Hi, everyone. My name is Carolyn Rim. Today I want to talk about words. Your words matter. Everything you say to yourself, everything you think is manifesting itself right now in your reality. Let me ask you a question: What would you hear if you listened to yourself for an entire day? People speak all the time but only a few realize how their thoughts, emotions and words manifest in their outside reality. Simply put, your words become your life.

"Let me say that again: Your words become your life.

"The words you choose influence your perception and shape your reality. You communicate in many different ways and improving your communication skills will help you change your entire reality. So I want us to put on our rockstar reality architect hats on and I want us to go over three tips that are going to really help you start the process of changing the way you speak to yourself and the way you speak to others.

"Tip number one is: **Practice positive mind programming.** This is huge. Thirty to 40 minutes each day, listen to something that is positive, inspiring, like a TED talk—you can get them free on YouTube. Every single day, listen to something that motivates you, something that gets you going, something positive. Let me ask you this: Have you ever thought about something you wanted but it seems so ridiculously out of reach that you talked yourself out of having it? This is where these positive messages really play a part, because those external voices start to play a part in the story. They start to override the negative voices in your head, so program yourself with positive messages, okay?

"Tip number two is: **Read 15 to 20 pages of an inspiring book every single day.** That's right, every single day. This is a seven day a week thing. Now you have two avenues: audio and visual.

"Two pathways are forming with really positive messages. Once you create these patterns in your mind you are going to interrupt your story of telling yourself that you can't do it, that you are not smart enough, and that you don't have enough money to go for it. It's all lies, all of them. You can be, do and have whatever it is you want in this world, anything. Don't think that you are selfish for wanting it, there is a reason that you want what you want—it's deeply connected with your purpose, so follow your heart.

"Tip number three is: Invest time in yourself. This is self-awareness, which is a crucial component to your leadership, and to your success, to being able to talk to yourself in a genuinely positive, loving way. Most of us talk to others in a positive, loving way but not to ourselves.

"Let me tell you, this is going to be a positive programming that you are doing to yourself.

"These are three easy tips that are going to start this process. Try to step outside yourself and see things from a new view. Close your eyes, step outside yourself and look at your life: Are things the way you like them to be? No? Change them. Write down the way you want your life to be. Don't give one speck of mental energy to how it's going to happen, just focus on what you want because we are fundamentally driven by our vision. You must see it in your mind and then it will manifest itself in your reality.

Start understanding how important your words are. Speak reality the way you want it to be, rather than the way it is and you will make your dreams come true."

Comments start pouring in from Facebook. Everyone loves the video. They love it because they say it is so relatable. I continue to humanize my brand. Just being me and sharing what I have struggled with is helping others.

THE BALL IS ROLLING

I then hire Ana Conlin, an *angel*. She stands up for me when I feel I am not able to myself. She gives me tips and tools about events and selling and speakers! She works every day with me for 30 days and helps me get in touch with some of the speakers and make this event a success.

I surround myself with amazing people like Matt Smith, Scott Niolet, Martin Ponce, Ryan Liberty, Elizabeth Taylor and Carmel D'Arienzo. My friend Martin buys $1,600 worth of tickets. Then my friend Carmel buys a ticket and even though I later ask her to speak, she never asks for her money back. All of these people just start to give.

Jairek Robbins helps me, too. He gives me amazing marketing techniques online. As soon as I have all Jairek's secrets, I go to work! He even runs an ad for me on his Facebook page. I start taking action. I make the front page of the local paper too!

I call everyone I know to get them to buy tickets. That's when I call Marie and Bill McAfee. They have been my friends ever since I worked at Mid Atlantic Waterproofing with them. "I need you and Bill to buy a ticket to my event," I say, and Marie immediately agrees.

To sell tickets, I message 10 people a day on Facebook I don't even know, inviting them to the event. Then I call Joe Malriat and Cherie. My mom calls every single relative. I mean everyone. I even call my ex-boyfriend Tim's parents, with whom I remained friends. Anna Conlin tells me to tell every speaker they have to bring five people to the event.

Orders for tickets slowly but surely start flowing in. I feel like I am in a dream and I'm selling tickets like crazy and when game day comes and we add everything up, I have $15K, so I borrow the rest.

My sister Marybeth gets me an interview with the local newspaper. Not only is she housing my child and me, she is helping me make sure this event is successful. And the day after my birthday, July 29, 2015, I get one of the best presents ever: I make the front page of the paper, the *Delco News Times*.

A WHIRLWIND EVENT AND A CHANCE ENCOUNTER

Then the event comes and I am grateful! Jairek flies in and speaks with everyone at the event. He even takes me to dinner on Friday night. We connect and we talk. He shares such valuable information with me, about the reasons some relationships don't work out: Everyone comes to a relationship with a different set of rules. For instance, a woman might come to the relationship with the rulebook to the game of Life, while the man might come with the rules to Monopoly. No wonder they clash, because each has his or her own expectations of the way life *should* be. This makes perfect sense to me. Jairek has been worth every penny and more. He evens pays for dinner.

After two long months of hard work, Saturday comes and Carmel kicks off the event and everyone comes on and crushes it! I walk everyone through the Empowering Dickens Process, which is going in to the future and seeing what your future will be like if you continue to do the same things you are doing today.

I ask everyone if they have the strength and the power to play full-out this weekend. I ask if people are willing to be vulnerable. I tell them:

"I have never been this vulnerable but I didn't come here to hide the most beautiful part of myself. If I fail, I try again, and again, and again, and again. I will never stop trying until I succeed and that's why this event is even taking place right now.

"But in my life, I fall down, and I feel like I don't have the strength to get up sometimes. And I pretend that everything is okay, and I keep striving forward, being pulled towards this destiny that awaits me, by this passion that swirls in my soul. I promise all of you, my Why—my little girl—and myself, that if I fail 100 times, I will get up 101 times. I will never stop getting up, it doesn't matter how many times I get knocked down. And every time I get knocked down, I experience pain, but it's actually good, because whenever I have jumped into action, I have had to change the way I view myself, I have had to change my behavior, I have had to change my discipline, I have had to change my focus, I have had to transform into something I wasn't.

"You all are going to embark on a journey this weekend.

"You can embrace your pain. You can make your pain spark your transformation, to elevate you. I am constantly evolving and it's bringing me more satisfaction then I can put into words. Happiness in life is not by what you get or the amount of money you make; it comes mainly from the person you become on your journey toward your evolution.

"I know what my destiny tastes like, what it feels like, looks like, sounds like, smells like, I am holding it in the palm of my hand without it being here yet. I have never been more grateful for this moment. I realize as I begin to feel like I deserve it, my passion and goal is so strong that the fears don't matter.

"What are the things that you fear, that have been keeping you from going for your dream or from doing things that you would like to do? You must dance with your fear and stop resisting it. Allow it to pretend it has you... And just when your fear thinks it has won, you continue to move forward, towards your greatness.

"This will not be easy, there will be moments you will feel like you just want to collapse and there will be moments you don't want to face the world but you need to just keep moving forward. You need to embrace the pain, because the pain will push you towards your greatness, towards your destiny.

"You can either live your dreams, or live your fears.

"Decide to dance. Decide to dance with your fears and move towards your greatness.

"Behind every beautiful thing, there has been some type of pain."

I tell everyone to grab their boards and write all the reasons they have not been successful—the reasons they are not in shape, they still smoke, they didn't take care of themselves. I ask them to go through the Empowering Dickens Process by going five years, 10 years, 20 years in the future. We look at where they will be if they continue on the same path and continue to not make changes. Would they be 90 years old sitting in their rocking chairs one day regretting not taking a chance on their dreams? Where will they be if they don't take action. I ask them to look in the mirror 20 years from now. Are they okay with their bodies, the baggage they carry?

Everyone in the room has tears falling. This is an emotional process but a necessary one for change. Then I have everyone stand up and get into a state of certainty. I ask them to remember a moment they felt confident. I ask them to remember a moment they were proud of. I ask everyone to stand like Superman and then we break those boards with our bare hands!

We break free from it all! All the beliefs that haven't served us, all the things we have told ourselves that no longer serve us are dissolved! It is a magical process! Jairek Robbins speaks and does an outstanding job, as do Ana Conlin and Elizabeth Taylor.

Sunday morning, Chris Voss, the FBI's number one negotiator for 24 years, speaks. Then, during Frank Clark's speech, I jump up to use the restroom and am stopped dead in my tracks. There stands my ex-husband, Mike, with tears in his eyes, hungover and probably still drunk. He walks up to me and says, "I support you, this event and I love you and I want our marriage to work."

Hugging him, I smell the booze, and my anger, sadness and fire rise. "Get out, Mike," I say. "We will not work together. Go. Go home." And he walks out.

In only five minutes, I must introduce the next speaker in front of 150 people. In the bathroom, I splash cold water on my face, plaster on a fake a smile, and say, "The show must go on."

I walk back into the event and tell no one about having encountered Mike.

I say positive affirmations to myself for the rest of the day. I will *not* crumble. I will succeed and rise. I will focus on the magic, not on the things that I think are crumbling. The event ends and I feel relieved and grateful at the same time.

ACTION LESSONS

That night after the event, I am reflecting back on the valuable lessons I learned from it. I made pretty much every mistake you can make and I learned from every single one of them. The best lesson I learned from this event is I can never ever fail. I either win or I learn. I realized if you want something bad enough, you can make it happen no matter what it is. Just know every mistake you make can either cripple you or make you accelerate. Remember you cannot fail if you learn from your mistakes. Whatever you want in your life, the universe will test you to see how badly you want it. Eighty-seven percent of people give up when it gets hard. They stop digging when they are only inches from gold. For myself, I know people will see me struggle, but by God, they will not see me quit.

And I have learned to never again focus solely on money. That was a big mistake on my part. When I start focusing on how much money I would make from my event, I stopped focusing on how I could help people. I love to create and help people and I started creating because I needed to make money. It became all about the money and not about helping others or doing what I love. This lesson ended up costing me a lot. I put this event before myself, my family, and before the things that truly mattered. I am grateful I pulled it off, but as I reflect, I will never do this again.

I will never again put a project before my own well-being and my family's well-being. I would work from the belief that when I do what I love, I am helping others and others will be attracted to what I do because my efforts come from love, not greed. I create not from a place of lack or needing money; I create from a place of love. Love what you do, do what you love, and the universe will applaud.

> ### *"Love is a very powerful antidote, especially when you start to give it to yourself."*
> ### —Carolyn Rim

Oddly enough, when I am done with this huge project, I don't want a break. I am more inspired than ever to help people and create things I love. Over the next few months I think about what Spark Your Rockstar was about. I know authenticity is such a big part of my Spark Your Rockstar brand and I never want to try to replicate or duplicate something. I think about the past year and the challenges and dares I have been part of. One of them was a 100-day challenge and another one was a 90-day challenge. I completed many goals while doing the challenges!

I want to create my own challenge but I don't want this course to be a challenge. I want it to be more of like a double-dog-dare. I want this course to be fun, sexy, daring. I want to make my own rockstar soup with my own spices and flavors.

Love is a very powerful antidote, especially when you start to give it to yourself. I want people to fall in love with themselves on the dare. Self-love is a part of my brand. If there is one thing I do well, it's moving others to take massive action. Loving ourselves is the quickest way to transform ourselves and the world. I keep thinking. and then say out loud, "I am going to start my own 99 Day Dare." The idea sparks like a firework! It's like someone has turned on the light in the dark. **I will create an online course.**

What would I want in a 99-Day Dare for myself? I would want to wake up earlier, meditate daily and have an accountability group. I would even want Joseph McClendon to come on the calls a few times and lead the group.

I call Joseph and explain my formula for the dare.

I will wake up every day on video with everyone at 6:30 a.m. EST and do five minutes of movement, five minutes of meditation and five minutes of mindset.

Every other Sunday at 11 a.m., Joseph will come on and speak to the group. He agrees, and in fact, he loves the idea.

And so, the 99 Day Dare is born. It comes straight from my desire in wanting to help people reach their goals—without a plan or accountability, most people give up within two weeks of establishing them.

I will sell my program for $359. It is my first course and I do not know what to expect. I put it out there on my Facebook page. This course takes me about an hour to create. Little do I know, I am reverse engineering course creation. Most entrepreneurs spend hours and hours creating a course before anyone even buys it. But I spend only about an hour putting the course together and the details. I will build this course as it goes along. Well, as soon as I put it out there, 25 people buy it. Within one day, I make $8,975. It is my first successful launch where I make money! Wow. Turns out my event, and the lessons learned, were just the inspiration and the momentum I needed to start creating magic in my life.

CONNECTING THE DOTS BACK

Joseph tells me to go over all my wins since the UPW event in Dallas 2014. I believe it's always good to connect the dots. After I sell my dare, I go over everything that has happened since the Tony Robbins event. Here is how I got to where I am. Joseph reminds me to continue to learn things as if I am going to teach them.

Start of the journey: I took out a loan and invested $5,000 in myself. I start listening to my heart. I start doing things that are very risky.

Day 1: Walk over fire with thousands of bad-ass Rockstars.

Day 2: After 15 years of a pack a day habit, I quit smoking. (I am a nonsmoker still.) Yes!

Day 3: Stepped into future self—magical Empowering Dickens Process.

Day 4: I decide I am not leaving this place without a mentor. I ask Joseph M. to be my mentor by a note that says "Ready, set, mentor me!"

Day 5 after the event: I get home. Everything has changed. I look at everything from a new mindset, a new perspective. I start seeing "problems" as "opportunities to scan for the positive & expand."

Day 6 after the event: Joseph McClendon agrees to be my mentor. Day 9 after the event: I give my two weeks' notice at work.

14 days after the event: I find a job paying double and one that will help me and support my other passions.

68 days after the event: My husband leaves me. He says his wife never came home from Dallas.

69 days after the event: I am vulnerable and post that I need support. Tony Robbins invites me to be his guest at UPW NJ.

75 days after event: Start my own business and don't let a lack of resources get in my way! Build my own website.

92 days after event: I am officially a motivational speaker! I hold my first event and 15 people attend.

124 days after event and one before UPW NJ: I hit the biggest pothole known to man (I know everyone in NJ/PA/NY knows about these holes!) and slide into a pole. I ignore those who say, "Don't you think it's a sign that you shouldn't go?" I say, "Maybe it's a sign you don't give up at every little bump in the road." I get huge support from people on Facebook.... (I had no idea how monumental these few actions/decisions were.)

125 days after the event: I get to UPW NJ and am not seated where I imagined I would be. But Tony comes out and tells the story of the woman who hit the pothole but didn't let that stop her. I have breakthrough after breakthrough at this event. Vibrates through my soul. I am a rockstar.

145 days after UPW Dallas and 20 days after UPW NJ: I am coaching people consistently and focusing on my next event. My boss recognizes my passion is in coaching. As Tony says, "You want to take the #*%#$ island, you must burn the boats!" I walk out of that office and feel like I can bend the walls with my mind if I wanted too!

169 days after the event: I start planning my next seminar event. Everything begins to fall together as if by magic.

186 days after the event: I hold successful second event for 40-plus people who bought tickets. I was shaky at the end with so much passion!

Everyone has something inside that they do better than anyone else. Mine is sharing my enthusiasm and energy and passion. I take on two beliefs. One: I exist to benefit everything I touch. Two: A thousand unseen hands carry me in every step I take! I am on fire with cosmic force.

270 days after my first UPW: Planning my event for August 8-9 with John Robertson for 150 people at the Franklin Institute.

330 days after the event: Hold a successful event! Lose $15K but learn valuable lessons!

360 days after the event: Sell my first online course, earning over $8,000!

Wow. Looking it over, I have accomplished and seen much. I send out gratitude for every good and bad moment so far. I am investing in my growth and failing forward. I am reprogramming my mind that I never fail. I either win or I learn. I am investing in me. My life is moving rapidly. Why? Because I am growing. I am expanding. I am living my dreams. When we are who we really are and do what we really love, the universe applauds.

> *"Giving up on your dream because of one setback is like slashing your other three tires because you got a flat. Keep moving forward."*
>
> **—Conventional Wisdom**

The following are posts from June until August:

June 29, 2015

You know that feeling when you know something amazing is about to happen? That take over the world, knock it out of the ballpark homerun, shake up the world, put a dent in the universe, feeling? That's how I feel. Right now, I am grateful I am getting the chance to create an event that will help people break through limiting beliefs and create a life they love.

When I started I was calling it 30 Days To Love Myself because I wanted people to fall in love with themselves. I hated myself and it wasn't until I started respecting myself, loving myself and valuing my unique gifts, that others started to treat me with that same respect, value and love.

162

July 12, 2015

Rise & Shine, Rockstars!

Do something today that your future self will thank you for. It's not certain when it will come to you, but if you are persistent and try to figure out your dream, it will come. Once you figure out what you want, the only thing left is to do whatever it takes to get it! Disregard the voice that says you can't, and go for it. This is your DREAM! You want it?! Go get it! Do something today your future self will thank you for.

> *"Believe in yourself! Have faith in your abilities! Without a humble but reasonable confidence in your own powers you cannot be successful or happy."*
>
> —*Norman Vincent Peale*

July 15, 2015

If you embrace the present and become one with it, you will experience a fire, a glow, a sparkle, of ecstasy. As you begin to experience freedom of the spirit, as you become intimate with it, joy will be born with you and you will drop the terrible burdens and chains of defensiveness, resentment, and hurtfulness. Only then will you become lighthearted, carefree, joyous and free! In this joyful simple freedom, you will know that what you want is available to you whenever you want it, because your want will be from a level of happiness, not from a level of anxiety or fear. Today, smile ... and let your strong happy heart shine.

July 16, 2015

From Abraham Hicks:

"You are the creator of your own experience and you must create your experience deliberately if you are to have the joyful experience you are meant to have. Unless, you, at any moment, are seeing the world through the eyes of source, then you are but a shadow of the being that you come forth to be. Which means, if you are doing less than loving whatever it is you are giving your attention to, you are not who you were really born to be. Negative emotion means you have pitched yourself off to some degree from who you really are. We talk about all these powerful positive emotions; ... I want you to reach for just one emotion, reach for relief. You are where you are regarding your relationships, regarding your finances, regarding your body, regarding your health. So in this moment, within your thoughts, accept where you are, and reach for relief. Talking about our problems is our greatest addiction. Break the habit and talk about your joys. Smile and start telling the story of your life the way you want it to be rather than the way it has been."

JULY 16, 2015

I feel as though my factory mindset has been replaced with a custom unique program. I am loving myself a little more each day.

JULY 19, 2015

Go to bed with this: Desire is the beginning of all creation. It is first thought. It's a grand feeling in the soul. It is God choosing what next to create. You want what you want for a reason. Do not talk yourself out of what you want. There are enough people for us all to have our dream and highlight each other's success. The soul usually knows what to do—the trick is to silence the mind.

JULY 21, 2015

Rise and shine, Rockstars! Today is the day you stop saying tomorrow and just go for it! Operate with complete faith and act as if your success is guaranteed. Do it! You deserve to be happy, to be supported and to be successful! You want it—Go get it!! You can't wait for the perfect time. Sometimes you just have to dare to do it, because life's too short to wonder what could have been.

JULY 23, 2015

Whatever relationships you have attracted into your life at this moment are precisely the ones you need in your life at this moment. There is hidden meaning behind all events, and this hidden meaning is serving your own evolution. Smile. Expand. Rise. Look at your life from a whole new perspective.

JULY 24, 2015

Today...smile and become your own superhero.

July 25, 2015

LOVE is the ANSWER.

July 27, 2015

So often we underestimate the power of a smile, a kind touch, a listening ear, an honest compliment or the smallest act of caring, all of which have the potential to turn a life around. Today ...Give the gifts that can't be begged, borrowed or bought. Give your love. People just want to be seen, heard and understood. I see you my friends. I see you.

JULY 28, 2015

Just in case no one told you yet today...

July 29, 2015

"The people that are crazy enough to think they can change the world, are the ones that do." —Steve Jobs

July 30, 2015

Follow the signs... The next quote you see on Facebook or Instagram you read, the next storyline in a movie you watch, the next person that calls you, it's the universe telling you something. Pay attention ... This is where the magic happens. So what if we followed the signs... Who would we meet? What would we learn? Who would we become? Decide to join the grind and come Spark Your Rockstar! Don't let *you* stop *you*! You want it—come get it! Don't let a lack of resources be the excuse for why you didn't pursue what you wanted! Come connect the dots to your destiny.

August 7, 2015

I am so excited about my Rockstar Transformations event tomorrow I can barely take it!! Not going to lie! I am shaking my ass and feeling joyous!

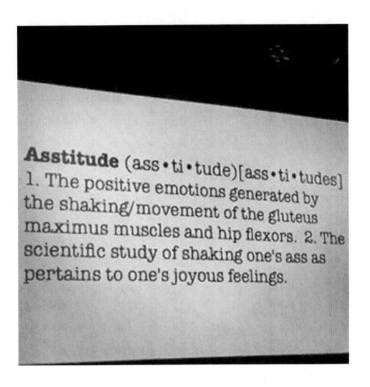

AUGUST 8, 2015

I was born for this day. Bring your legend to life!! Jairek Robbins and I demonstrating the arrow break for everyone!

AUGUST 8, 2015

We had an incredible time and the speakers were amazing today! I am so grateful for all the speakers today and tomorrow!

AUGUST 9, 2015

Jairek gives me a shirt at the end of the night that says, "The people who are crazy enough to think they can change the world are the ones who do." —Steve Jobs. Next to Jairek and me is Matt Smith, a friend who is very supportive. This event didn't just take place because of me; it took place because of all the people who helped me get there. Thank you to all the speakers and audience who came.

AUGUST 9, 2015

You see this man? That's my dad, John Anthony Rim. My event would not have happened without him. When I wanted to quit and give up because it was hard and I didn't think I could, he lifted me up and told me I couldn't give up. He said I would make it. Scan for the lesson, keep moving forward, and make it happen! Here's to my hero, for pushing me to succeed especially during the moments I wanted to crumble. I stayed strong, Dad. I made a promise to him that I would never stop following my heart,

I would never give up and would continue towards my dreams!!

AUGUST 9, 2015

My little girl handed me a note during my event with a simple message, while I was speaking and doing board breaks with everyone. It said, "Mommy, you have love all over your hands." She is my hero.

AUGUST 11, 2015

Give yourself permission to dream big. And then decide to make it happen. Your life does not get better by chance; it gets better by change. Go confidently in the direction of your dreams and live the life you've imagined.

AUGUST 11, 2015·

Make yourself epic. There's nothing more attractive than someone who believes in themselves and their greatness! Make yourself epic! You are so worth it!

AUGUST 12, 2015

What if you were sent here to be someone's miracle? It is a gift to be able to contribute to someone else's life. Everything you do and say matters. There are people in your life who need to know you care. Telling someone that they are amazing and to stay off the well- worn path, may seem small to you but it may be that little spark the person needed, to push forward through to the next level.

AUGUST 12, 2015

You! Yes, you! The one reading this. You are beautiful, talented, amazing, and simply the best at being you. Never forget that.

AUGUST 15, 2015

Be an original. Every rockstar differentiated themselves from The Herd and marched to their own drumbeat.

AUGUST 16, 2015

Smile. You have been created as one of a kind. The rarities that make you special are no mere accident. You have been created in order that you might make a difference.

AUGUST 20, 2015

I truly believe everything happens for a reason! It's never too late to start creating a new beginning to your story. You are the author, the star of the story and you are the only one holding the pen. Make today the day you become the hero of your own story.

AUGUST 22, 2015

When you go for your goals, especially the big ones that really count and fit in with your purpose in life, it is inevitable that people will discourage you. There are many reasons for this: concern, jealousy, ignorance, etc.

The people who try to talk you out of a life of greatness, is because they have already talked themselves into a life of mediocrity. Follow your heart and don't try to talk yourself out of wanting what you want just because it looks ridiculously out of reach. You want what you want for a reason. Surround yourself with the believers, the doers, the dreamers, the movers, and the shakers.

AUGUST 24, 2015

Be the best possible version of you. Along the path towards success, there will be people who try to tear you down and try to criticize you. You must keep moving forward and be the best possible version of you. Keep your eyes focused on your goals and what you are creating.

AUGUST 27, 2015

So for all you parents out there, spend some one on one time with the little one. It doesn't have to be anything extravagant. Have a dance party in your living room, read a book, tell a funny story, or just color. Celebrate your kids because they truly are amazing and so worth it.

SEPTEMBER 2, 2015

Your secret power lives within you. It whispers to you each day to spark it and turn it up. Turn the burning desire to succeed!! Beam your light on the world and smile! When we be who we are, and do what we love, the universe applauds! Today, turn up your power, and move towards your burning desires with cosmic force!

Photo by Ana Conlin

Chapter 13
A Nudge and
Becoming a Messenger for the Universe

"Try to see the good in others. When you're tempted to judge someone, make an effort to see their goodness. Your willingness to see the best in people will subconsciously bring it forth."

—Marianne Williamson

It's Friday night and Marybeth has my little girl. I am currently sitting alone in my home making movies. Mike is out of the house away for a week and I am here taking care of the cats and working. I am posting in lots of groups on Facebook now. Light workers' groups, Namaste groups, Tony Robbins groups and all kinds of groups. The more visible I am, the better, my mentor said. I am working on my dreams. I normally don't go out on most nights anyway. l am strict about that recently. I feel as if I have become obsessed with my dreams. I go out once in a while, but I am working on something that moves my spirit. It moves my soul. I feel so pulled by what I am doing.

People can make their dreams come true. If you want success you have got to believe it, you have got to eat it, you have got to sleep it. Sometimes I am up for two, three days in a row, working. People ask, "Is it worth it?" My answer? Hell, yes, especially when I am on fire on a project or a course. I am learning the most powerful weapon on earth is the human soul on fire.

My passion and soul has me up hours later than most people working on social media, on my book and on marketing, my online courses, my seminars, my events. The worst bankruptcy is when a person has lost his or her passion for doing something they love. How many people in the world talk themselves out of their dreams? Going for it the scariest thing. Once we take responsibility for our dream and decide we are going to make it happen, it's like we leap into the dark, but if you keep leaping and having the faith, then the magic will start happening. We are all made of the same stardust and we were all sent here for a reason, and it always serves us.

There is a reason that most people who set goals do not achieve them. My mentor told me to have some certainty, knowing that if you see a vision in your mind, it's because it's already created in the future in some other dimension. That was a little deep but it's true.

My phone ringing breaks my train of thought. My sister has my little girl and she wants to keep her overnight so I can work. I work late into the night, determined to finish the coding of the website for the dare program I have coming up. I am doing it all. Website design. Facebook pages. Facebook ads. I am doing everything myself because at this point I cannot pay anyone and sometimes it is overwhelming. I am typing away on the computer and as I am typing I realize how incredibly tired I am. Maybe I can just put my head down for a few minutes and I will be okay. 11:11p.m. I keep seeing all these numbers like 11:11 or 3:33 p.m. The angels are watching me. Guiding me. I put my head down at my feet.

I wake at 7:33 a.m. Shit. I quickly shower and get ready. I need to meditate so I silently sit for 10 minutes and allow all the noise to fade away. I ask for the power, the strength, the love, the patience, the endurance whatever it takes to go to the next level. I ask the universe to use me in helping others. I am ready to receive the gifts.

I only have a few weeks before the first 99 Day Dare opens and only a few hours before I am supposed to meet my sister for lunch so I work hard on creating the first few pieces, coding the website and helping stay connected with the people who already have signed up to the secret Facebook group I created.

AN AMAZINGLY LOVING ENCOUNTER

About two hours later, I leave to go meet my sister. Grace, my other niece, and KK are best friends, holding hands in front my sister. "My loves!" I say with a huge smile. They practically jump on me and hug me tightly. "Hey Marybeth," I say. I give her a big hug, too. We walk down State Street in Media, Pa. and are having a beautiful afternoon together. We stop and get a few air balloons made for the girls. Then we walk a little more and we come to the restaurant and order lunch. I notice that there is a woman with her two kids sitting near me. The one boy is maybe seven years old. The other one looks about three years old. They are sweetly trying to get their mother's attention but she is fully focused on her phone. I turn my head back around to be aware and present with my own family.

Within a few minutes, we hear the mom start screaming, "You two, I hate coming out to eat with you, you little shits, I don't want to talk to you two right now. All you do is bug me all day long. I am never gonna take you out to eat again because you can't just sit still in peace for one minute. Just leave me alone for God's sake!"

The seven-year-old has tears in his eyes and his face is red. The little one starts to cry and the mom keeps yelling. The whole restaurant is silent, but no one is doing anything. I receive a feeling I never have felt so strongly. It starts in my core and streams up to my heart: "Carolyn, go help those kids and that mom. Tell her everything is going to be okay and then hug her. Breathe with her."

I don't have a choice. There is one seat empty directly across from the mom. I sit down next to the younger child. The agitated mother looks up at me, phone still in her hand, and says, "Who the hell are you and what the hell do you want?" I look at her without answering for a moment so she can feel my energy. I do not judge her; I accept her and I love her for right where she is. I see past her mistakes. My love melts her anger. I see past all the features of her outside features and for a moment I can see her soul. She sheds a tear. She feels seen. She just needs a hug and so do her boys.

I continue to stream acceptance, love and connection into her. I reach my hand out and gently touch her hand that held the phone and I say, "My name is Carolyn Rim, I received a message from the universe and the universe told me to come over here and tell you to breathe and to put your phone away." She takes a deep breath. I can see all resistance leaving her. Then, she puts her phone in her purse. Her shoulders drop, and it looks like she is taking her first deep breath in forever. The two boys look at me like I am some sort of angel. I send love into them with my energy and my eyes. The little one giggles. I look back at the mom.

The restaurant was still in silence watching and listening. I say, "The reason that you got so upset with your kids right then is because you were on your phone. You were giving your phone all this energy, attention and love. You were getting your need for significance met

177

through the phone. You need to get your significance from your kids—they need you and when you are not giving them attention the only way they know how to get it is through negative emotion. See them for how amazing they are. They are perfection, and all they want is your attention and love. Truly, we are not separate. We have all been in that situation where our kids are driving us nuts. But, right now, they need your attention and your love."

Then I stand up, and I motion for her to stand up with me. I gave her a huge hug. She tried to hug me on the other side but I said, "No, let us connect heart to heart. Most people hug the other way because their hearts are closed and walls are up." So we connected heart to heart. I breathed in and out with her in unison. I whispered in her ear, "The universe really just wants you to take more deep breaths in and love your children. But most important, love yourself. Get significance from your children because they will give it to you. You are a beautiful person and a beautiful mom."

The kids were smiling and the seven-year-old jumped up and hugged me. I wrapped my arms around him and let the love in my heart overflow into every cell of this boy's body. I bend down and whisper into his ear, "You are so unbelievably enough. You are beautiful boy, a beautiful soul and you will make it through this. Everything is always happening *for* us, not to us. I promise." He pulled away, happy tears in his eyes. I looked at the three-year old boy and gave him a huge high five and a little kiss on his cheek. I told them they were both little super men and to never stop believing in themselves or each other.

I turned around to walk back to my table and the whole restaurant was just looking at me in silence. A few people were smiling at me, with tears in their eyes. A few still stunned by what just took place. It was as if I had shifted the very vibration in the room.

As I went back to the table, and sat down. I gently closed my eyes for a moment and thanked the universe. It was such a blissful feeling to be kind. To show love to someone who everyone else in the restaurant would have judged and showed hate towards, I showed love.

HATE WILL NEVER FIX HATE

The lesson I learned was that more hate will never fix hate. Only love can dissolve hate. To truly change someone, we must first see them right for where they are at, then love and accept them for right where they are at without trying to change them. They will then shift organically out of where they are when they feel seen, loved and accepted. Turns out loving yourself was the truest way to change someone.

When I sat down, my beautiful daughter looked up at me and said loudly, "You told that lady to be nicer to her kids, right Mommy? Or do you want me to go over there?" We all burst out laughing.

Our food arrived and we all starting eating and for a moment, I looked back the mom and the two boys. She was giving the older boy a dollar to put in the jukebox. She then turned to the three-year- old and gently swept her fingers through his hair. He giggled. I could not help but feel this incredible joy spread through me.

I realized I have always felt like the universe wanted to use me as this vessel. Ever since I was a little girl I always felt like I had this gift to give but I was so afraid to truly embrace it. Today, I made the conscious decision to accept the gifts that the universe has been trying to give to me. So, I have these messages for people and I am just going to start giving it to them because that's what this world is about. Connecting and helping one another. Showing compassion and kindness to another human being.

I have never been more grateful in my whole life for where I am right now. Today was a turning point for harnessing that energy to be a vessel for the universe to spread love and kindness. I am also learning the truest way for others to change is just loving and accepting them for right where they are at. Loving and accepting them without trying to change them, without judgement, just loving them. I am now able to harness the energy, becoming a receiver and cultivating the magic within.

Love has become my religion. I am a vessel for the universe. My desire to be used as a vessel to help others has finally come true. I know who I am. I know why I am here. Let the magic continue.

> ### *"Today, I made the conscious decision to accept the gifts that the universe has been trying to give to me."*
>
> ### *—Carolyn Rim*

That night, my little girl and I snuggled up under the blankets with a good book. I then turned on the ocean waves on my phone. Ever since she was very small, I have turned on soothing sounds on YouTube on my phone and we were both lullabied to sleep by the sweet sound of the rolling waves.

I look at my little girl and I say with 100 percent certainty, "One day, KK, we won't have to listen to the waves on Mommy's cell phone anymore, because all we will have to do is open the window, and we will hear the waves right outside our window." We smile as we close our eyes dreaming about the big beautiful window we will one day open to our beach house.

These are Facebook posts from this time.

SEPTEMBER 5, 2015

You are enough. Stop the voice of doubt and realize how unbelievably worth it you are.

SEPTEMBER 7, 2015

The average adult now spends up to three hours on social media a day. It's easy to get our needs met through social media. We get significance, love/connection, contribution, certainty and uncertainty. I know how important this message is to spread. My little girl is my everything and I feel so good when I put the phone away and read to her. We have a new rule, every night 30 minutes before bed, all electronics and phones get turned off and we grab a flashlight, a few books and then we snuggle and read together. I think awareness on this is huge. Kids today have it a lot harder than we did growing up, I believe. When you wake up tomorrow and see this, I hope it brings awareness to you as it did to me.

SEPTEMBER 9, 2015

Wow! More than 100,000 views! My videos have officially reached over 100,000 views and climbing! THANK YOU to all the people following me and how grateful I am for all of you! I feel as though I have discovered a proven system for achieving BIG GOALS! In the past 11 months, I have quit smoking, quit toxic relationships, quit drinking the 9-5 Kool-Aid and built the life of my dreams! When most people set out to achieve new goal, they ask, "Okay, I have my goal; now what do I need to do to get it?" It's not a bad question, but it's not the first question that needs to be addressed either.

The question should be asking ourselves is: "Who do I need to become?"

A great quote by Jim Rohn to go along with this post. "If you want to have more, you have to become more. Success is not something you pursue. What you pursue will elude you; it can be like chasing butterflies. Success is something you attract by the person you become."

You can have, be, do, become anything you want in this world! When I understood this philosophy, it revolutionized my life and personal growth. You got a dream? Follow it, protect it, feel it, own it, and most importantly, see it in your mind as if it's already done. Be grateful. Don't focus on the "how" focus on the end result of what you desire.

At Spark Your Rockstar, Dreams do come true.

> *"If you want to have more, you have to become more. Success is not something you pursue. What you pursue will elude you; it can be like chasing butterflies. Success is something you attract by the person you become."*
>
> *—Jim Rohn*

SEPTEMBER 9, 2015

New school clothes at Target: $249.97

Two new pairs of shoes: $68.47

SuperFlash socks to make her run faster: $5.99

The look on my daughter's face for her first day of school: PRICELESS.

SEPTEMBER 10, 2015

As Deepak Chopra says, "Today, make sure to factor in uncertainty as essential ingredient for success and happiness. In your willingness to accept uncertainty solutions will spontaneously emerge out of the problem, out of the confusion, out of the disorder and chaos. The more uncertain things seem to be, the more secure I will feel because uncertainty is my path to freedom. Through the wisdom of uncertainty I will find my security."

SEPTEMBER 11, 2015

It's official... I was accepted as a BNI Member full of entrepreneurs and business owners! First meeting, first 30 Second Commercial! Nailed it! Immediately Booked 3 Paid Speaking Gigs after the meeting! Yessss! This is a Game Changer!

"Step into the field of all possibles and anticipate the excitement that can occur when you remain open to infinity of choices. Experience all the fun, adventure, magic and mystery of life."

—*Deepak Chopra*

Do you like yourself? I remember when I didn't like me because of my behaviors and actions. Today, I can look in the mirror, send myself love, a wink and smile. In the past year, I have transformed every area of my life. I believe the biggest thing that has truly changed my life is practicing gratitude. I am so grateful for every experience and I get on my knees at night and I thank the universe for every good time and every bad time in my life, because I needed every valley in my life, so that my mountain top would taste better. Today, say to yourself I am where I need to be for right now; I am enough for today; and I love myself regardless of anything that happened yesterday, because Today is a fresh new opportunity to take a step in the right direction practicing gratitude and self-love.

Chapter 14
Surrounded by the Greats, a Visit to the Past, and Awakening a New Me

"For what lies inside the human being is the whole spiritual cosmos in condensed form. In our inner organism we have an image of the entire cosmos."

—Rudolf Steiner

I fly to Canada for a weekend with my tribe for the Power Of Success Event in Canada and it's incredible. At this event, a few people came up to me and were telling me they watch my videos and they were inspiring them. My life is changing as I continue to build my brand and surround myself with the right people. When I get to the event, I realize I have one ticket to sit up front, or I can sit in the back with the tribe of friends I came with. My standards were completely set on I sit in the front, no matter what. I ask them if they mind. They all say no, but I still feel a tinge of bitterness from one or two of them. Most of them are happy for me, but some are not okay with it. I cannot sit in the back though. It is a standard I set for myself.

When I walk to the front I see Les Brown, Bob Proctor, and Tony Robbins all standing up there and I feel so inspired. I know I will get to shake hands with all of them today, I say to myself. I will shake hands with these great men who have inspired me so much and who have inspired the world. I have absorbed what they said to me like sponge soaks up water. Recently I had been listening to Les Brown motivational videos and it will be just a beautiful gift to hear him live. He has a beautiful aura around him the whole time he speaks.

Then 12 p.m. comes and someone who knows me and works there comes up to me and says, "Carolyn, you're going to VIP lunch, right?" I don't know that I even have an invitation to a VIP lunch.

I say, "Yes of course." Then, he escorts me into a room with about 20 people. The event speakers are there. I walk up to each one of them and hand them my card. Where most people would be scared, I take massive action.

"Hi, Mr. Brown, my name is Carolyn Rim and I am a rockstar. Here is my card." Then I go to Bob Proctor, I introduce myself and I breathe them all in. Then a man comes in with a mic and asks, "Who wants to ask a question to these guys?" I jump up and practically scream, "ME!"

He comes over and I grab the mic. I ask them all, "How can I spread more love and compassion in the world?"

Les Brown says, "I can see the passion and love you have in your eyes for spreading your message. Carolyn, I believe with all my heart that if you keep taking action and surrounding yourself with people like us, then it will most certainly continue to happen. You are changing the world just by being here and being you. The biggest gift you can give to the world is being yourself and doing what you love."

Later that night I jump on video on Facebook in front of thousands of people. My videos are starting to get a lot of views.

I feel so inspired after today's events and being surrounded with such game changers. I jump in front of the camera with no outline or script. I just start speaking.

"I don't want to have meaningless conversations anymore. I am done pretending to be someone else. I am done with people- pleasing. I am Carolyn Rim and I came here to change the world and that is exactly what I am going to do. I am going to create a ripple of love and compassion in this world. I am on fire with passion for my dreams, for my love and what I have to offer to others.

"Our souls were sent here for a purpose. Wake up to the gift you are. You are anything but average. You were born to shine and to be your beautiful self. Be your beautiful, amazing, gifted self and never, ever try to be anything that you are not. When you are yourself, you bring in the people who are supposed to be in your life. When you are yourself, you surround yourself with greatness and you become great.

"Start being okay with being *you*, start making the decisions that your future self is going to thank you for. Stop saying tomorrow You can start *right now*, you can start by accepting where you are. Accept where you are, decide where you want to go, and then decide to make it happen.

"Take all this energy and let it be the spark that says today is the day that you decide No More. I am going to have better relationship with more intimacy. I am going to have more fulfillment in my life. Let today be the day you step over that line in front of you. Take that step and hug your kid. Look someone in the eyes and say, 'You are amazing' and mean it. Grab your husband or your wife and say 'I am so grateful for you. Thank you for being you because you're absolutely amazing and I love you.'

"Let today be the day you hold the door for someone. Let today be the day you smile at someone without a smile because they are the ones who need a smile most. Let today be the day that you *listen* to people. See them with eyes that don't judge, see them with eyes that love. Let today be the day that you have compassion and love in your heart because people will feel it, and so will you.

"I want the parents in the world to put their phones away and connect with their kids. I want the world to know that gratitude, growth and contribution is the only way to get that fulfillment you seek. I want people to have more gratitude for the little things they have, like clothes, your body, your breath. I want us to educate our hearts to fall in love with our reality right now. Start saying 'I am grateful I woke up today.' Take it all in!

"My hope for you is that you let today be the spark that you see the light and that you make today the best day of your life.

"I was talking to a client on the phone recently and they said, "I don't want to go to work today."

"I said, 'You don't *have* to go to work today! YOU *GET* TO GO TO WORK TODAY!' Saying that vs. I *have to* go to work makes such a big difference.

"Let's turn that attitude around and say, 'I am so grateful.' I am so grateful that I get to go to work and light everybody up, get on the phone and talk to people. We get to choose how we see things. We can focus on what's wrong or on what's right. We can choose to see the good.

"You can move towards what you want. You don't have to be happy with where you are right now but just accept it. Accept where you are and then move forward. That is the key to our success: You must accept where you are and you must decide where you want to go and decide to make it happen.

"As always, I am sending you mad love and light."

DEFINING MY TRUE SELF, AND MY CLIENTS

Within a few hours, hundreds of comments and thousands of views poured in. I remember what Les told me. The best gift we can give to the world is just being our true selves. The more I invest in myself and go to events, the more I am learning and the bigger impact I am having. The more I give, the more I receive. The more I invest, the more return I get.

Later in the week, I receive a message saying I was accepted into the Business Networking International Association. Every Friday from now on, I will get to wake up at 7 a.m. and do a 30-second commercial on who my perfect client is and what I do. It's incredible to see my coach David Kauffmann and the way he works the room. He really knows what he's doing—he's in charge of 186 BNI chapters all over Pennsylvania. I jump in feet-first and start to understand how the universe works with give and take. You see, in BNI, you give referrals and you also get referrals. If you do not give referrals, then others stop getting you referrals. It is a beautiful give and receive system. I really like how everyone cares about each other.

Later, when I return home, I get a call from a woman named Erica Franco. She would like me to do the Empowering Dickens Process at her Center for Healing in Ewing, N.J. for her clients. I am smiling from ear to ear that I will get to walk these amazing individuals through such a powerful process. I agree and a few weeks later I am driving to New Jersey with 30 boards for the breaking. I get my needs met on such high levels by public speaking and helping others.

A few weeks ago, I spoke to 30 architects and ever since BNI, I have been getting a ton of speaking gigs. I get certainty, uncertainty, love/connection and growth/contribution. I take groups through a guided meditation and provide them with a visual of what their future will look like if they continue with the destructive behavior patterns. I help them connect with their hearts and their souls. I explain to everyone there is no chemical that can fix a spiritual problem. It's only a few-hour process but I walk out of these groups feeling so happy and fulfilled. I meet some amazing people.

After I connect with Erica from the Center for the Healing, she tells me I can have my firewalk event at her place if I want. So I have to start to sell tickets for that event.

I continue to learn about social media marketing and how to market myself and my brand to the world. I contact Joe White, a motivational speaker in the Wilmington, Del. area who I know does firewalks. He could lend me one of his guys to help me. About 50 people show up. The firewalk is never about the fire—it's about overcoming something you thought was impossible. It's about dancing with your fear instead of letting it control you. I learn something about myself each time I walk over fire.

After the event though, I get a message from someone on FB saying I am different from Tony Robbins and I should really do something different from a firewalk because I have my own magic and my fire is within me.

I think for moment about this. It is critical that I differentiate myself from the thousands of other people online. I am going to have to continue to expand the Spark Your Rockstar brand and the community. I agree with some feedback I am given and I am not resistant to it. Although everyone who came to the event got a lot from it, it wasn't my style. It wasn't my magic. I had to find my own gift and start learning how to market it and how to evolve it.

The following Friday at 7 a.m., I talk to a few people in BNI about it. I explain I am glad I held the firewalking event but I want to do something different from Tony Robbins. I want my own rockstar soul with my own spicy secret sauce.

As a few members take a liking to me, and one beautiful blonde woman, Renee Girifalco, asks, "What do you love to do that really helps others make things happen?"

I think for a moment and then say, "Well, I love vision boards and manifesting and meditation."

She returns my smile and says, "Let's do it. Can you come out for my team on Sunday?" I instantly say yes and shake her hand.

So, within 24 hours of joining this group, I have my first paid speaking gig booked for a vision board party with Renee Girifalco and her Nerium Team.

From David Kauffman, I learn how different paid speaking gigs are from staging my own event. He asks if I need help and I am absolutely willing to accept. He tells me to use everyone in the room as my own personal salesforce—but the most important thing with BNI, I have to inform them of who I am looking for. Just saying I am a life coach who changes lives isn't detailed enough. Who do I love to work with?

David asks me things like, "What does your client say a lot? What is the wording they use?"

I joke with him, "Well, they say 'should' a lot. 'I should have done this.' 'I should have done that,' and they end up shoulding all over themselves! My clients say 'should' a lot because they feel their ship has sailed but the truth is, they can become an 'I am glad of the past failures I had because they were all lessons in disguise to help me grow'-kind of person by working with me. So, listen for anyone in this week in your business saying the word 'should' too much!"

David laughs and says, "That's is good first start on a 30-second commercial. Let's keep expanding on who your perfect client is."

MOVING INTO MY NEW SELF

I walk out of the BNI meeting feeling filled up with good energy. Being surrounded by 70 plus entrepreneurs every Friday is going to change the game for me. I drive home and grab the mail at my door. I see a statement for my car payment. I put my stuff down and take my coat off. I open the statement.

> Dear Carolyn,
>
> You have one final payment of $859.45 remaining for the BMW 2011 3 Series Xi. Thank you.
>
> Sincerely,
> Otto's BMW of West Chester

I am sitting in my home with a pen in my hand smiling. I am staring at my check book in front of me. With the money I made from my online course, coaching, paid speaking gigs, and events, I am finally able to make the last payment on my car. I have been making a few double payments over the past year. The car is officially mine! It was a $50,000 car I bought three years ago. The decision was not the best one but at the time I was in sales and my number-one need was significance, so all I thought about was material items that would bring it to me.

I didn't know there were so many beautiful ways to meet my need for significance by giving to others. Today, that is how I get that need met. I have had a car payment since I was 23 years old, when I bought my first 2003 BMW 3 series. I had high standards even then.

Wow. I wonder what it will be like not to have a car payment. My car payment was what most people's mortgage statement was. I look on my 2015 goals list and sure enough, one of my goals in 2015 was to pay off my car two years early because I didn't want any debt. All I did was write down my goals and decide to make it happen. I write the last check, put it in the envelope and stamp it.

> *"The problem with most people is, they just review past mistakes without seeing the lesson or the gift in it."*
>
> *—Joseph McClendon III*

When I meet a goal, I feel like I meet a new version of myself. A better version. I feel like I keep learning more about myself. It is starting to become less about the actual goal itself, and more about who I become in the process of completing that goal.

Jesus. I start thinking again how far I have come. That is key, my mentor always says. To go into our mind and think about all the things we are proud of ourselves for. He says that's what builds true confidence because no matter what anyone says we can revisit the times we are proud of in our life.

He says the problem with most people is they just review past mistakes without seeing the lesson or the gift in it. Rarely do people go back into the past and connect the dots back to where they are. I told him the other day I still sometimes doubt myself. I doubt what am I trying to prove, I feel pulled by something greater than myself that is very hard to describe. He told me to continue to just allow myself to be pulled and attracted like a magnet to my destiny.

TWO FEET FROM GOLD

I am working on so many things right now and I barely have a moment to come up for air but that is most likely what I need more of: More deep conscious breaths in and out.

I think about all the people who have been to the place I am now and given up. I think about those who gave up right before they hit gold. Whether they stopped or they pushed forward, what made the difference?

Of course, it's not always easy to share openly, honestly and be raw with people but I 100 percent believe our vulnerability is something to embrace, not hide. I feel a hint of sadness. I have all these beautiful things and changes happening to me, so why do I feel sad? I am so close I can taste it but there is also so much more to do and make happen and it takes an overwhelming amount of energy.

Then I figure out where I need to harness it. Self-sabotage, doubt and fear sneak in slowly. I think about how much more I have to go on my book I am telling people about and I think about how far away I really am from where I want to be. So what if I paid my car off? I still have a lot of debt to handle from the failure before and not a lot of time to figure it all out.

It would be so easy to just pick up my feet and move with the masses and stop, two feet before gold. But I won't. I will never give up on the vision that I envision and I will never give up the passion swirling in my soul.

Today, I will keep moving forward. I feel the feelings and I move forward anyway. I embrace and dance with the pain, with feelings instead of trying to resist. I will allow the emotions to flow through me. I decide to get on camera with my followers and make a quick five-minute video. I cry. I show my skin. I become vulnerable and share that I am sad and even though at times I feel like giving up, I will never give up.

"My new life is both expecting and appreciating the wide rainbow of emotions humans go through every day and then choosing what emotional home or set point I want to live in. I have had to start waking up and start actively choosing to see the good."

—Carolyn Rim

Someone asked me on my video the other day, "How are you always so happy?" That was the thing. I am not always happy. I just make a conscious decision when I wake up to see the good. There will be days like this when there is an overwhelming amount of work to do, or when I feel anger or sadness. The best thing I have learned so far is not to judge my emotions when I am going through them, but just to be with them instead. Embrace them and dance with the painful ones and you will organically shift out of it.

Maybe I feel a hint of sadness because I am Spark Your Rockstar's only employee. I am doing it all myself, I am promoting, I am building my own websites, I am trademarking my own stuff, I am doing everything. Some days I am lonely and it is freaking hard, but it is okay. I can handle it. Hard forces me to grow. I am grateful for the chance to grow and expand.

192

We all have unconquerable spirits and I am not going to give up, I will never give up my dream. I am following my heart and I have gotten so much joy, so much immense joy and a fire in my heart. But I accept and understand there are going to be days where I feel strapped to a roller coaster of emotions and I feel like I have no control over the ride but I do.

No, of course not every day is amazing and sparkling with unicorns and magic. There is no right or wrong answer. It's finding magic little moments that I can just be overwhelmingly sad and happy because I feel as though, "Yes I have come so far, but I still have a wide gap in between where I am and where I want to be."

At the same time, I am grateful that something is guiding me to help bridge that gap. I am almost there, I try to convince myself. My company is exploding. I see my business expanding far and wide. I see the dream of owning a company with purpose and having a huge ripple of love and energy through the world.

That's when I hear Tony's voice: "All you need is within you now. Remember when everything around you is crumbling and you feel like you can't seem to find a way out, celebrate, because victory is near."

I smile at this. I have programmed a voice within that helps me through the doubt. Though the fog. After I get off the video speaking to everyone, again comments pour in even faster than normal. Vulnerability is an incredible gift when harnessed for good and authenticity.

HOW DID THIS HAPPEN?

As I look on the calendar, I realize we are already in October and it is getting close to the one-year anniversary when I decided to invest in myself and go to that Unleash The Power Within event with Tony Robbins and my whole life changed. Who would have thought a year later, I would have my own firewalking event? I shake my head. Sometimes I still can't believe it. I feel like someone is about to wake me from a dream. I start thinking about all I had to do to get where I am.

I have had to drastically change my attitude and my perspectives on how I see the world. I had to communicate effectively with people and explain I wasn't just some person high on being, saying, "Oh, everything is great and wonderful" when it wasn't. I had to explain that it is both expecting and appreciating the wide rainbow of emotions humans go through every day and then choosing what emotional home or set point I want to live in. I had to start waking up and start actively choosing to see the good.

A lot of people at first told me I was living in a fantasy world and that it was impossible to have my dreams come true. They would say things like

"Be realistic." I believe every time those words are uttered, a fairy falls down dead somewhere. Those words are the type of words that peck at your soul. "Be realistic."

I say, "Hell no, don't be realistic." I had to start looking at the naysayers in my life differently. I had to tell myself that the only reason other people tried to talk me out of what I sincerely wanted or what I was going for was because they had talked themselves into a life of mediocrity. I believe everyone when they first start going for something great goes through the internal and external voices of doubt. Twelve months ago it wasn't here. Twelve months ago I had $36 in my pocket and I wanted to die.

> *"Over the last 12 months, I have built my dream life, I love what I do. What would the world look like if everyone gave themselves a chance to take a moment today and give their dreams a chance and gave themselves permission to dream big?"*
>
> *—Carolyn Rim*

It's a good time to visit my old past self to see the contrast of my expansion and growth. I keep having these beautiful visualizations and I feel like I am meeting new versions of myself from future and from past, and every time I close my eyes a new adventure awaits me. I just allow my creator to guide me, my higher self.

I have started something very special: The Transporter. It is a red door meditation I created and through this red door time doesn't exist. We can be transported into any time and space in our minds.

We can travel at the speed of light to any moment of your life in your mind. There are no limits or boundaries here.

I close my eyes as a new adventure awaits me and I am pulled into the space I feel most comfortable and expansive in. I just let go and allow my creator to guide me, my beautiful higher self.

THROUGH THE RED DOOR AND INTO GRACE

I lick my lips as I transport myself back in time. I see the seven stairs in front of me, leading me down to the big red door into the past. Visualization is a beautiful thing because science has now proven that when you close your eyes and visualize, your subconscious mind cannot

194

tell the difference between something real and something actually happening, so it becomes just as certain.

I walk down the steps and I see one word on the vivid crimson red door. It's the color of blood and I can almost taste the color.

I see the word RELEASE. It has an almost hypnotic ring to it, doesn't it? A loose, limp, relaxed feeling. A feeling of total lightness. R E L E A S E. The red door opens. I take a deep breath in and out. I relax even deeper and I step through the red door to see what my creator has waiting for me.

I go back to the grey cube in my mind's eye. I am above my past self looking down on the Carolyn of the past. I read into her mind and I see her thoughts as if they are going by like a CNN crawl on the screen. I hear them, too, as if she is reading them out loud.

"I am 30 years old and there is no way that I can get another job. I feel stuck. I will be here forever. I will never be good enough for what I really want. I feel like I will be in this call queue and this cube for the rest of my life. I want to die." I see the speed pick up on the screen and it slows down on one thought. "I will die before I spend another 10 years in the fucking cube. I hate myself. I hate my life. I am not *enough*. I can't take it anymore. I want to get out of this place." I then notice my past self type the words into Google: Golden Gate Bridge. My old past self is researching bridges to jump from so she can finally escape the pain.

I have an impulse to hug her. I float down beside my past self.

I stare into her. Her eyes are tired. Her eyes are sad from masking the pain. From putting on this façade for so many years. So many different masks this woman wears. She is scared. Led by her fear. God, I love this woman I am staring at so intently. I softly caress her sweet face with my hand. I gently pull my past self into me and I hug her deeply. I tell her without words that we are gonna make it, that she can't give up now because I need her. I love her. I wonder if she can feel me. That's when I remember. I slowly let her go and I see she has tears coming down her face.

I remember. My God. I remember. I think back to what was happening in my past self. That was when I felt the presence of something unseen. That was the first time I felt the divine presence of something greater all around me. I felt the presence of grace. I felt the presence of love. I felt the presence of love.

For a moment, I am blown away. Does that mean I was the one who helped myself in the past? Could it have been my future self that gave her love and a hug that made her feel a feeling like she wanted to live? She *wanted* to live. So, what is real anyway? What is time, anyway? Was I in *this* moment or *that* moment? I stop questioning and just trust. I take a step back away from my past self as I see her typing the name Tony Robbins into the screen. I smile because I don't need to watch the rest of this scene. I know the rest of the story.

I float up and back towards the red door, feeling like a light that keeps rising higher and higher. I take a big deep breath. As I step through the red door and see the beautiful steps back to the Now in front of me, I am walking out of here knowing my power, my gifts, my strength.

As I walk up the steps I start shedding layers of skin that don't serve me almost like a snake would shed its skin, I am now shedding my old skin and a new me is emerging. Each step I take back into the Now evolves me. I am light. I am love. I am expansion. I am the universe. I am one with everything and everyone.

I open my eyes. I am crying. I grab my journal and pen. I write down, "EVERYTHING IS CONNECTED. Every moment and everyone. Connect the dots to see and create the future ahead. TIME DOESN'T EXIST IN A SENSE. Time is expanding. You, and you alone, have all the power within you at this moment to shift everything."

I have a new superpower. The power of time travel in my mind. I am excited to expand this outwardly and give it to others. However, I sit and I allow myself to absorb the deliciousness of this moment right now.

The following are posts from this time.

SEPTEMBER 16, 2015

Come on baby... Say it with me... Say it as Les Brown says it! "It's Possible!!"

—Dreams Do Come True—

SEPTEMBER 15, 2015

"Let that person who makes you smile again, be you. Ever love someone so much you would do anything for them? Yeah? Well then, make that person yourself and do what makes you happy."

—Harvey Specter

SEPTEMBER 18, 2015

One thing I learned from listening to Wayne Dyer is to listen to intuition. Something is on my heart to share. You see, my mission is to spread more compassion and love in the world. My mission is so people can start to see that what they receive will never make them happy. If you're not happy now, you won't be happy when you get what you get. To feel true happiness is when we are grateful. The universe supports us, because we are grateful for what we already have, no matter how small or little it is, we realize that the real gifts in life can't be begged, borrowed, or bought. The real gifts in life come when we wake up to the gift we really are. Go ahead and love yourself like the gift you really are.

I want to tell you secret. Do you know why it's so hard sometimes to get started tapping into to your greatness? Because of the people you surround yourself with consistently. Sometimes, it can even be your own family and friends.

They constantly review what you have done in the past, and throw it in your face. They put themselves on another level and feel high and mighty after putting you down for your past mistakes. *Do not allow anyone to put you down.*

You must remove yourself from people who are stuck in the past, who constantly bring up negative emotions and situations. You are not your past!! So many times, our family and our friends can influence our decisions on who we are supposed to be with, on where we should live, and what we should be when we grow up.

You must surround yourself with people who see the light in you and what you are trying to create. Some will get mad that you are striving for greatness, some will be jealous, some will resist because they fear change but you must continue to move towards your destiny! It doesn't matter what happened yesterday! You must realize how powerful your thoughts are.

If you continue to focus on yesterday and the past and all your mistakes... Guess what starts moving towards you? The same experience over and over again. Break the pattern and start thinking that you really are great! And that you are benefiting and refreshing everything you touch!!

You can start being a better mom, a better dad, a better employee, a better business owner, a better friend, a better sister, a better wife, a better husband, a better person today! Don't allow other people's opinions of you to become your reality. You are amazing and you are a gift. You are whoever you decide to be. Make the conscious choice of who you want to be daily and don't allow others to influence you.

September 23, 2015

Are you ready to rock this day, baby? I am excited! I am visualizing greatness in my heart, seeing my future and bringing it towards me with cosmic force of the universe. One day, I will have a whole building's-worth of employees who I treat like gold and they serve with me as a force for good in the world and help me transform people's lives.

September 24, 2015

Keep moving towards your greatness and don't let anyone talk you out of going for your dreams. The only people who will ever try to talk you out of a life of greatness will be those who talked themselves into a life of mediocrity. Lift off towards your dreams like a 747 in full flight.

September 24, 2015

I invite you to take a moment to think of something that happened today that you can be grateful for. I know is easy to sometimes focus on what's wrong in our lives, on to-do lists and all the other tasks we take on daily. Yet, I promise if you think about one or two things you're grateful for, in 21 days of doing this, your happiness levels will increase by 20 percent and you'll start seeing the positive everywhere you look.

SEPTEMBER 25, 2015

You are such a gift to the universe.

Sometimes I know for myself in the past, I had this voice in my head that said I wasn't worth it and that I wasn't loved and that I wasn't enough. That my dreams were out of my reach. That I would be judged. That I was joke. That my past and my dreams didn't match. The voice told me I was part of the masses, part of the herd. But I can say with 100 percent certainty: These are all lies. They were lies that I told myself for so many years.

Today take a deep breath in and say out loud," I am worth it and I am loved and I am enough. I want what I want for a reason and purpose and I am going to stop talking myself out of what I want and I am going to start going for it." After all, there is nothing more sexy and inspiring than someone following a dream that no one else can see but them. That's where it all starts. Imagining the life you want. Envisioning it daily.

What if we all thought like that? The world will be a completely different place. I woke up this morning grateful, grateful for the air that I breathe. Grateful that I gave my dreams a chance. Grateful I didn't listen to my doubts. We can transform the world by starting with ourselves and expanding outwardly. It all starts with allowing your heart to lead and seeing the vision, because the first one that sees it and believes it is you.

SEPTEMBER 28, 2015

Do you believe in magic? No? Yes? Whether you do, or don't, either way, You're RIGHT. Today, believe in magic.

SEPTEMBER 29, 2015

So I found this picture going through some old things today. My sister Marybeth was like a guardian. I always remember her watching over me, defending me and making me feel loved. I didn't grow up in a perfect family. But you know what? I love my Dad and Mom because they did their best and continue to guide me, help me and believe in me. I am so grateful to have them in my life.

Guess who I am!!? Yup! The one in the heart shirt: the littlest bambino, a.k.a. Lil General. Today be somebody who makes everybody feel like a somebody. You are an amazingly caring person and you help others daily. Don't ever let anyone put you down or make you feel less than. You are special. Inside and out and you are right where you are supposed to be. Let your soul shine and be grateful for what you have in your life. This world is a beautiful place. Your soul is begging for a chance to speak its truth. Speak *your* truth.

For those of you that signed up to WAKE UP NEXT TO ME for 99 days .... Prepare to be ignited within your soul! We are going to apply the Rockstar M3 Equation and the results will be out of this world! Private FB group with Joseph McClendon III Ph.D. being set up now. I need you to think big with me, okay??

"Welcome to Planet Earth... There is nothing you cannot be, do or have. You are a magnificent creator."

—Abraham Hicks

OCTOBER 2, 2015

Okay, here I am again. I've been using the app "Facebook Groups" (which I still will use) instead of FB because of the hurtful things that can be caused from social media. But I have found such an amazing group of people and I need their encouragement, love and support and they need mine, too. I am a relevant person and I intend on behaving that way. I can't let the negative outweigh the positive. I want to thank Carolyn Rim for throwing gas on the fire that Tony Robbins lit. And also to Joseph McClendon (Tony Robbins' right- hand man) for directly talking to me today and throwing more gas on the fire!! And to my fellow "99er's" YOU. GUYS. ARE. AWESOME!!

OCTOBER 3, 2015

Yesterday's call was amazing!! So grateful for those who signed up for the 99 Day Spark Your Rockstar Dare! They are all in and ready to lift off towards their dreams like a 747 in full flight!! Amazing!! Messages are pouring in about the 99 Day Dare.

OCTOBER 3, 2015

I have a community I am building of positive people and today in our group, it's Sexy Smiling Selfie Saturday! Name three things you love about yourself! Believe it or not, when I go to businesses and schools to speak, and ask this question, people don't know what to do! They are like, "Wait, you mean talk nicely about myself?" Yes!! Be your own best friend and give yourself some love, baby! By smiling and giving yourself love, you consciously let others know how to practice self-love.

Start smiling and practicing radical self-love and keep shaking that... well, you know.

OCTOBER 6, 2015

Break the rules today, baby! Let your soul shine, laugh and be your ridiculously amazing self!

"The only way to deal with an unfree world is to become so absolutely free that just your existence is an act of rebellion."

—Albert Camus

OCTOBER 9, 2015

Today .... Start telling the story of your life the way you would like it to be, rather than the way it is. I have transformed in the past 12 months. I have gone from $36 in my bank account to building a six- figure business that I absolutely love and am so passionate about. You can be and do and have whatever it is you want!

The only thing that stops you is the bullshit story you keep telling yourself. What if today you allowed your heart to take you off the well-worn path? Blaze a trail with your dreams and I promise the universe will support you! It will have your back with a cosmic force of positive energy!! Have faith, baby! It's possible! Come catch the SPARK!

OCTOBER 10, 2015

The nice thing about a smile is when you give one, you normally get one back. Are you smiling back at me yet? Because even if you don't feel like smiling, the very act of smiling starts to make you feel better! So just give it a whirl! Smile even if you don't feel like it and you will start to feel happier!

OCTOBER 11, 2015

Today, I am doing a vision board party for Renee Girifalco's Nerium Team! If you had told me 12 months ago that I would be getting paid to help others achieve their dreams and goals by doing what I love (speaking, meditations, group coaching, visualizations), I would have told you that you were crazy. Well, turns out, folks...

At Spark Your Rockstar Dreams Do Come True.

OCTOBER 11, 2015

DO YOU KNOW MY STORY?

What if I told you that you could have, be, and do, whatever you want in this life? Like I mean make as much money as you want. Have and be with whoever you want, and of course, work wherever you want! Whether it's a movie star, astronaut, or a writer.... if you can dream it in your mind, I can show you how to make it happen faster than you thought possible.

Sound too good to be true?

I bet you're saying to yourself, "No way. What's the catch?"

No catch. No gimmicks.

I WILL SHARE HOW YOU CAN QUIT TOXIC RELATIONSHIPS, QUIT ANY NEGATIVE HABITS AND LITERALLY BECOME THE REALITY ARCHITECT YOU WERE BORN TO BE.

You could be living your dream life—sooner than you ever thought possible. There's only one thing. The first one who has to see this dream, and believe this dream... IS YOU.

I can help you get the clarity, the drive and the motivation to ignite your dreams because At Spark Your Rockstar, Dreams Do Come True.

OCTOBER 12, 2015

I see a world filled with love because I love myself.

OCTOBER 13, 2015

Today wake up and decide to just rock it! Stop saying "I will tomorrow" and just go out and do it! You must operate with complete faith that your success is guaranteed. :) The first one who has to see it and believe it is you. Never forget who you are! A mother-f&@$*ing ROCKSTAR!

OCTOBER 13, 2015

Today is the day you stop saying tomorrow! If you do what you did yesterday today, you will always get tomorrow's same results! Take massive action Tuesday!! Operate with complete faith and act as if your success were guaranteed!

OCTOBER 13, 2015

Someone just came up to me at the gym and was in tears saying I didn't know her, but she felt like she knew me, and that my videos make a huge difference in her life. This is why I do what I do. So grateful right now.

OCTOBER 16, 2015

This goes out to all the people who were ever told they couldn't do something. Either by someone else or by themselves. One year ago today, I had $36 in my pocket. I worked in a cube and I had one thought: "I will die before I spend another 10 years in a cube." Click play to find out what step I took to create the momentum in my life.

OCTOBER 17, 2015

"I would rather be hated for who I am than as someone who I am not." I believe that we should all be true authentic self. I have never been happier in my whole life because I'm finally doing things that make me happy. Why not do things that make you happy? People wake up every morning and do things that they hate. STOP doing things you hate and START doing more of the things that you love.

OCTOBER 19, 2015

The Law of Attraction will continue to give you and repeat giving you what you are thinking about. Deepak Chopra says 95 percent of the thoughts you had today are the same as the thoughts you had yesterday. So if you continue to think about that stressful job, that tense relationship you're in, all the things you don't like in your life or maybe even financial stress, then you will continue to experience it. What if you could release all that and feel amazing? Feel like avalanches of abundance rather than stuck between a rock and a hard place? Go ahead and step into my...Universe.

OCTOBER 20, 2015

Today, let's make it simple. Wake up and remember what a gift to the universe you really are.

OCTOBER 21, 2015

By now, you all know I am bottling up the spark! So how can you ignite and awaken yourself? How can you shed another layer of skin to the next level of your awakening?

October 21, 2015

One of my beliefs is all breakdowns lead to breakthroughs! I got more comments, likes and views than I normally do and tons of private messages. People told me I was their inspiration and that I wasn't allowed to give up. Showing that I am human and not secret sauce, baby. I will make mistakes and I will fall down but I promise that I will keep moving forward. I will never give up on my dreams. I am a visionary and I will keep on keeping on!

October 23, 2015

Stop. Take a deep breath in through your nose and allow your stomach to expand and fill with air. Breathe out for four seconds. Think of one thing you are grateful for no matter how small it may be. Just one thing. Practice gratitude. Why? It has the same positive effects as Wellbutrin and Prozac. There is always—always— something to be thankful for.

October 24, 2015

I believe we can help others just by leading them to the feeling they desire. However, just like the old saying goes, you can lead a horse to water but ultimately it's the horse that must drink it.

October 24, 2015

Today is my first FIREWALKING EVENT! I have never been more nervous or excited in my whole entire life! Believe!! Last year on this day I was at Tony Robbins and if you had told me I would be holding my own Firewalk event one year from now, I would have told you that you were crazy!! I am a reality architect and I can build the life of my dreams. It's never too late to rewrite the story of your life the way you want it to be, rather than the way that it is! It's not too late to get your ticket!

OCTOBER 25, 2015

Officially held my first Spark Your Rockstar Firewalk! So grateful to all you Rockstars who experienced the amazing transformation of the Firewalk! I will never forget my first Firewalk... I quit smoking, finally put my two weeks in at work and got a job making double what I was making all within a week of my first Firewalk! That was exactly one year and three days ago today. I reminded people tonight, it's never about the fire! It's about overcoming fears and taking action in your life. Keep being amazing, world.

OCTOBER 26, 2015

Practice gratitude. Avalanches of abundance are moving towards you at this very moment. In all ways, not just financially, avalanches of spiritual abundance and physical abundance. The only one that can stop flow of abundance is you. You get to wake up today and be either of two mindsets. Abundance or lack.

A man can stand at the edge of the ocean and worry about all his issues in life. He can barely see the ocean if his mind controls him and he focuses on the past hurts and future worries. Or a man can stand by the ocean and allow himself to be recharged by it, the fresh sea salt air and sound of the waves moving in and out. He absorbs the energy of the ocean and appreciates the ocean. The moment. He is completely present and in the now. Same scene. Same ocean. Two people, however. One found abundance and one found lack. Choose wisely, my friends.

OCTOBER 26, 2015

It's proven you become like who you hang around. Look around you...
You okay with becoming that? Be true to you. You can decide to rewrite
your life any time you want.

OCTOBER 27, 2015

I made over $10K in one month from my first program launch I created!
I am now teaching my coaching clients how to turn their ideas into
programs and successful launches! I will be launching the secret formula
step by step in my next program! But for now... This is only for my
coaching clients! And the amazing thing is I will only be doing one-on-
one for one more month! Excited to see their results! Be a maverick.
Give yourself permission to dream big, baby!

Keep sparking www.SparkYourRockstar.com

Chapter 16
Get the Fuck Over It

"Write this down, doll. Get the fuck over it."
—Joseph McClendon III, Ph.D.

I can't stop thinking about my ex-husband. For some reason, this is the one thing in my life I can't seem to get a handle on. Business, fitness and success, all wonderful and expanding but this whole let go and get a divorce thing was killing me. I still want him in a way, even though I don't want him. It is the strangest feeling after being with someone 10 years, it is hard to let them go. I still am having thought patterns and feelings that are not serving me at all. I think about him sexually and I am telling myself it is wrong.

I grab my phone and dial my mentor, Joseph. He has been dealing with this shit for a year now. I knew he most likely is not gonna like me calling about it but I need his advice. He picks up in his usual tone, "Hey, doll, what's shaking?"

I clear my throat, "Uh, hey, Joseph. I am uh, really struggling right now," I say, trying to hold back the tears. "I am really struggling with my ex and I still have like this emotional tie to him. I have just been going through it. I am in pain and I don't know what to do and I am really emotional. I am suffering."

He takes a deep breath and says, "Carolyn, I need you to do me a favor. Go run as fast as you possibly can and grab a pen and paper. Now, I am gonna time you, so run fast."

I run as fast as I can to the kitchen and I grab a pen and paper. I say, "Ready, boss, hit me."

"Are you ready to write? This is really important and I want to make sure you really allow your mind to comprehend this and grasp what I am about to say to you so listen very carefully because the next words I say are magic kid.

"GET THE FUCK OVER IT."

He then hangs up on me.

"Um, Hello? Joseph??" OMG I cannot believe he hung up on me!

Okay, well, good, I am glad he hung up me. He is tired of my shit, and you know what? I am tired of my shit, too.

I deserve love. I deserve happiness and so does my ex, Mike. We both deserve to be happy. I am so upset. I jump in my car and I start driving in the rain. All of sudden a burst of inspiration hits me for a video and I quickly pull over. I grab my phone and I hit the record button. I feel like the universe is streaming right through me. I say:

"Hey Rockstars, I was so inspired to speak with you today that I actually had to pull over and make this video for you. I want to know, have you decided yet on what you wanted? And most important, have you decided to take yourself there no matter what? Success doesn't happen the moment you make the goal, or allow yourself to dream big. Success is born when you decided you are going to take yourself there no matter what. Don't give one speck of mental energy towards how it will happen.

"You can fail at what you don't want, so why not go for what you do want? Life is a beautiful contrast. Find out what you want and go after it like your life depends on it. Make love to it. Make it your obsession. DON'T LET YOU STOP YOU.

"There is one guarantee. If you don't take action, then you will never get what you want in life. Understand, failure is a step in the right direction. It may be painful going after your dreams but I can tell you the dreams and ideas come to you for a reason. You can act on them or not.

"Divine inspiration is coming through you when you get the sparks of inspirations or an idea for something. If they come to you, it's because you have what it takes to make it happen. Anything that is worth it will not come overnight. KEEP MOVING FORWARD. NEVER STOP.

"You can fail at what you don't want, so why not go for what you do want?"

—Carolyn Rim

"Remember, anything is possible and the first one who has to see it and believe it is you. I have a dream I speak in front of thousands and help them transform their dreams into a reality. I believe it with everything in my soul. The most powerful weapon on earth is a dream that you allow to ignite within your soul.

"Take a chance on yourself. You are ready and able to do amazing things in this world. The world would not be the same without you. What is your dream? Allow it to rise up in you ....and SPARK YOUR DREAM. SPARK YOUR ROCKSTAR. SPARK YOUR PASSION. SPARK YOUR BELIEF. SPARK WHATEVER YOU NEED, TO MAKE IT HAPPEN. THEN.....DECIDE NO MATTER WHAT TO MAKE IT HAPPEN!

"So, I will ask again, Have you decided yet?

"Do you know how powerful you are? You have the power to create any reality that you want. I was thinking about how each of us in the world are reality architects and we have the chance to build our life, the life of our dreams, the life that we only dream of. And it was only just right now that I realized just how powerful each of us are.

"Do you all know how bad I want my dream?"

I am starting to choke up on the video. Tears. Jesus, so much emotion.

I continue:

"They say in Napoleon Hill's book *Think And Grow Rich* that the most powerful energy in the world is desire—when you desire something, when you want something bad enough, you will get it. A burning passion for what you want.

"And guess what one of my secrets is? I have it. I was thinking about how my dreams are going to come true. I was thinking about how my dreams are coming true, right before my eyes, they are already in the process. They are happening. So many amazing things are going on right now in my mind and in my world. I was thinking about how the only one who can truly stop me though, is me.

"The only person who can truly stop you in following your dreams is you. See, I want you to think about what you are thinking about when you say you can't do something. Seriously, think about what you are thinking about. Are you thinking about all the problems? Are you thinking about financial stress? Are you thinking about relationship stress?

"What are you thinking about when you are telling yourself that you can't do something or that it's not possible? Because I was just thinking about it and one constant thought stream has been, 'I will not fail. I either win or I learn. I will not quit and I am going to get my dream.'

"I truly believe that I will be the top motivational speaker in the world one day. I want it so bad. Like there has got to be a reason I have this desire in my heart to help people and to really let people see that they can be and do and have anything they want. I want people to understand what a gift they are. You are a beautiful gift, if no one has told you that today. If your heart is beating, that means you have a chance. You have a chance to make a difference in someone's life today. You have a chance to just give yourself some love.

"Any failures I have had, and all past experiences have been stepping stones so I can continue to move towards my dreams and my own evolution. I am grateful for every single lesson and I am grateful for every person. I am realizing that I need to take time to allow things to cultivate, to grow inside of me. That's what one of my teachers, Sifu Terryann DeAngeles, told me, and I agree. She said I needed to allow things to grow within and allow them to bloom.

"I am learning that if you want something bad enough then you can make it happen. But you have got to *want* it. If you *kind of* want something, like if you *kind of* want your dreams to happen, then they *kind of* won't happen. But if you want it with your whole soul, if you are putting your mind, body and soul into it and you are cultivating that energy and harnessing that energy to put a freaking dent in the universe, then you will succeed.

"I am feeling the passion for my dreams, the fire for making something magical and amazing happen. I am feeling the swirling, twirling energy of love in my soul. Most people tell me my dreams are impossible. So, I decided from this point forward, the only people I am surrounding myself in my life right now are people who are saying, "Hey, you can do this! Hey, you got this, we believe in you."

"It's so important to surround yourself with people who believe in your dreams.

"Just remember what a beautiful gift you are, just remember that you have the power, you are a reality architect, you can create whatever life you want.

"You have to make a decision about what you want! What do you want? Most of us are not crystal clear on what we want so we waffle all the time back and forth. You have to get clear on what you want and then you have to decide to make it happen no matter what.

"I am not saying it will be easy because it won't, you will make mistakes, you will fall down but what do we do when we fall down, guys? You just keep getting up, you gotta keep getting up, you can't give up when moving towards your dreams, you just have to keep moving forward no matter what.

"Choose what patterns are making you happy and *focus* today on deciding what it is you want because I made that decision yesterday. I decided what I wanted in my life. I decided what thought patterns I was no longer willing to accept for myself, the thought patterns I was putting myself through with my ex. I decided that I was a gift and that this dream of mine is going to happen."

I am shaking by the time I end the video. I hit the post button. Within two hours go by, I have more than 90 comments and 7,000 views. By the end of the night there are 12,000 views and hundreds of comments. Just in a few short hours, I receive more than six messages asking about my private coaching, I sell three of those people on a coaching package.

That night as I sit in bed with my book and hot lavender tea, I allow myself to feel proud. I believe I am starting to have more self-worth and confidence—before, I would not have celebrated myself for my successes because I really thought that was being arrogant or overconfident.

But truthfully celebrating yourself is the best thing you can do for yourself because that means you can celebrate others' successes. The book I am reading is called *Think And Grow Rich* and I am reading it for perhaps the tenth time but each time I read it I learn something new.

I am reading the chapter on sexual desires. It is so fucking fascinating and I wish they had taught this shit in high school to me. This would have helped with many of the urges I had back in high school and how to get my needs met in healthier ways. Now let me explain the sexual transmutation definition in Napoleon Hill's Think And Grow Rich, Chapter 11, The Mystery of Sex Transmutation, which is the tenth step toward Riches, according to the book.

Breaking it down, "the meaning of the word "transmute" is, in simple language, "the changing, or transferring of one element, or form of energy, into another."

"The emotion of sex brings into being a state of mind. Because of ignorance on the subject, this state of mind is generally associated with the physical, and because of improper influences, to which most people have been subjected, in acquiring knowledge of sex, things essentially physical have highly biased the mind. The emotion of sex has back of it the possibility of three constructive potentialities. They are:

1. The perpetuation of mankind.

2. The maintenance of health (as a therapeutic agency, it has no equal).

3. The transformation of mediocrity into genius through transmutation.

"Sex transmutation is simple and easily explained. It means the switching of the mind from thoughts of physical expression, to thoughts of some other nature. Sex desire is the most powerful of human desires.

"The transmutation of sex energy calls for the exercise of will- power, to be sure, but the reward is worth the effort. The desire for sexual expression is inborn and natural. The desire cannot, and should not, be submerged or eliminated. But it should be given an outlet through forms of expression that enrich the body, mind, and spirit of man. If not given this form of outlet, through transmutation, it will seek outlets through purely physical channels.

"The transmutation of sex energy calls for the exercise of will- power, to be sure, but the reward is worth the effort. The desire for sexual expression is inborn and natural. The desire cannot, and should not be submerged or eliminated. But it should be given an outlet through forms of expression which enrich the body, mind, and spirit of man. If not given this form of outlet, through transmutation, it will seek outlets through purely physical channels.

"A river may be dammed, and its water controlled for a time, but eventually, it will force an outlet. The same is true of the emotion of sex. It may be submerged and controlled for a time, but its very nature causes it to be ever seeking means of expression. If it is not transmuted into some creative effort it will find a less worthy outlet.

"Fortunate, indeed, is the person who has discovered how to give sex emotion an outlet through some form of creative effort, for he has, by that discovery, lifted himself to the status of a genius."

I just had to figure out a way to channel all the sexual energy I had. I have had an abundance of sexual energy ever since I could remember. I loved my sexual energy but I had no one to share it with and I needed to find a way to use this as a creative outlet like the book said. It advised that when one harnessed this sex energy that I could literally tap into my sixth sense. It said that I would receive messages from infinite intelligence. I chuckle. Already happening, I think to myself. He talks about how fortunate the person with a high sex drive is. I chuckle again.

I think back to a moment in high school where I am in ninth grade in Catholic school at O'Hara and I am in the library. I am here making up time and barely anyone else is in here, I am 14 years old. I see a very attractive senior walking into the row I am in. I look up at him and my knees go weak. Jesus, he is so hot, I think. I want to just hook up with him right now. He comes over towards me and says, "Hey, don't I know you?" I look at him and smile,

"I am not sure, I know I have seen you around this year at the games." I was totally lying. I had never been to one of the football games but I wanted to impress him and I wanted to have something in common and I could tell from the varsity jacket that he most definitely was a football player.

"Oh, you watch me at my games?" he says smiling back at me. I literally could not even make up what happens next.

I must have had a look on my face like, "Oh please take me right in this library and slam me right up against these books." I licked my lips and it was like I was unconscious speaking to him. Oh, how easy these boys were. I bet they thought the same about me. Oh, how easy Carolyn is. He licked his lips and grabbed my hair pulled me into him. His kisses were messy and sloppy but still I was kind of living out my high school girl fantasies so I was okay with the inexperience of his kiss.

Back then I really only knew how to escape the pain and fill the void with a few things. Drugs and sex. I think back to all the ways I treated myself and my body, with such a lack of disrespect. I have learned to respect myself and my body but my past still haunts me. I often have flashbacks of moments I can't remember clearly. It is like my mind is hiding the past from me. It won't let me see something because it is so painful but I have learned to be with and embrace my pain. Its constant evolution for me. Growth will never stop for me.

Napoleon Hill goes on to talk about what constitutes a genius:

"Some wiseacre has said that a genius is a man who 'wears long hair, eats queer food, lives alone, and serves as a target for the joke makers.' A better definition of a genius is, 'a man who has discovered how to increase the vibrations of thought to the point where he can freely communicate with sources of knowledge not available through the ordinary rate of vibration of thought.'"

I start thinking about it and I realized that I may have been already harnessing sex energy. I was not having sex with Mike but did feel an abundance of energy to make things happen and get things done. I also had the ability to listen and receive the messages from the universe of infinite intelligence and be guided.

However, I use this transmutation sex energy differently. I think about my dreams coming true when I am having sex with myself. So when I am orgasming I literally think about my dreams coming true. I know this sounds really strange maybe, but it works. But I have gone three to four weeks at times with no orgasm, which for me is quite long.

I stop thinking about sex energy and want to rest my eyes. I put my book away and turn out my light. I flip over to see the empty bed next to me. I still sleep on one side of the bed. After 10 years of sleeping on the right side, I got used to it. I smile and move over to the middle of the bed. I create a new thought pattern before I rest my eyes to bed.

I imagine a train going by and on this train my thoughts go by one by one. I love myself. I love my life. I will always love Mike because he gave me the greatest gift I could have ever asked for. He gave me Kaylee-bear. Our relationship served its course. Two vibrations in different places is all. Turns out I was able to get the f— over it after all.

Thank you. Good night, God. I close my eyes and slip away into the darkness of sleep.

I wake up to the little barking alarm on my iPhone. I stretch, walk into the bathroom and get ready to go speak at this charity. I am excited and nervous. I speak in front of people on video all day long but not in person. I think about the day I have ahead of me. My ex still comes to mind. Mike. Kaylee has asked if he and I could go see *Inside Out* tonight. I had agreed and so had Mike. This separation is a process. I allow myself to feel how I am supposed to feel. I allow the emotions to move through me.

At the charity event, when I arrive, all the women are taking their seats. My mom is there and greets everyone, and then Peggy introduces me to the group of about 40 beautiful women. I look around before saying a word.

"Stand up!" I tell them. Everyone does and then I turn on "Jump" by House of Pain and tell everyone to jump with me. The women, from 20-somethings into their 70s, all join me in jumping, even a woman using a walker! Everyone is out of breath and laughing hard by the end of the two minutes. I then tell everyone about my progress on the book and what I have learned. I tell them how reading this book and going to events has changed my life. I share all the tips and tools I have and 45 minutes later I have everyone in tears. We do a gratitude exercise for people, for family, for love— the things you cannot buy.

Afterwards everyone wants to talk to me. It makes me feel so good. My mother has probably picked up none of what was said. She has a hard time letting go of things. I have compassion for her and I hug her. I even take a picture with her—a rarity. I feel incredible, starting to understand giving and contribution.

I walk to my car to go home, finish up some work online, then go see a movie with Kaylee and Mike. This may be a bad idea, our hanging as a family, but I still miss him and the way we can laugh together as a family.

A few hours later I pick up Kaylee at school. We jump in my BMW and we are on our way to meet Mike at the movie theater. We pull up and he is standing outside, smoking. He had quit but after our separation, he picked it up again. Kaylee and I jump out of the car and run to him. We are so excited to see this movie. We get tickets, popcorn and a drink.

As soon as the movie starts, I start to tear up. This is going to be a beautiful film. I think about my relationship with my ex-husband and how I miss our family. The movie walks you through the everyday emotions and how they affect us. It reminds me of when things change and people have to pick up the shattered pieces of life and start over.

Sometimes we can get stuck in a repetitive cycle of thoughts. Some people are stuck for years, reliving a painful situation over and over. It serves no purpose but to cause you to feel uncomfortable and pained. I believe that by fully allowing ourselves to feel the feelings from the beginning instead of resisting them, pushing them away or only feeling a little at a time, we can release the patterns that no longer serve us much faster and live healthier and happier lives. Boy, I need to start taking my own advice.

Feel the feelings. Pick up the pieces, and then cultivate the gratitude for every situation that has occurred in your life. Embrace the feelings. Soak in sadness if I must. Dance with my fear. Get mad if I must and then let it dissolve into compassion for better understanding and evolution of my life. Let myself feel all the emotions I need to feel. Most of all, embrace happiness and sadness and allow the sunshine in. Sadness can end up saving the day.

At the end of the movie, Mike and Kaylee are both crying happy tears. Who knew we could learn so much from a film?

Saying goodnight to Mike is awkward. Why are we hanging out like this? Part of me knows that Kaylee, Mike and I will all be happier if we just stop hanging out together. I forgive myself but learn the lesson. Listen to the intuition within. My intuition said I should not go but I went anyway.

> *"Listen to your gut and intuition.*
> *That bitch knows what's up."*

> —*Carolyn Rim*

The following posts are from this time.

OCTOBER 28, 2015

I raise my arms up mid-way and tilt my head back, I roar with energy that can be felt around the world. Shudder. Ripple effect. I am not leaving anything to chance. I am creating my own destiny.

Are you?? Not tomorrow. Not next week. Right now. Take matters into your own hands and live in a world you create rather than the world that was given to you.

OCTOBER 30, 2015

What if today you started with one thought.... I will focus all my energy on being a light, an example of the absolute joy that is available to us at every moment. Smile—TODAY'S the day magic happens.

OCTOBER 31, 2015

Here's looking at you kid—smile... You're beautiful.

NOVEMBER 1, 2015

I used to be someone who didn't want to frazzle those around me, or make big waves. Now I can't stop thinking about the ripple effect that I am having around the world. I want people to love their kids more, be kinder, take life less seriously, laugh a little, stop holding grudges, let it go, live your dreams now, and believe. I want people to put their hands over their heart and be grateful that it's still beating because as long as you feel a beat that means you're alive. It means you have a chance to make a difference today. You were created for a purpose. Everything would be different if you didn't exist. You beat unbelievable odds to be here. Look around. Most people are on autopilot. They live in a world created by other people's thoughts. Wake up. Take off the mask. Realize it's much better to be hated for something you are, than loved for something you're truly not. Just be you, and I promise the right people will love you too.

November 2, 2015

The law of attractions states that what you want is also seeking you, what you seek is seeking you. Anchor that in today, that belief of knowing what you want, wants you too.

November 2, 2015

Wake up and hug someone today for eight seconds. When you hug someone for eight seconds, or more, a chemical gets released into the brain called oxytocin. It's the love chemical. It makes you feel good. Then add connection to this. Ask the person you are hugging to take a deep breath with you in and out. Whether it's a sister, husband, child, or friend, give them a hug and take a deep breath.

When's the last time you had a bear hug? Come on, bring it in.

November 2, 2015

Let the world know why you're here and do it with all your heart, and of course, a smile. :) Here's looking at you, kid.

November 3, 2015

Put your hand over your heart right now. Take a deep breath in and out. As long as that heart beats you're alive and you have a chance to make a difference in the world. You were created for a purpose. The last chapter of your life hasn't been written yet, but you have to take back the pen and stop letting other people tell you who you are and what you can and can't do! You are the only one writing your story. You are the only one holding the pen. It's never ever too late to begin again, to start over, to jump in, to lift off towards your dreams like a 747 in full flight. It's never too late to take a big juicy bite out of the world, like the ripe juicy peach it is.

NOVEMBER 3, 2015

This is exactly what I am talking about. I just woke up. Had a nightmare. Went down to make some tea. And I saw this video about an entrepreneur and it hit me like a truck going full speed. My success in the end will speak for itself. I am working my butt off. I wrote for seven hours today. Apparently, it's a lot harder than I thought to publish a book. You need editors and resources and the ability to harness massive focus and energy. One of my goals is to finish my book. *I* am in the zone. Come hell or high water. I will finish my book! I will go after what I want and I will continue living with passion. I will become a best-selling international phenomenon and my story will inspire millions of people to start living their dreams instead of their fears.

NOVEMBER 3, 2015

Make your light so dim with humility that it's luminous. Today I am grateful for all those who have supported me, believed in me, reached out to me, bought my courses/coaching program to events. Thank you for loving the crazy me. The real me. The one that has the real value and is packing lots of BIG BANGS and tons of Bada Booms! You all make me shine. I am just a reflection of you all. Thank you and cheers to all the energy that's putting positive powerful dents in the universe.

NOVEMBER 4, 2015

You can dance with your fear, you can eliminate the voice of doubt and fear, by just dancing with it. Next time fear shows up, instead of resisting, take that bitch by the hand and twirl her! Say, Yes, I am scared but I have never been more excited. Today is the day I become the reality architect I was destined to be and build the life of my dreams! Yes!

NOVEMBER 5, 2015

Love wins. Love always wins.

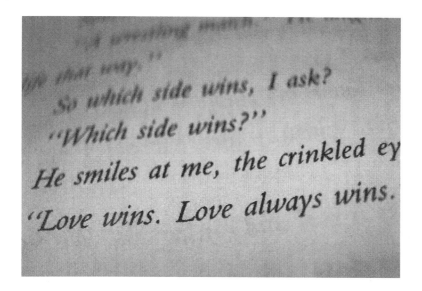

NOVEMBER 5, 2015

Are you an incredible coach that lacks one thing—clients to help? Wish they would line up at the door? Think about it. Right now. How many *amazing* coaches have part- or full-time jobs because they don't know what they bring to the table and don't know how to package themselves correctly? I have gone through many failures and breakdowns in the past year. One thing I kept doing and thinking: What I have to offer has tremendous value and I know what I bring to the table! I know my worth and continue to add and subtract to the success formula. I have and will continue to constantly look at the formula used to create the avalanches of clients I have cultivated and teach other great coaches the same.

NOVEMBER 6, 2015

Does this spark joy? That's it. One secret question to help you literally transform your living space and make your life better! I will be speaking in Media, Pa. for a local charity this Sunday! Hope to see and connect with you there! Peggy Rowe, it's absolute honor to be speaking at this event, especially since it will help people who are not as fortunate as us. We can make a difference! Together we rise!

November 8, 2015

Today, I had my first special date with my little girl. I wanted to set a time each week that was just the two of us. We have been through a lot of change the past year. Lots of uncertainty. Through it all, she is still the strongest little girl I know. We went for a hike, fed horses and enjoyed each other's company today. Sometimes, you just have to disconnect from it all, so you can reconnect.

November 8, 2015

So everyone who really knows me knows I have had—ummm, how do I put this—issues with my mother. As I grow I realize that she is one of the greatest teachers of my life. Today I am speaking for a charity group, Horizon House. It's all about decluttering space. I have spoken at 30 speaking engagements in the past year. This is the first one I invited her too. It's a big deal for me. Trust me. Our greatest evolution for growth lies with our biological family (the family we are born into).

Follow me on My Facebook page—we are going straight to the top!

NOVEMBER 8, 2015

Today I was privileged to speak at my first charity event for Horizon House. Every penny went to charity today. Feels so good. I have one goal when I speak: To help the people in front of me realize the absolute joy we have available to us at every moment! Does this spark joy!? You bet it does.

NOVEMBER 9, 2015

Today, I want you to realize the absolute joy we have available to us at every moment. In my opinion, it's the little simple things in life that matter most. A smile of a child that you helped create, a good laugh with a friend, a quiet moment to yourself, a journey or adventure. If you constantly are saying the grass is greener on the other side, stop looking and become laser focused on yourself and your own lawn! Make the best of it because you are so freaking worth it.

NOVEMBER 13, 2015

The law of attraction works. The problem with The Secret is they didn't break it down far enough. Many people watched The Secret and still have trouble creating financial abundance in the universe, and still don't have the job they have always wanted and still live in toxic relationships. You see, you are a vibration of energy and you broadcast like a loudspeaker and it acts like a powerful universal homing beacon. Like energy attracts like energy. So what are you broadcasting? Thoughts of the past? Thoughts of how it could have gone differently? How it really should have gone? Are you shoulding all over yourself? Continuing to relive that moment over and over?

How do you stop this rinse and repeat cycle, you might ask?

We open our hearts and create clarity with what we want in our life. We start feeding our faiths and starving our fears. We start balancing out the yin and the yang. The masculine and the feminine energy. Start tapping into our magic.

Think about all the ideas that you have "shelved" because you think it would not work or think about how hard it would be. The time for massive transformation is now. The time for waking up from autopilot is now. Stop letting other people create your life. Wake up! You are brilliant! Most people in life don't act on their dreams because they say, I will tomorrow, or I have time or I will wait and see. Too many people close their eyes for good with dreams and goals and purposes not lived. Million-dollar ideas trashed because they could not find a visionary who thought big enough.

November 14, 2015

Let the world know why you're here and do it with all your heart, and of course, a smile. ;) Here's looking at you, kid.

November 15, 2015

I want to create a spark for people. I am not the coach that sugar-coats everything. I don't always say what my clients want to hear. Sometimes, when we are knee-deep in our own bullshit and excuses, it's hard to see that. So that's why having a life coach is so crucial. They can see what we are blinded to. I always look at people and see them as they could be, not as they are.

November 16, 2015

Think about it. People who have no aim in life are sure to get there. If money didn't exist, would you still get up every morning and do what you do for a living?

NOVEMBER 18, 2015

Life will give you whatever you ask of it. Truly. You can have any amount of energy level you want, make any amount of money you want, be in any type of relationship you want, be a movie star, writer, or an astronaut even. There is one part of the formula people miss when it comes to Law of Attraction. You must be crystal clear on what you want—then your actions must also speak in alignment with that. The universe is always watching and listening. It knows you become like who you surround yourself with. So if you want to be a millionaire and surround yourself with people who are broke... Guess what you're not going to become? If you want to be an astronaut but you are partying and drinking every night, guess what you will not become?

Your actions and words must align with what you are wanting and you must take consistent action to get there. This a magnificent world we live in and everything in your reality at this very moment is made from invisible energy. You are a loudspeaker of energy and you are broadcasting vibes into the universe that create your reality. Like energy attracts like energy. So ... What are you calling into your reality??

An even better question: Do you know you hold the power to change it?

NOVEMBER 21, 2015

Bye-bye, old rules. Hello, new amazing rules!! I am a sexy sensual woman and I embrace my feminine energy and I listen to my heart. I own my space and I don't need to have it all figured out to be happy! I create my reality and everything in front of me is a choice! Want to change your life? Check out Joe White. I love giving credit where it is due.

NOVEMBER 22, 2015

Stop making up so many rules in order to be happy. How easy would it be to take a deep breath, smile, and become grateful for all the beautiful things you have in your life?! Happiness is an inside job. Your happiness doesn't depend on who you are or how much you have... It has to do with what you think.

"Today, plant seeds of love!! Love is the most powerful cosmic force in the universe!"

—Carolyn Rim

November 23, 2015

Remember, it's not what you have, or who you are. It's about what you think. The poorest person could feel the richest. The richest person could feel the poorest. The Law of Attraction is easy, really. If you want financial freedom, success, happiness, and fulfillment, you must cultivate the feelings within. You are more than money, more than fame, more than success. You are a gift to the universe and an eternal being. Wake up & live.

November 24, 2015

STOP! LOOK & SMILE. Did you know just the simple act of smiling even if you're in a bad mood actually sends a message to your brain to make you feel happier? It takes 48 muscles to frown and only four muscles to smile. Let's start a ripple effect of smiles today and it begins with YOU.

November 24, 2015

I believe everything happens for a reason. Everything. Every day you wake up with a choice. You get to choose how you treat people. But know one thing. The way you relate to anything is how you are relating to yourself in that moment.

November 26, 2015

Today, plant seeds of love!! Love is the most powerful cosmic force in the universe!

November 27, 2015

Start taking care of the most important relationship in your life— the relationship with yourself.

November 28, 2015

Just let go. Cross out all the rules that you put in your life to be happy. Through the power of your mind, you can create prisons or palaces, wealth or poverty, joy or suffering. The thoughts and images and what we repeat in our mind like a personal mantra, are what our very powerful minds bring into reality.

NOVEMBER 29, 2015

Want to get rich today INSTANTLY? Count Your Blessings.

NOVEMBER 29, 2015

What if instead of trying to be history teachers and telling the stories of the past over and over again, we begin to feel grateful for every moment because it has brought us to where we are!? Imagine how amazing that would feel. Yeah, it's just that simple to reach for better-feeling thoughts. Activate the creator within. Wake up and live.

Chapter 17
Disconnect to Reconnect

"We can inspire others not by being perfect,
but by being real and by being raw."

—Carolyn Rim

"Mom, I just wanted..." Kaylee was trying to get my attention. "KK one second." I am on the phone.

"Mommy I love you. I feel like when we are together, you are here in this room, but you are not really here in this room."

I stop. She's right. I had become very self-obsessed with my phone. "Kaylee, I am so sorry," I say, and I put my phone down. I hug her but a few minutes later, I am back to my phone.

I am on my phone almost constantly. I can tell my little girl and my family are starting to notice. I am starting to feel guilty for being on the phone and computer so much but I need to be for my job.

Or do I? There is not one reason I need to be on at 8:30 at night while putting my little girl to sleep but I feel constantly pulled to it. Why? I do research on this. Turns out, phones have the same effect that sex and drugs do on the brain. They activate the same place, the pleasure center of the brain. I see. Now I understand. I can't stop looking at my phone because I am addicted to it. The average adult spends over three and a half hours on the phone a day. The average person checks the phone 118 times a day. What is this doing to children and their families? They say ignoring your child has effect as physical harm. I feel like I am going to be sick.

Are you addicted to your smart phone? Take the quiz to find out at http://www.psychguides.com/guides/signs-and-symptoms-of-cell-phone-addiction/ Here's the text of the quiz:

This self-assessment is not meant to officially diagnose you with cell phone addiction. If you are concerned about your problematic behaviors, speak to your doctor or mental health professional about possible treatment.

- Do you find yourself spending more time on your smartphone than you realize?

- Do you find yourself mindlessly passing time on a regular basis by staring at your smartphone even though there might be better or more productive things to do?

- Do you seem to lose track of time when on your cell phone?

- Do you find yourself spending more time texting, tweeting, or emailing as opposed to talking to real-time people?

- Has the amount of time you spend on your cell phone been increasing?

- Do you secretly wish you could be a little less wired or connected to your cell phone?

- Do you sleep with your smartphone on or under your pillow or next to your bed regularly?

- Do you find yourself viewing and answering texts, tweets, and emails at all hours of the day and night, even when it means interrupting other things you are doing?

- Do you text, email, tweet, or surf the internet while driving or doing other similar activities that require your focused attention and concentration?

- Do you feel your use of your cell phone actually decreases your productivity at times?

- Do you feel reluctant to be without your smartphone, even for a short time?

- When you leave the house, you ALWAYS have your smartphone with you and you feel ill-at-ease or uncomfortable when you accidentally leave your smartphone in the car or at home, or you have no service, or it is broken?

- When you eat meals, is your cell phone always part of the table place setting?

- When your phone rings, beeps, buzzes, do you feel an intense urge to check for texts, tweets, or emails, updates, etc.?

- Do you find yourself mindlessly checking your phone many times a day even when you know there is likely nothing new or important to see?

I keep feeling that really gross feeling in my stomach. I just don't like the way it feels. I have just answered YES to every one of the questions. Yuck.

I look down at the phone, the very phone that is making me sick, and I see my friend Jonathan Centeno is calling me. I pick up even though I am on the verge of tears. "Hello?" I say.

"Hey Carolyn!" He says. I then start crying. I feel comfortable in front of Jonathan because he started out as a client of mine and had referred a ton of friends to me. He also came to my event in Philadelphia where we became friends. He is a film maker.

I get a great idea. "Jonathan, I need you to come film me for three days. I need you to film my smart phone addiction." I tell him about the smart phone addiction, and about Kaylee and about what seems to be happening in my life. Even though he lives in Florida, he agrees to come to Philadelphia over Thanksgiving weekend, which is only a week away.

I start working again. Horrible habit, to be so utterly addicted to the phone. A week passes by and Jonathan shows up at my door with a tripod and camera. He is ready to film. He is an incredible human being. He is not even charging me for this. He just wants to help. Over two days he films me and Kaylee. He films me at times I do not know he is filming me. He films us in the morning, in the evening and pretty much anytime Kaylee and I are spending time together.

We both work on putting the film together. On the third day, we work until 3 a.m. making edits. Many times through the editing process, I stop and break down emotionally. To see myself ignore my angel child makes me sick to my stomach.

When the film is finally done, I hesitate posting it. Jonathan says, "You should post this. People will understand, Carolyn. We have all been there."

My mom is on her way to pick up KK from my house and when she comes in, I ask her if she wants to watch the film with me and KK. We all sit and watched it for the first time. KK, Jonathan and I all start crying.

231

My mom makes a face: She's sick, having a hard time watching it.

I feel sick, and I grab my daughter and say, "Kaylee, I swear this phone is going in the trunk when I am in the house with you."

She says, "I forgive you, Mommy. It's okay."

My mom says, "You can't post this video. What will others think of you, Carolyn? You do not want to put yourself in this type of light."

I say, "Mom, this video is going to bring awareness to thousands of people. I am posting it. Yes, it is vulnerable. Yes, it is raw. Yes, it is real. But it is the truth." I cannot let my mom's judgment of this get in the way. I go to the computer and post the video described below:

NOVEMBER 29, 2015

This is something that was not easy for me to post. I asked Jonathan Centeno to film me when I was on my smartphone. For two days we filmed. When I watched the final video, I could not believe how much my phone was stealing me away from my own life. I decided to shine light on this ever-growing problem. Becoming aware of this issue helped me to put the phone down and become present when I was with my little girl. Please share and help me bring awareness to this issue. I am not saying social media is bad. I am just saying we need to set boundaries with it.

Within 24 hours the video has 50,000 views. I am blown away. People are responding with comments like:

Brenda Sisson: It's like that everywhere... I try and take breaks... But, you get sucked back in!! Thanks for the reminder...

Jasmine Corri: What a wake-up call! We must be more present in the real world & in our children's lives if we have children & be a better example to them not to depend on the smartphone but instead be more present as well. Needed this thank you for sharing!

Steffany Kirby: Thank you Carolyn Rim. This makes me sad but it's what I needed to see...I'm guilty of doing this.

Amanda Lea Waldt: I don't have kids but I do this to my husband all the time and he just feels like I'm ignoring him, so he ends up sitting right next to me with no conversation because I'm so caught up with my smart phone.

Vesna Terzich: Yes let's share and realize the addiction to our phones. We need to reconnect with human beings that are right there in front of us and not virtual connections. That human connection is vital to our existence!

Jennifer Vinita: I've known this is a huge problem for me, something I keep meaning to deal to with. What a fantastic video! I was watching it as my three kids were playing in front of me, instead of being involved with what they're doing. This made me so sad to see, to think about how I make my kids feel. I'm going to start a no electronics time during the evenings and outings. It's not just me, but my older two kids who are always on their phones as well. Thank you.

Lulu Frazier: Excellent!! Ever wonder why they call it a "cell" (u are locked in & can NOT get out) Turn OFF ur cell & turn ON ur heart. Thank U Carolyn. I applaud U 4 posting!! U opened up "a can of worms" that DEFINITELY needed to be addressed! This cell phone addiction is a RAGING fire that is OUT of CONTROL! Help put out the flames.

As I look through all the comments and see the views keep climbing I think about how grateful I am that I have shared it. My mom calls me to apologize. She says she is so sorry for saying anything and making me feel like I should not share it. She says she only did it because she loved me and she didn't know how everyone would respond. I forgive her of course. My mother is the sweetest kindest person you will ever meet. She would give her heart for anyone. I know in my heart she was only trying to help me. Protect me. Just like all moms try to do, I guess. Or the good ones, anyway.

A few days later, the video has reached 100,000 views. Hundreds of comments, messages and emails pour in from all over the world. I am totally blown away by everyone's response. I had to make sure I am not saying social media is bad because it's not. Social media is the only reason you are reading these words right now, a wonderful tool but boundaries must be set for this one.

So I decide to capitalize on this. I call my infusionsoft rep. I tell her how many views and she says she we should definitely be linking a campaign (Email Content) with this.

So I whip together the content. I create a quiz for people to take to see if in fact they are addicted and then I create the top 10 ways to disconnect to reconnect! I send the following over to my rep at infusionsoft, who puts the campaign together for me:

Top 10 Ways to Disconnect to Reconnect! Ready to recharge your mind, body and soul! This will make you SMILE ...OHHH YES!!

1. Go to an Event or Retreat
Going to an event or retreat is a great way to disconnect and re-connect to your soul. Oh—I have an idea: You should come to a Spark Your Rockstar event! Join the rockstars and me for an exclusive one-of-a-kind

weekend. Allow us to help you unwind, relax, detox, recharge and cultivate inner stillness at a Spark Your Rockstar Event.

2. Cultivate Stillness—Meditation

Second on the SYR list is SEND your brain on a little all-expense paid vacation! There are so many ways to disconnect but one thing is for sure... Silence is one of the best. When is the last time you remember stillness? Been a while, huh? Commit to a daily meditation practice even if it's just for 5 or 10 minutes, as soon as you get up. Once you become silent you will have to take a look at your inner state of being and sometimes this can be crazy and chaotic. Just take a look within and allow yourself to focus on your breath in and out. For me, this was very hard at first because I had all these thoughts, "Why am I just sitting here?" "I have to pee." "My leg itches." All these thoughts came into my mind but once I just continued to focus and become silent, I had profound answers come to me. If you're ready to make a longer commitment, consider trying a silent retreat, one where meditation and quiet contemplation are the main events. HINT... Go back to #1... A meditation retreat may be just what the Spark Your Rockstar doctor ordered...

3. Who Wants a Quickie? ;)

Are you ready to be excited, turned on....and whoa?! Wait a second! I thought we were relaxing! Yes WE ARE! That is exactly what THIS quickie will do for you! I am talking about the one and only...Quickie Body Scan. Are you starting to melt yet? By now, I should have helped create a small smile on your face which always helps relax the face muscles. To help quiet your mind, and boost awareness of the sensations in your body, sit or lie down in a comfortable position and close your eyes. Start by drawing your attention to different parts of your body, and checking in with how they feel. you can begin at your scalp and then go to your eye lids, and then down to your shoulders and neck, and feel any tension just dissolve. Then start working your way down the body and continue to notice tension and release it. A thorough body scan might last about 10 minutes, but you can make this a quickie anytime you need to distress and just relax.

4. When You Are Off Duty, *Mean* It!

Make weekends and vacations true relaxation times, not just lighter versions of your weekday workdays. Use the-out-of-office notification setting on your office email and resist the urge to respond to emails until just a few hours before your scheduled return. If not checking your email makes you nervous or puts your livelihood at risk, politely inform colleagues that you'll be checking emails at specific times, for example 10 a.m., 3 p.m. and 7 p.m., and will be able to respond only to the most truly time-sensitive ones. If you value your off-hours, so will they.

5. DANCE ...Like You *Mean* It.

Turn on some music and just dance. When is the last time you just *danced?* I mean just let your freaking hair down and started to move your hips? The free motion and stretching of movements of dance can help release tension from the body and lift your spirits. Exercise in any form can act as a stress reliever by pumping up endorphins and dancing can be particularity enjoyable to blow off steam for many people! I guarantee this will boost your mood! NOW SHAKE THINE ASS!

6. Listen to Nature Sounds

I bought a machine from Walmart for around $16 and it has all- nature sounds. Before bed, my little girl and I listen to the ocean waves. I tell her one day we won't have to play that anymore because we will be living on the beach and all we will have to do is open our windows to listen to the sweet sounds of the rolling waves in and out. I recommend getting a machine like this, because they are small and compact and you don't use your phone for it. When relaxing or going to sleep, you want your phone turned off, turned down, and downstairs. It's important to start disconnecting from needing the phone by you at all times. At least place it on the other side of the room.

7. Laugh

Even if it doesn't feel natural at first, making time for a quick laugh, whether it's by watching a silly animal video or reminding yourself of a funny joke, can help bust you out of a stressful head space. Laughter releases endorphins in the brain and relaxes the muscles in your face. So, go ahead. I dare you...make an inappropriate joke and don't take life so seriously all the time. "That's what she said." It makes no sense, I know, in this reference, but it gets me every time!

8. Breathe In and Out...Bada-Boom...Bada-Bing.

I remember I was sitting in traffic a few short months ago and I realized, I was not breathing. I was holding my breath. Why? I connected the dots and realized anytime I was nervous or feeling tension I would start to breathe in a very shallow way. My shoulders would slouch and my eyebrows would furrow in. Then I decided to breathe in and out. Just focusing on the breath and the cool inhalation when I breathe in and the warm exhalation as I breathe out has helped tremendously. You try. Try to focus all your energy on the breath, and it can take you from good to great very, very quickly! I have some priming I do daily and would love to share it with it you as well! Reach out to me if you are interested in rewriting your mornings with less stress and more love, energy and team spirit!

9. Have Sex (with or without Your Partner...)

So just to name a few benefits of sex, whether you have a partner or not, sex can help boost happiness and self-esteem levels and decrease stress levels instantly. You may nod off more quickly after sex too and for good reason. After an orgasm, the hormone prolactin is released—it's responsible for the feelings of relaxation and sleepiness. So, you can now make the big OOOO without feeling guilty! What the hell, right?! Grab your partner and give them the sexy eyes. By yourself? No worries. That makes it even easier. Grab a mirror and go ahead and be irresistible.... to yourself. Can anyone say: H to the O to the T?!

10. Take a Walk! A What? A Walk Outside!! A Hike! Yes! Get Sunshine!

I think it's so nice, I will go for a walk. Do you ever get the winter blues? Feeling a little holed up staring at the computer screen, to the rectangular screen, and back and forth from your iPad, to your Mac, to your iPhone and then you realize, you have not been outside, like really outside, in nature in a really long time. You are human and whether you say you like the outdoors or not, it is in our human nature to love the outdoors. I know every time I am feeling a little under the weather all I need to do is take a little walk and I feel so much better! Grab your dog! Grab your husband! Grab anything you want except your phone or laptop! Leave technology at home and disconnect2reconnect!

Please Share in the Rockstar Community Which One You Liked and Which One You Did to #Disconnect2Reconnect! Looking forward to hearing some of your answers, whether they are on this TOP 10 list or not!

People are eating it up. I love that this is all coming from my intention to truly help others and myself. I allow the information to be sent for free and tell people to come to my next event, a Poconos, Pa. Mindfulness Retreat in the mountains with a monk and myself. More than 30 people sign up for it. Connecting the dots back, the reason I bought tickets to my first retreat was because I was real and raw. We can inspire others not by being perfect, but by being real and by being raw. People love real and raw because it's rare.

So I decide to just make this my DNA. I create a plan for myself and I share it. I leave my phone in the trunk of my car for a specific time of the day, from 5 p.m. until Kaylee goes to bed, and I am present with her. She is so worth it. It feels good to be a mom first and foremost, because when I serve from this place, it feels damn good.

I serve from my overflow rather than my cup. Bottom line, sometimes the best way to find yourself is to disconnect to reconnect. I continue every day to find balance between work and just meaningless scrolling and surfing.

The following posts are from this time.

NOVEMBER 30, 2015

Hey, YOU! Please, yes, you, the one reading this. I wanted to say how grateful I am for every one of you who watched, liked, commented and shared my video to help bring awareness. It is now over 50,000 views in the first 24 hours. I have gotten so many messages that I wanted to respond to some of them here. So people have been asking and messaging me how they can start setting boundaries with the phone because they have the same issue. Just know that technology isn't bad! It's a great thing and I have built practically my whole business using social media. However with that said it's important for us to take time away from constantly checking updates and messages and phone calls.

So here is what I am doing. I have decided to put my phone in my car trunk from 5 p.m. until 8:30 p.m. (at least on nights when I have my little girl) because if I have it in the house then I will just reach for it because it's become a habit for me. But if I have it in my trunk. I will not reach for it. I played cards and games with KK last night and I set up something called KK TIME. This means for one hour, no TV, no tablets, no smartphones. It's just one-on-one time with KK and me so we can connect. We played good old-fashioned checkers, Spot It, Flapjack, and a memory game. We laughed so hard together and it gave me so much joy to connect with her.

Those are just a few things I am doing. I still have to use social media for my business but I now see that I need to set boundaries with this as do many parents, spouses and just people in general.

NOVEMBER 30, 2015

We can inspire others not by being perfect, but by being real and by being raw. People love real and raw because it's rare.

DECEMBER 13, 2015

What if I fall?

Oh, but my darling, what if you fly?

DECEMBER 15, 2015

What if the greatest achievement of your life was to enjoy your life?

December 15, 2015

Today's forecast will be extra sunny in your day, with some light lifting off towards your dreams in the early afternoon. Bring your umbrella just in case, because you bite in this day like the ripe, juicy peach it is. Around every corner today, something wonderful is about to happen. Followed by some bliss and gratitude in the evening.
www.SparkYourRockstar.com

December 17, 2015

All I need is within me now.

December 18, 2015

Four sayings that hold the power to change the world. I am sorry. Please forgive me. I love you. Thank you. Just saying them out loud or internally will instantly change your state. Trying saying them and take full responsibility for where you are in life.

December 19, 2015

#1 Goal this January 1 will be to work out and get healthy. Most people will quit a mere 15 days into January. New Year's Resolutions have become somewhat of a joke to people. Here is your chance to jump in! I dare you to wake up with me for 99 days! This is accountability to a whole new level! Your year-to-date results provide undeniable proof as to the effectiveness of current strategies, as well as the quality, consistency, integrity and intensity of your efforts. Question: If you continue doing things the same way these next 99 Days as you did in 2015, what type of results can you realistically expect?

December 19, 2015

Success happens the moment you decide to make it happen. Not actually when the goal happens itself, but the moment that you decide, I am making it happen no matter what. So: Have you decided yet?

December 20, 2015

You are the controller of your destiny! You get to decide how today goes. You! When I wake up in the morning, I visualize that the entire universe is cued up to give me everything I am wanting. You must believe that your success is guaranteed no matter what, that the universe is on your side. Remember though, a chisel is just a tool to carve wood but in the hands of a craftsman, it can create beautiful things. Grab the chisel and Create your own destiny.

DECEMBER 21, 2015

It's quite possible to attain great wealth, the best education, and an exceptional life & still be unhappy. This occurs when people live with an absence of gratitude. Success is a process that includes both peaks and valleys but the one consistent in a truly successful life is gratitude. A special kind of magic happens when you are grateful.

DECEMBER 22, 2015

It's never too late to start telling the story of your life the way you want it to be, rather than the way it is.

DECEMBER 23, 2015

Remember what you focus on you will get more of. You are like a loudspeaker broadcasting a signal. Like energy attracts like energy.

When you have clearly written, time-bound measurable goals... you will bring into your reality the people and resources to help make that dream come true. All you have to do is focus on what you want....and see it, feel it as already done.

> *"A dream written down with a date becomes a goal. A goal broken down into steps becomes a plan. A plan backed by action makes your dreams come true."*
>
> *—Greg S. Reid*

DECEMBER 25, 2015

In life we have two choices: We can be sad, cranky, and focusing on everything that's wrong about others and ourselves; or we can be happy, excited and focused on all the beautiful qualities about others and ourselves. What's wrong is always available and so is what's right, we get to choose where we put our focus! We have the choice! Join me for the 99 Day Dare and come catch the SPARK for life!! Say yes! By now, you know it's the 2 mm shifts that you make in your day that make all the difference! See what meditation and working out daily can do for you! It transforms everything!! Smile!! Wake up every morning with me! Yes!

DECEMBER 27, 2015

You can fail at what you don't want, so you might as well take a chance and do something you really love. Greatness comes when you allow yourself to dream big and think big. I am so grateful for the Tony Robbins seminars because they put me in touch with powerful positive people. It's sad to even say this, but it's so true: It's your closest friends and family who will try to talk you out of taking a risk on something that you love. You must let your own voice guide you. But this voice is not loud, it whispers the answers but you must quiet your mind to hear it. And you must surround yourself with people who believe in you and force you to be the best possible version of you. Cut your excuses in half and double the amount of action you take... It's time to step up.

DECEMBER 27, 2015

My little girl is my Why. She had me from Hello. Her heart is pure, and so many of my smiles start with her. She is the reason I don't give up most days. She pushes me to be a better version of myself daily and hold myself to a higher standard. Her smile makes my heart sing. What makes your heart sing!? Don't know?! Find out! Start doing things that make you happy.

It's never too late to start telling the story of your life the way you want it to be rather than the way that it is. You are the author and you are holding the pen.

DECEMBER 28, 2015

At any moment you can say this is not how my story ends. Just start writing Chapter 1 of My New Life. Then rewrite the story the way you want it to be rather than the way it is.

December 31, 2015

Happy New Year, you amazing gifts to the universe! Smile and shake thine ass into the new year!

January 6, 2016

Shift happens when you plant a seed of abundance and love in your mind. Make your joy a top priority and watch how fast your life changes. My life is not even recognizable from 12 months ago!! What an amazing adventure!! Spark your Rockstar within and join me. You can be, do and have anything you want on this life. You control your destiny. Now let's blow this Popsicle stand and go make it happen. I'm out.

January 8, 2016

Try this belief on for size in 2016: I don't need a reason to feel good! I can feel out-freaking-standing anytime I want!!

January 8, 2016

Good morning! Today's forecast is here and it looks like we are in for another amazing day here on earth. You glide easily through your day today as you focus on solutions and not problems. Late afternoon some clouds roll in, but don't worry, it's only to rain down avalanches of abundance on you!! Later into the evening, you relax and spend time in gratitude for all the little things you can be grateful for. You realize that the whole universe is cued up and ready to give you

241

anything that you're wanting.

Start your day with a different type of forecast... You will have a different day.

> *"To laugh often and much; To win the respect of intelligent people and the affection of children; To earn the appreciation of honest critics and endure the betrayal of false friends; To appreciate beauty, to find the best in others; To leave the world a bit better, whether by a healthy child, a garden patch or a redeemed social condition; To know even one life has breathed easier because you have lived. This is to have succeeded."*
>
> *—Ralph Waldo Emerson*

JANUARY 10, 2016

Are you happy where you are? Getting all the results you want and more?! Plugged in, turned on, powered up? Then, awesome! Most people are aimlessly floating with no goals or passion. Most people quit their goals by Jan. 15! What if I told you I found a secret that would help you stay on course? Wouldn't you like to spark avalanches of abundance in your life? Have a healthy body and mind? Reach your goals this year once and for all?! It's possible. In fact, once you realize that you created everything around you, whether good or bad, and stop blaming anyone else, and just accept full responsibility for where you are, a vibrational shift happens and you are ready to take over your ship and start towards a destination instead of just floating aimlessly through your life!! It's time to cut your excuses in half and double the amount of action you take!

JANUARY 10, 2016

You have ideas unique to you, a specific rhythm and perspective that are your strengths, not your weaknesses. You must not be afraid of your uniqueness. There is a reason you want what you want. It's deeply connected to your purpose. Embrace Your Uniqueness because the odds of finding another you, are one in 400 trillion. Go ahead give yourself permission to dream big.

JANUARY 11, 2016

I am unique. I am special and I am worth it. I am a child of God and I deserve to be happy. I am naturally a joyful person. I am legendary and the whole universe is cued up to give me everything I am wanting and more. I am a giver. I empower and help those around me. Remember, you get to decide who you are. Stop listening to the opinions of others and drown out the voice of uncertainty and listen to the sound of your own rockstar heartbeat. Incantations are the easiest, fastest way to recreate who you are.... And the first one who has to see and believe it is you.

"Personal development is the practice of whom we wish to become."

—Jim Rohn

JANUARY 11, 2016

Close your eyes and think of three things you are grateful for every day. You will sleep better. If you want abundance in any area of your life, whether it be business/finance, spirituality/faith, or relationships, you have to start getting into the alignment with abundance. Once you are in alignment, you will find yourself embracing avalanches of abundance and joy. You must practice gratitude daily for it to have the amazing effect it does. Thank you all for being unique. Thank you all for shining & being your own kind of beautiful. Goodnight.

JANUARY 12, 2016

Accept full responsibility, you take your power back, that you create your reality. I was born to squeeze people's hearts. I want you to feel again. Wake up! Wake up! I want to feel it pump within my hands. I am calling to the whispers in your soul that tell you it's possible to be, do and have anything you want. It's possible to love more and judge less. To open your eyes to the gifts and avalanches of abundance all around you. You are meant for greatness!! Stop getting your needs met on low lying levels. Stop settling for less than the best possible version of you. Draw the line in the sand, my friends. Say no more. No more turning on autopilot and lifting up our feet and moving with the crowd. We plant our feet fully on the ground. We fight for a world with kindness, compassion, gentleness, and love. We laugh out loud, and we sing like Angels and by God, we dance. Like stones thrown into the pond, we have this ripple effect all around the world of peace and love. I am coming for your heart. I am here to awaken... And to let the light shine through. I have sent my arrows of desire into the universe. It's only a matter of time. Watch out world: You ain't seen nothing yet. Wings are spread and I am ready to fly.

> *"Every dark time in my life made me who I am today, therefore I am just as grateful for the dark moments in my life as I am for the brightest ones. I needed every low valley in my life to make my mountaintops better. I keep moving forward toward my dreams regardless of the setbacks I have. My passion points the way. I know my path is one of great honor."*
>
> **—Carolyn Rim**

JANUARY 13, 2016

The picture on the next page was taken almost 10 years ago. I sang at a friend's wedding. Sandra Moore Boyd's. I will never forget it. I sang "Making Whoopee" by the great Frank Sinatra. My whole life I have been on stage and making events.

When I was eight years old, I had all the kids from my neighborhood do a play in my garage. I wrote about a fortune teller, a prince and an evil queen. Of course, as the director, the writer, and the casting personnel, I cast myself as the lead. But what's even funnier, tonight I remember not letting my neighbor's parents in until they paid to come in to my mom and dad's garage to put on a little show! I even made some flyers selling tickets! I made about $50 and bought the whole cast Pizza Hut after the play (not by my choice; my sister, Mary Beth Rim, who helped co-direct at the time, made me. I wanted to keep the money and invest in props and the next show).

I have been doing this all my life: and I love it. I remember opening a store in my dad's office when I was nine years old. And then when I was in ninth grade I tried out for the play *Annie* and during my audition I started dancing and everyone started clapping and getting excited. The casting director quickly got on the mic and said, "This is a singing audition, not a dance-off." I remember saying, "I will go direct and write *my own* play." Mic drop...

I love what I do today. Why? Because I follow my heart and damn... It feels so good when I listen to my higher self. Yes, it's hard work and yes, I work more than a full-time job but that won't be forever and the better

I get at this, the more I will rise. I am currently rebranding. I am creating my new website right now called www.CarolynRim.com. Why?? Because I am a star and I will shine bright. All the greats do it! Model Success, baby! Brand yourself with your business.

Here's to finding your purpose, and having the CONFIDENCE to move towards it.

Yours truly here, signing off with big hugs, high-fives and pattern-breaking ass slaps....

January 18, 2016

Keep moving forward. Your dreams are worth it. Leave the B.S. stories you tell yourself at home about why you can't have what you want. You can be, do and have anything you want in this world. Giving up on your dream because of one setback is like slashing your other three tires because you got a flat. Keep moving forward.

JANUARY 19, 2016

Today I lead a call of 30 people through a workout and meditation on a zoom call at 6 a.m. EST. Then I jump on my community call at 7 a.m. and host while Missy Loy shares her incredible story! Now, I just got done speaking at Horizon House with Peggy Rowe and her team! I am so grateful to be able to do what I do!! I love speaking and inspiring others to create the vision in their mind! Their goal is to raise $250,000 by June 30, 2016! I know they will get there! I helped create a custom visualization for them reaching their goal! It was amazing! Excited to work with amazing teams like Peggy's!

JANUARY 20, 2016 BLOG POST

I woke up at 4 a.m. today with no alarm. As I drink my water and get ready to start my day, I pull up my laptop. I have been working on my book for five months now. It's my journey from 2014 to 2015 and how I went from broke, unhappy, and dying, to starting my own business, finding my passion, and being awakened within. As I go back over the year, all the posts on FB, I find one post from a month ago, by Cynthia Savage and it catches my eye. The question on the video she posts from Tony Robbins is "What if enjoying your life became your greatest achievement?"

I stop. I sit. And Instantly I think about stopping to meditate on this one sentence. It seems so simple, doesn't it? To enjoy one's life. To be filled up with overflowing light and love. To be shining bright.

If it's so easy, then why are so many people stuck, complaining, and unhappy? People tell me all the time, "I love your energy." "You shine brighter than the sun." Recently I had one woman say, "Your presence is brighter than any room you are in." I do not say this to boost myself up or brag. I say this because I think I just found the reason why. I let that inner child shine through me as much as I can. I laugh too much and at ridiculous things. I don't take myself or anything too seriously. I play hide and seek, tag, and all the childhood games with my little girl. It's a beautiful privilege to be her mom and brings back moments from my childhood. I love to sing and have random dance-offs.

I believe that every dark time in my life made me who I am today, therefore I am just as grateful for the dark moments in my life as I am for the brightest ones. I needed every low valley in my life to make my mountaintops better. I keep moving forward toward my dreams regardless of the setbacks I have. My passion points the way. I know my path is one of great honor.

My intention is to squeeze your heart to life, to awaken you, to believe that you are enough. You are special. You do deserve love and happiness. Life is meant to feel good. Celebrate the little things, smile through the dark moments, play with your children, and most of all, love yourself, absolutely love every fiber of your being. You are more worth it than you will ever know. I hope you feel the energy I am sending to you in this picture. And open your eyes: Every day is a blank slate. Make today the day, that you believe enjoying your life is the greatest achievement of all. Watch how fast the world around you changes in magical ways.

I put the words, "Life will never be the same" in honor of Tony Robbins and Joseph McClendon who sparked me awake. I will be forever grateful. Thanks, Cynthia, for posting a beautiful video and post. Obviously, it inspired me.

Sending you hugs, high-fives, and pattern-breaking ass slaps,

Carolyn

Chapter 18
Life Doesn't Happen *to* You, It Happens *for* You

"Love always wins. Love is the most powerful cosmic force in the whole universe, and when you add it to what you desire, and fall in love with your dreams, the unseen is all of sudden seen."

—*Carolyn Rim*

I am staring at the ceiling smiling. It is still dark outside. I look at the clock. It's 3:03 a.m. I am wired. I can see the headlines now: "America's Top Confidence Coach meets Top Strategist Tony Robbins." I can't stop thinking about what happened in the past 24 hours. It's almost like a dream. Not sure what's real and what's not. In less than 12 hours I will be on a live interview in front of thousands of people with a man I admire more than Superman: Tony Robbins. He is the only man who has ever held a candle to my real father.

Yesterday, I received a message from Anthony Conklin. "Would you like to ask Tony Robbins a few questions tomorrow? Thought it would be a nice thing to do for you. I will be interviewing him."

I had to re-read the message a few times to make sure I wasn't hallucinating.

I replied, "OMG That would be incredible! Thank you so much! I don't know what to say other than thank you! I am so grateful."

He replied, "I know you are. I see you fiercely impacting people. I am watching you. See you tomorrow at 6 p.m. on Blab." (Blab is a social media platform that allows up to four people talking at the same time. It allows thousands of people to chat about what everyone is talking about on the screen.)

I could only sleep a few hours last night. I get up and start my day. I share with all my followers and friends I will be live on Blab tonight. I am finally going to get my chance to talk to Tony Robbins and thank him for everything he has done for me. I have never been so excited in my life.

I am rolling through a few questions thinking what I will ask Tony. I will ask him, "How can I spread more compassion and love into the world on an even more effective level?" I wonder what he will reply. Oh, just thinking about speaking with him gives me the chills. I am finally going to get to thank the man who has helped ignite the matches and sizzle within my soul!

The hands on the clock cannot move any slower. I do my usual work, meet my clients, and meditate. I pray to God. I visualize the interview. I ask God to please help me. "Please God let me do your will and not my own. Let me be a light in the world for others and myself. I am light and I am love. Allow the light within me to expand and ripple outward. Thank you. Thank you. Thank you." (I end every prayer or visualization with three thank yous.)

I want to be super-prepared for tonight's interview so I set up three computers just in case. I set up lighting. I test my audio, my Blab link and everything is running smoothly. I do Blabs all the time so this isn't my first rodeo!

About 10 minutes before show time I jump into the Blab and see Anthony Conklin and his coach, Vicki. They are letting everyone know that Tony Robbins will be on shortly. Then, the magic man himself, Tony Robbins, jumps on. I am connected to his every word. I can't believe how calm Anthony is. He is calm, cool and collected. Tony shares some wonderful information, about making changes and taking massive action in life and what is needed to do that.

And then before I know it, Anthony says, "Carolyn Rim—this girl is a Rockstar life coach—come on in!"

I jump in and I see myself and Tony and Anthony and Vicki on the screen. It is incredible. It is like a dream come true. I am beaming.

I am smiling so big at Tony. I am flying. I open my mouth to speak and the most horrifying thing I can imagine happens. He can't hear me. Tony Robbins says, "I can't hear you." Tony is looking at me and giving me such a warm smile, but meanwhile I am panicking, and I am shouting at the screen, "No No No!"

Anthony jumps in, "Carolyn, try logging back in and out." I feel worms in my stomach.

I see everyone's comments in the chat room. "Sucks for that girl." "Awe, that's a shame." I see the number of people on. My audio doesn't work in front of 4,000 people. How could this be happening? I log back in. Nothing. They still can't hear me. Anthony even lets me try a third time. Nothing. No audio. I am practically in tears. I cannot believe this is happening. I turn my camera off. Unreal. How could this happen? I tested *everything*. Tony Robbins says, "Tell that girl I said sorry and I must go. Thank you, Anthony, for having me on." I watch as his face disappears from the screen. Here was my chance and I blew it.

I am still watching the interview on Blab and all of sudden, Anthony gets a message on his phone and says, "Oh my God. Carolyn Rim, try coming back on. You will not believe this." I jump back into the Blab on video and try to talk and now they can hear me! My audio suddenly works!

Anthony says, "Carolyn, Tony Robbins felt so bad that your audio didn't work he wants you to be his and Sage's special guest at West Palm Beach at the next Unleash the Power Within Event."

I stop breathing momentarily. I am blown away. I start to cry. I explain to everyone watching, to Anthony and Vicki, that the past two months I have been working with Dragan Trajkovski and Kelly Phillips with my Rockstar group. We have sold about 30 tickets and I have 30 Rockstars going to West Palm Beach but I haven't the money to buy my ticket. I cannot believe Tony Robbins is going to give me a ticket to be his special guest.

I am a little bit in shock and I am starting to connect the dots. If my audio had worked, I would not have been invited to UPW Palm Beach as Tony Robbins' guest. I had three computers set up and I tried from three different sources, and not one of them let my audio work until Tony Robbins jumped off!

To me, that's a sign. Destiny. That is grace. That is something much bigger than me helping me.

I chuckle to myself. Here I thought the worst thing happened by my audio not working, but it turned into a huge gift. I start to think back to all the dark moments in my life, about how grateful I am for them because they brought me to this moment. I think about how those moments of trials and tribulations made me who I am today.

> *"Where are you looking to fulfill your needs or seek answers from others? Where are you looking for the answers? Outside yourself? Does a certain situation seem to keep happening to you? Take a deep breath, stop for a second, just stop and look within yourself, because I promise you if you look within, the answer is there. You just have to quiet your mind and the soul will speak. It points the way to your destiny."*
>
> *—Carolyn Rim*

This past year has been the hardest and the most rewarding year of my life. I wonder if other people connect the dots in their life, if they would find that everything that happened to them that they labeled bad was instead a gift in disguise. I share this with everyone in a video. I get messages and emails like crazy about what has transpired. It seems almost surreal that these things keep happening to me. I must start saying that these are my new normal.

I meditate after this and I am crying tears of deep appreciation to my

Father in Heaven. I feel so surrounded by a force I cannot see, I cannot touch—but I can feel it's an invisible presence all around me. I go to bed that night and have a deep restful sleep. I sleep all night long.

The next morning I start thinking about what I need to do to make West Palm Beach happen. I need to find a hotel room and flight. Laurie Strough Smith messages me on Facebook to see if I want to stay in her room.

I review the list of people going. Missy Loy doesn't have money for a room so I give my last $250 to Laurie, a.k.a. "Rockstar Red," for Missy Loy's share in her room. Missy is part of my Rockstar group and I am so excited she is coming to West Palm Beach. She is an incredible human being. Mike Peppler, a friend from the Rockstar group, ends up paying for her flight.

I only do this because I have faith God is going to provide for me if I give.

Then, within about three hours of my making this transaction and giving $250 for Missy's room and giving up my spot, Carolyn Cole, a friend in my 99 Day Dare, asks if she can buy my ticket since we will both be flying out of Philadelphia.

I message her back, "I would appreciate that so much."

She buys my flight and messages me three more hours later saying, "I am sure you probably already have a room, but I have an extra bed in my hotel room if you do not. Want to stay with me?" I feel like I am manifesting now at incredible speeds. The thing is, I know it's not me, and it is me. It seems the more faith I have in others and myself, the faster things seem to be speeding towards me. I have no doubt within me. I feel as though I am walking with an invisible net underneath me. I feel so close to God.

I immediately thank Carolyn Cole: "I will accept your gifts. You have no idea how much this means to me."

"Love is the oxygen of life."
—Tony Robbins

At the moment, my business and I are in serious trouble. On the outside, I am making it seem like they have never been better, but I feel even if I do make some money with the 99 Day Dare, or coaching clients, I am constantly playing catch up with everyone I owe money too. Carolyn Cole seemed like an angel who swooped in out of nowhere.

So, the more I seem to expand, the more certain people seem to leave my life. I have a few people who are no longer my friends, because they say I care only about myself. This hurts to hear but maybe they are right in some ways. After some meditation and some serious looking within, I realize I have the answers inside.

I admit and accept responsibility that I have done things that were selfish but I don't believe I don't care about others. I care deeply for myself and my company. However, I care about others, too. That is the whole reason I am doing what I am doing. I must allow the people who were knocking me down, or saying things I found untrue about myself, to fall away from me. Not everyone is supposed to be on my journey with me forever. I have to be grateful for their presence while they are there and just move forward.

My integrity and character have to change. I have to learn the lessons from past mistakes but also not idolize others. Just in the past few weeks I have learned so much. I have learned that when I think something bad is happening, it is for my own highest good. What if we were all grateful for all the bad moments in our life because it made us who we are today?

What if life weren't happening *to* me, but was happening *for* me?

That thought has a different vibration, a vibration of love, of trust. I learned the lesson by not searching outside for the answer but instead moving inward to look at my own truths. I accept the things I have done wrong in the past, decide not to beat myself up for them, and move forward. I know the world is big enough for us all to make our dreams come true.

> *"Not everyone is supposed to be on my journey with me forever. I must be grateful for their presence while they are there and just move forward. And when I think something bad is happening, it is for my own highest good."*
>
> **—Carolyn Rim**

I understand the Law of Attraction and I am currently applying it to my life and getting dramatic results with it. I decide to share this lesson with everyone on camera. I go live to my whole audience:

"Hi guys, my name is Carolyn Rim and I am your confidence coach here to talk to you about the greatest lesson that I learned over the past year. I believe successful people share information and knowledge.

The Law of Attraction states that the same experience will continue to happen to you until the lesson is learned. I had the same experience happen three times over the past 12 months. Today I finally learned the lesson.

Right now you have a gift. There is so much content and knowledge out there for you to be resourceful.

"A situation has happened three times over the past year and today I realized why. What happens is, I meet these incredibly amazing strong women and I latch on to them and I am like, 'Okay, give me your knowledge and I will give you mine. Let's share tips, let's inspire each other, let's empower each other, let's change the world.'

"It's amazing to be with these women and they inspire me and from each I have gotten so many lessons. I am obviously not going to say their names but I can tell you that over the past year three incredible women came into my life and I idolized them.

"I felt like some of the people I met just wanted to change me. I know they only wanted me to grow but the way I was being treated was not okay. One of them even tried to get me to change my brand name, Spark Your Rockstar, because she didn't connect with the word rockstar. My brand is my brand, Spark Your Rockstar—it sparked me. Carolyn Rim *is* Spark Your Rockstar, Spark Your Rockstar *is* Carolyn Rim. You are a Rockstar if you are watching this—a Rockstar is someone who believes the impossible is possible. A Rockstar is someone who is compassionate and loving towards others and themselves.

"I realized I was searching for these answers in these incredibly strong women. I am searching for these answers and asking them, 'What's the answer? Give me the answer, come on, give me the answer! What is the secret to life? Tell me!'

"Here I am searching for the answer in all these women when the answer was within me this whole time. I was searching for it outside of me for so long, trying to find something or someone outside myself with the answer, but I had to learn that *the answer was within me all along.*

"There will come a time in your life where you are aware, when you have an *aha!* moment. That's what I feel like I experienced today.

"So, I want you guys when you are watching this to apply this to your own life. Where are you looking right now in your life to fulfill your needs or seek answers from others?

"Are you getting your needs met on a lower level? Where in your life are you looking for the answers? Outside yourself? Does a certain situation seem to keep happening to you? Take a deep breath, stop for a second, just stop and look within yourself, because I promise you if you look within yourself, the answer is there. You just have to quiet your mind and the soul will speak. It points the way to your destiny.

"I believe it's truly one of my greatest lessons that I have learned this year. The Law of Attraction states that the same experience will continue to replicate in your life just in a different way until you learn the lesson. Life is always happening not *to* you, but *for you*.

"A time will come when you must come face to face with who you are, the good, the bad, the beautiful, the ugly. And when that time comes, accept where you are, and then decide where you are going to take yourself. Others can help light the way, but ultimately, you must decide to take the leap and look within for the answers.

"I promise, the answer is within you, my friends. Remember, as Tony Robbins says, 'All you need is within you now. Connect the dots back and learn the lesson to expand and move forward.'"

I love making videos and speaking to others. Within a few hours the video has 4,000 views. People say in the comments they keep listening to the video. They can relate to the same situation repeating in their lives until they learn the lesson from it. They can relate to the answer being within them.

That is what is connecting me to others. Being real and raw. We don't connect to others by being perfect. We connect with others by being real and honest and sharing our story and our growth. I am just absorbing all the magic right now. I am in appreciation frequency.

I continue for the next week to consistently share where I am and make videos. I just can't stop sharing all my magic. I decide to get more visible than ever by sharing a video every day.

> ## *"What if we were grateful for all the bad moments in our life because they made us who we are today?"*
>
> ### —Carolyn Rim

The moment I decide to become more visible than ever, I make this video. Ever since the Tony Robbins interview, I am more inspired than ever to do what I must:

"Hi guys, my name is Carolyn Rim and I am a Rockstar speaker and transformation expert. I have faith this will reach the right people. Watch until the end and let me know what the message was for you. You have a choice right now. You have a choice to allow the words I am about to say and the message that I am about to say to enter your mind and allow yourself to, like a sponge does to water, absorb it.

"Or, you can just watch this video and then get off and do the same shit that you always do. So you have a choice. There is always that choice. I am just so inspired to tell you it is not easy to get to where you want to be. If someone tells you, 'Oh, it's easy it's peachy keen, it's awesome, yeah it's very, very simple,' that's a lie. It's not authentic. It's bullshit. I am sorry that I am cursing—I just get so passionate about my dream, about making this happen, about getting my message out to people that we need more compassion and love in the world. That stepping into who you need to be to reach your dreams is going to be really hard, but it *is* possible.

"We need more people who believe in themselves. We need more people who believe in themselves so their children believe in themselves. Who do you think is watching you right now? Your children, your husband, your wife, your family—you are constantly setting an example for those in your life by your actions.

"Imagine if you weren't here. All the people you have talked to, all the people you have touched and connected with would not know your love or your magic. Think about it. Think about how valuable your soul is. Everything would be different if you didn't exist.

"I truly believe that we were all born for a purpose. We all have a mission in life. And we can either choose to listen to that and follow that because I believe in our curiosity and our passion. That is where all the answers and the magic are. I was on my 99 Day Dare call today, and Missy Loy said something that struck a chord with me. She said my faith in her made her believe in herself. I believe with my whole soul.

"I don't care how it's going to be done, but I need to get the message across that it's not going to be easy just to go out there and make it happen. You are in a battle with your old self and the new you that is trying to emerge. Don't let who you were talk you out of who you are becoming. You are in battle with an angel and a devil, and you have to know how to keep pushing forward.

"I have faith that if I take the leap, something will catch me. I don't know what it is, but I know it will because it has—*it just has*—my whole life. Think about all the times you were scared you wouldn't make it or something would happen. Think about all the little miracles that have "

"You have a choice today to say, 'You know what? I am going to go out there and make today *amazing*. I am going to light up everybody I see. I am going to spread smiles everywhere and show people what it means to shine bright. I am going to smile through the bullshit. I am not going to spread negativity. I am going to inspire people with it. I am going to make my pain my price and make it a gift to the world.'

"All my painful moments—they weren't for nothing. I had to go through the pain to make me who I am and I am inspired to share that with you.

"Know that the universe is on your side and there are angels surrounding us and we never know when we are going to meet one who carries the message for us.

"With that said, go today and really be aware, be aware of the people around you and what they are saying and know that it's possible.

Signs and angels are *everywhere*."

—Carolyn Rim

After my videos, I get a ton of messages about how inspiring I am. I even have people wanting to fly in to work with me. Mike Peppler messages me first. wants to come fly into Philadelphia and work with me for three days. I have never had a client who came from afar to work with me.

We agree on a price and a few weeks later he flies in. He is staying at The Inn at Penn on the campus of the University of Pennsylvania. I have now worked remotely with clients all over the world, but I normally work face to face only at my events. Everything else is done on video.

I didn't know what to expect with Mike Peppler but I know he and his wife are good people. On Christmas Eve, they showed up on the Dare calls with reindeer antlers on. Matt Smith and the Pepplers were on the Dare calls consistently. I have this feeling I know Mike and his wife from somewhere, as if I have met them perhaps in a past life, as crazy as that may sound.

I have no idea what is about to transpire. I know I only want to help Mike. I set the intention that we both grow. Mike had recently posted something on Facebook, and I could not wait to speak with him about it. He shared that his mom was emotionally and physically abusive, and she touched him when he was little. He was so raw, open and vulnerable.

I still am not where he is, but I know I want to be. How refreshing to just share it into the world—be so open about my past, not ashamed.

"Signs and angels are everywhere."

—Carolyn Rim

I pull up to the Inn at Penn an hour late. Traffic was so bad today and I got lost on the way here. I walk into the hotel and up the winding wooden staircase. So much rich history here. I meet Mike, who is making an older woman at the front desk laugh. She reminds me of a grandma who always makes sure you're taken care of. When I see Mike, I feel like breaking down and crying. I feel like telling him, "Hey, you. I have searched for a longtime for you, my friend."

But I hold myself together. For some reason I want to keep my cards close to my chest. He greets me with a hug and says, "Hey you. Good to see you. Tell me something good." He is my soul brother. He feels and smells like *home*. I cannot describe the feelings I have for this soul—not a sexual feeling but a big bear/little bear feeling. It reminds me of who I really am. It reminds me of home. From where I came from before I was streaming into my body now.

We are led to a conference room Mike has reserved and a tall man named Trinity comes in to see if we want refreshments.

Mike asks the man, "What does your name stand for?"

The tall man explains, "It means the power of three. The Father, the Son and the Holy Ghost."

Mike gives me a look, saying "Pay attention."

I still can't quite see what the big deal is but I do my best to stay open. Mike asks Trinity, "We would like some tea. I wanted to also ask if you had a message for me?"

The man stops and looks as if something physically takes over his body. "Yes," he says. "It is better to teach a man to fish than it is to just give him a fish. When I was a boy in Jamaica, I went into the water and taught myself to fish with a sharp stick. It made me who I am, and I am that I am." Then Trinity walked out of the room.

I look at Mike and say, "Okay tell me what just happened? Why did that man say what he said? What just happened?"

Mike takes a deep breath, places his hands over his face and starts to cry. He tells me stories of signs and angels everywhere. He tells me he was brought here by God and that people have messages for him all the time as long as he asks the right question. When he later asks the person why they said what they said, the other person has no idea.\

*"One smile can light up someone else's world.
Smile at the world today and it will smile
back."*

—Carolyn Rim

For the next two hours, he tells me all about what's been happening and how most days he feels like some spiritual Indiana Jones on an adventure.

He says, "God speaks to me. Sometimes it is louder than others. Ever since you got here, I keep getting chills. Do you remember who I am?"

I try to put on a mask so he can't read my face. I am so resistant for some reason. Why? I am not sure. I say, "Mike, I am not sure. I guess so. Maybe I feel like I know you, too. Not sure how to take all that you just told me. It is not often someone tells me they have a direct communication to God."

He shakes his head and says, "I know, sometimes I don't believe myself and then someone will show up with a message from Him. Or He just comes to me."

I am angry at Mike for this but I do not know why. I am resistant to the signs. I want to test this. "Mike, can you prove to me that God talks to you?"

He says, "Yes but be prepared for the next three days to have some messages come through me to you that you may not like, okay?"

I shake my head yes, even though in my heart I am resistant. Then he says, "Follow me." We go to a place in the city to eat and order way too much food. I do not why; we just do. We have leftovers.

After we are finished, Mike says a man with a red collar around his neck is hungry and we have to get the food to him. I think that's strange but I allow myself to just go along with what he says. As we get into a cab, we start heading back to the hotel.

A few minutes into our trip, he turns and says, "Look to your right."

We are at a red light and a man with a red-collared shirt is sitting on the street. He is holding a sign that says, "Please help. I am hungry."

I open the door with the leftovers in my hands and hand the man the box of food. I get back in the cab. I say, "It's a coincidence. Show me something bigger."

260

Mike looks at me, "We should not test the Lord." I can't help it. I want proof. Like solid proof that God is speaking to Mike.

We then go into the campus bookstore, which is in the same building as the Inn at Penn. Mike says, "Go into the bathroom. Something on the wall. It is a message for you."

On the bathroom wall, I see an old clock ticking slowly away. What does this mean? Time? What about it? I walk out of the bathroom and back to Mike. I say, "What does this mean?"

"This means that time is running out. He wants you to know it's time to be real honest and just share yourself with the world openly. Do not be ashamed of your past, Carolyn. Your past makes you who you are today. I know you know this, but there is a part of yourself that is resisting. You don't show up on time. You need to make friends with time."

This seemed to be more than I could bear. "Mike, I am done for the day. Have a great night."

I walk out of the bookstore and give my ticket to the parking attendant. As I am driving home, I have so many unanswered questions. I start thinking about time. I have always struggled with it. Felt like there was never enough of it. Maybe I do need to change my beliefs around time.

I pull up home and I am so tired, I walk into my house and fall asleep on the couch.

"Do not forget to show hospitality to strangers, for by so doing some people have shown hospitality to angels without knowing it."

—Hebrews 13:2

TIME TO SHED ANOTHER LAYER

I am up at 6 a.m. the next day. I am going to take the train into the city today, I say. I get to Mike about two minutes before our scheduled time. I am stressed but do my best to show up with energy. He is there speaking with a hotel employee, Bethany, as I walk up the steps. I smile at them both. I do not know why I feel so resistant to this man, but I do. He looks at me with a big smile, asking, "Ready for more adventures?" I look back at him. This is going to be an interesting next two days.

Over the next two days, Mike and I explore Philadelphia and we have so many signs and unbelievable things happen. More coincidences and things happen. We see signs and speak with people. We follow the signs.

It is our final day there. I am sitting across from Mike. I finally believe him. I finally break down. We are sitting in the library at the Inn at Penn. I start to cry. I tell him about the money situation I am in. I tell him about my past. He looks at me with compassion and understanding. He says, "Carolyn, you have to do it. Be real with the world and they will fall at your feet. The time to shed another layer of your awakening is upon you."

I see Mike, but I feel God. Mike says, "May you know just how incredibly blessed you are today and every moment of the rest of your life. You are never alone. I have sent people here to protect and guide you. Mike is one of them. You feel at home around him, yes? That is because you both come from the same place. Trust yourself. Don't avoid. Pay attention. Be patient. I love you."

I see the glaze over Mike's eyes vanish. I just spoke to God through Mike. I get up and say, "Mike, you are an incredible soul. I am grateful you came to Philadelphia. You have given me a gift that words cannot describe. I thank you for that."

Mike says, "Carolyn, you have given me a gift too. I grew and expanded from this too."

I walk away from Mike and feel my energy level swirling upwardly again. I go home and decide I don't give a fuck who knows about my past. I am not ashamed about my past anymore. I love every part of story.

I write the following post and decide to share the ghosts of my past with the world:

FEBRUARY 7, 2016

I was 16 years old in this picture that follows. If you look hard enough, you can see the pain in my eyes. I am going to share some things that I normally would not share on Facebook, or for that matter with anyone else. I know many would rather I hide the truth, but honestly, I have nothing to hide anymore. I am not ashamed of my past anymore.

My client, Mike Peppler, was the one who inspired me to write this. He just kept saying he had nothing to hide, and that he was who he was, and he didn't care who knew it. I kept thinking how liberating that would feel just to let it all out. Say screw it. This is my truth. This is me. Come here and take a look at the wounds that I have turned into scars. Take me or leave me.

I feel so strongly to share who I used to be to who I am now. I want everyone to know that it's okay to make some mistakes and get back up. Your past does not have to equal your future, unless you live there.

Deep breath in... Here goes:

I was 14 when I first had sex. I am not going to mention any names because is not necessary but I remember feeling that freedom for a moment that everything faded away and I didn't feel the pain. I had finally found a way out of myself. To numb the pain I was in. Not physical pain but emotional. I felt alone. I hated that alone feeling and always had to be doing something, which is quite ironic now because my alone time is by far my favorite part of my day. When I am meditating in stillness.

I remember I went searching for anything to fill the void I felt within my soul. I felt so empty. So spiritually dead. The only time I felt alive is when I was doing drugs. Or when I was lying to those I loved. Or when I was selfishly seeking attention from men who were taken. I lived for the rush. The rush of the adrenaline of doing something so wrong and naughty. I didn't know how something could be so wrong but feel so right at the same time.

This is how I saw myself for years. As a piece of meat. A whore. A slut. I had no real value, I thought. I went through high school getting into fights because other girls would be mad I slept with their boyfriends. I switched schools a few times because of this.

I clearly remember a vivid moment that I do not think I will ever forget. I was called into the office one time and one of the teachers said several students were worried about me. They saw me smoking pot on school grounds, snorting in the bathroom, doing whip-its in my mom's van in the parking lot. I remember the message from this teacher.

He looked at me as I stared at him with glassy, stoned eyes. He leaned in and said, "Carolyn, while others are being voted for prom queen and who will be most successful, you're being voted as most likely to die of an overdose. *Wake the fuck up.*"

That comment stopped my racing thoughts dead in their tracks. He walked out the office and slammed his door. I sat for a moment. Not making a move or a sound. OMG, I think, how did I get here?

I went from bar to bar with my fake I.D. pretending to be someone else. I felt like I could smell the alcohol seeping out of my skin, and all I could feel was this sense of hate for myself. Here I was addicted to drugs and alcohol and men. Anything not to feel inside. I felt my cheeks get hot as the tears streamed down my face and felt the churning in my stomach like worms. Ugh. I wiped the tears away and put on my best facade to face the world outside.

You see, that *aha* moment isn't when change happens. It's awareness that comes with the *aha* moment. I must give a shout-out Joe White for bringing this to my attention at one of his seminars. Action is what breeds change and at that point I was not ready to squarely face the woman I was. I could barely even look in the mirror anymore. Just looking in the mirror would make me sick. I hated me. I hated that I felt like a whore. That's all I felt like anymore. There was no more twinkle in my eyes. Just a dead zombie and my drug of choice was more. More.

More. More.

I went home that day to numb the pain just like any other day but this time, I decided not to wake up.

That night, I went out with these guys. I drank way too much. Vodka. I kept thinking it wasn't happening fast enough so I kept slamming shots and then all of sudden... It hit me like a ton of bricks. Like to the point where I blacked out. I woke up on the curb the next morning to a guy shaking me. He said, "Hey, you alive?" I looked up and realized I was face-down on the pavement out front of my mom and dad's house on the sidewalk.

My one thought: "Shit. I can't even kill myself right."

I could tell you many more moments that lead me deeper and deeper down, but then one day, I was gifted with grace.

I was caught. I was caught making $65K a year with no bills and yet I was still broke. I remember stealing from my dad and he had finally had it. He called me. He said it is done. No more. I wanted help. I was grateful that finally the chase was over. No longer would I have to wake up every morning and find a way to fill the void. I would do anything to stop the lies, the guilt, the shame.

I went to rehab and started going to NA meetings. It wasn't easy. Many days, I felt different and not like them but I just kept focusing on the similarities instead of the differences. Slowly but surely I fell in love with myself and my life again. They advise you not to get into a relationship the first year of recovery. I was pregnant one month after entering the NA program (you all know by now rules are not my thing). I ended up marrying the father of my baby two years later. But NA saved my life.

Life was good for a while but then I just started to once again feel bored. Unfulfilled. I was married, steady 9 to 5 and had a little girl who I adored, but I found myself asking, Is this it? Is this why I came here?

I found myself looking up bridges to jump from. And instead, by divine grace...My fingers type in the name Tony Robbins. I could not help but connect instantly with his energy as soon as I saw him on video. I guess most people can, but this seemed different.

This felt like ... Destiny. My story continues, as most of you know. My story continues to become more amazing and bizarre and outrageous. All the things they said were impossible... I just kept doing.

I keep leaping into the dark and having the faith that my feet will hit the ground. I keep sharing honestly and being vulnerable. I keep saying, "Hey! This is who I am and I love me! I am not what happened to me. I am not my past. Now when I look in the mirror, I see a fallen angel. A fucking warrior, a wise, strong, humble, compassionate woman who I love so much. I am so grateful for the hand I have been dealt in my life because it is that hand that makes me who I am today."

So thank you to the people who have hurt me the most. Thank you for making me the woman I am today.

Remember if you want to truly love yourself, then you must love your past too, no matter how difficult it may seem. All those struggles made you who you are today.

Don't ever give up on you. Especially when you think you have no way out... that's normally when the door appears towards your new priceless magical beginning. Big. Bada. BOOM.

Sending you hugs, high-fives and pattern-breaking ass slaps,

—Carolyn Rim oxoxo

BONDING AND CONNECTION THROUGH PAIN WITH OTHER ROCKSTARS

Within a few hours, my post has nearly 300 likes and comments, emails and messages pour in. So many stories. People are sharing their stories with me. They tell me what they have made it through. They tell me the pain they went through. I connect deeply with all the stories. I reply to them and build a stronger connection with them. My people. These are my people. These are the souls I admire and surround myself with. Even though sometimes sharing these private things is uncomfortable, it is that type of vulnerable honesty that is needed in the world. I realize my stories are the key that unlocks other people's prisons.

The following are posts from this time.

JANUARY 27, 2016

In less than 47 minutes I will by jumping on and participating in a LIVE Blab with Anthony Conklin and Tony Robbins. Yes, you read that right. I am pretty much freaking out but I have never been calmer in my whole life...it's the calm before the storm.

"Someone should tell us right at the start of our life that we are dying. Then we might live life to the limit, every moment of every day. Whatever you want to do, do it now. There are only so many tomorrows."

—*Tony Robbins*

JANUARY 28, 2016

What's your Why? Before I became a mom, I was scared I would not know what to do. But then she came out, and all the fears just faded away. My little girl became my Why, pushing me every day to be the best possible version of me. Today, think about the top five people in your life. Are they pulling you up or pushing you down? Do they support and encourage or break you down and make fun? KK is definitely one of my top five and she reminds me to let my inner child shine and not take life so seriously. She reminds me to smile often. One smile can light up someone else's world. Smile at the world today and it will smile back.

JANUARY 29, 2016

Whatever you're doing right now.... STOP! and ask yourself this: Is this bringing me closer to my final outcome or away from it?

I was upset over something little and was running a certain thought pattern. I stopped, and asked, Does thinking about this get me closer to my final outcome of becoming the world's top speaker and best- selling author? To helping others light up and awaken from within?

No or yes?

I love it because it's an instant pattern break. Try it on anything that doesn't feel right and I promise it will be an instant shift to set you on the right course! Shout out and thank you to John Robertson for this little light bulb twisted in the right way that changed up my life!

JANUARY 31, 2016

There is something about the beach that just makes the whole world fade away. I take my 99 Day Dare group to the beach all the time in our morning meditations. All they have to do is close their eyes and step through the red door onto the crystal white sand and start to hear the waves going in and out. They breathe in the sea salt air as the wind kisses their cheeks.

Every morning for the past 120 days I have done a live meditation and visualization with incredible groups of people in the 99 Day Dare. Being able to see everyone on camera really connects the group, as most of us are visual learners. Plus, it gets us outside our comfort zone. It's a judgment-free zone!

I love infusing my energy, my desires, and my heart into these visualizations and meditations. I always say to myself before any meditation I lead, "Let me be an open vessel and give them exactly what they need." I have never been more certain that this is exactly what I am supposed to do.

Because I continue to focus on being an author of the unseen, I know what I want to create, be and do. Mark my words, it's only a matter of time before what I see in my mind is right here in front of me. Anything is possible with enough desire and belief. The first one that has to see it and believe it is you. I do feel as though I am getting dramatic results because I am adding another ingredient: Love.

The best piece of advice I can give you is to fall in love with the process of life. Fall in love with right now. Be an example for others of the absolute joy we have available to us in every moment.

Faith and desire are great (and are needed) and will get you many things in life, but without love, you are only hollow inside. Love always wins. Love is the most powerful cosmic force in the whole universe, and when you add it to what you desire, and fall in love with your dreams, the unseen is suddenly seen.

The magical threads are all around me. I see how everything in my life is interconnected like a web. The beautiful web of life.

Can you take a step back and see the invisible? Those who can see the invisible can make the impossible happen.

FEBRUARY 4, 2016

People with no dreams or goals will wake up every day trying to talk you out of yours. No matter what you have experienced in your life, it's never too late to step up and decide that this is not how your story is going to end.

FEBRUARY 8, 2016

https://carolynrim.leadpages.co/create-grow-monetize-fb-co.../

I have empowered and inspired more than 73 people to build their own FB communities. The ones that put the time, energy, and effort and followed my step by step strategies are now reaping the rewards of leading their own community! Whatever your PASSION is ... You better BELIEVE there are others who will take an interest in you! So many ideas! You could create a single mom group or a meditation group or a reading group... The possibilities are absolutely endless!!

For those of you who are interested or curious about starting your own communities, and learning HOW TO MAKE THEM THRIVE ...here is an article I wrote! Top 5 Reasons to Start a Facebook Community! Plus get more info on the upcoming online course I will be releasing: How to Create, Grow and Monetize a FB community!

I learned an extremely valuable lesson in the above post. I learned never to work on a course before I offered it to my audience. No one bought this. I do help clients individually build their audience but this program was a flop. It was an extremely powerful lesson for me. I learned to reverse engineer every course from that point forward. Shout out to Derek Halpern, who also helped ignite this lesson. I decided I would offer my course before I spent hours building it. That way I knew what my audience did and didn't want.

"Can you take a step back and see the invisible? Those who can see the invisible can make the impossible happen."

—Carolyn Rim

FEBRUARY 10, 2016

Shout out to all the kind people in the world. Imagine if one act of kindness was done by every person in the world every day... Imagine what type of world we would live in.

When I grow up... I am going to have that be a part of my brand and community.

Every Wednesday will be an act of kindness. Today, support someone's dream, pay the guy's toll behind you, or purchase the coffee for the person behind you. Give $10 or $20 to charity once a week. Connect with your kids and spouse without the use of electronic devices for an evening.

Every act of kindness counts... sets into motion evolution for humanity and pushes the human race forward. Just remember, what may seem little to you may be monumental to someone else. Now Go be a rainbow in someone else's clouds. Brighten up their day. Be kind.

Over and out, Rockstars.

xoxo
Carolyn

FEBRUARY 11, 2016

"Magic happens at the corner of I believe in myself and I don't give a fuck what anyone else thinks." —Andra Popescu

FEBRUARY 11, 2016

What is fear? Fear is thoughts about the future that at present don't exist. You know what worrying about the future does? It robs you of the present moment. Come to the now and live and enjoy the moment.

FEBRUARY 12, 2016

The universe is constantly delivering exactly what you want. You are telling the universe what you want at *every moment* based on the feelings, thoughts and beliefs you have. The universe is always giving you more of what you want. You have the power, no matter what happened yesterday, or 10 years ago—every single day is a new day to take a deep breath and start again.

FEBRUARY 13, 2016

Today, try not to take life so seriously. Every day you are faced with hundreds of little traps that encourage you to take your life way too seriously.

The frustrations can come in many forms such as money issues, slow internet connections, long wait times, people who drive at a snail's pace, and endless to-do lists. It's easy to get caught up in perpetual flow of decisions and events that make up our lives and to forget that most of the challenges we are faced with are only as stressful as we choose to let them be.

So... Next time you are tempted to smash your computer or throw yourself a pity party or even lash out in a fit of road rage (because we have all been there!), remember not to take life so seriously. Take a deep breath in and break the pattern! Live in a beautiful state of mind!

Happiness and laughter are a choice, and genuinely happy people make the choice to be happy, every day! It's possible to have a life filled to the brim with laughter, light and a positive outlook. You just have to make the decision to. Practice.

Have a great rest of your Saturday, you amazing gifts to the universe!

Sending hugs, high-fives and pattern-breaking ass slaps,

Carolyn Rim

> *"I freaking love seeing others succeed. The more I see others succeed, the more I know it's possible."*
>
> *—Carolyn Rim*

Chapter 19
One Cold Night

"She doesn't have to worry about being cold anymore."

—Audrey Laye

It is the day before my daughter's birthday. Her father has her tonight. I am sitting at home on the couch. It is below freezing outside and with the wind-chill it feels like minus 15 degrees. All of sudden, I feel that presence around me. Whether it is God or the universe or whatever, it wants me to go online.

I go to my computer desk and sit down. I put my fingers in top of the keys. I do not know what is going to come through me. In the search bar I start typing, "Homeless people in Philadelphia freezing to death." I click on the first link that comes up, and article by Scott Keyes.

Source: https://thinkprogress.org/at-least-five-homeless-people- froze-to-death-last-week-5dee49bb6a6d#.2j26s2po1

"She died where she lived: at the bus stop.

"Willie Mae White loved to dance. She told stories about her boyfriends. She treated everyone with kindness. She was homeless.

"On Tuesday, White froze to death at the Joliet, Illinois bus stop she called home. She was 55 years old.

"'She doesn't have to worry about being cold anymore,' an acquaintance, Audrey Laye, told the *Herald-News*.

"Living on the streets is dangerous any time of year, but that's especially true when temperatures dip below freezing. In this past week, as a cold front swept through the Midwest and Northeast, at least five homeless people have died from the cold.

"They include:

"Willie Mae White, 55, of Joliet, who died in sub-zero wind chills Tuesday morning.

"Glenn Donovan, 53, of Highland Falls, New York. He was found in the woods near the Hudson River on Friday night.

"A Philadelphia man in his 30s. His body was found in the freezing cold Thursday morning. Officials have not been able to determine his name yet.

"A Jersey City man in his 40s. 'Even the people who saw him on a daily basis said they did not know his name,' wrote *The Jersey Journal*. He slept in abandoned junk cars. His body was found Wednesday morning as the temperature hit 5 degrees.

"A Chicago man who remains unidentified after dying from hypothermia on Tuesday.

"As parts of the country have experienced deep cold snaps this winter, homeless lives have been at risk, and last week's deaths came after several died from the cold earlier in the month.

"It doesn't have to be this way. Some states, including Colorado and Oregon, and cities including Phoenix and Salt Lake City, are making great strides in getting their homeless populations off the streets and into homes."

I am crying thinking about the homeless people in my city freezing. I read another article about a mom and little boy sleeping in their car. Freezing. I do not understand.

We are spending millions of dollars trying to reach life on other planets but what about the lives on *this* planet?

I want to make a difference. I decide I am going to take massive action

273

but what? I ask God or the universe whatever was connecting with me at this moment. I say out loud, "Tell me what to do. I will do it. I am here to serve."

Then it hits me. This is not going to be easy. The answer I receive is to go outside with them. Go be an example of what is possible when one includes the emotion of love and compassion. I create a post on Facebook: "I am going to go sleep outside for money. I am not coming in until we raise $10,000 and pull 150 souls off the street."

My sister Marie calls me a few seconds later. "I saw your post on Facebook. Carolyn, this is a dare-devil stunt and its stupid and you are going to get yourself hurt. You need a fucking intervention." She is worried for me.

"I love you. I promise I will be okay," I say and hang up.

I call Peggy Rowe at Horizon House. "Peggy, can I have a link please where people can donate? I want to get hundreds of people off the street please."

She pauses for a moment and then says, "Carolyn, I do not know if this is a good idea——"

I cut her off, "Peggy, I am doing this with or without your help." She sighs. "Okay I will have a link within an hour."

I text my business coach David Kauffman. He calls me and says, "This has nothing to do with your brand. We will hold an event to raise money if you want—but things like this take time. You don't have to do this. This is nuts. Do you know how cold it is right now?"

I tell him, "David, I need your support. I just wanted to tell you what I am doing. I love you. Bye."

As I start putting on my jacket, gloves and hat, I think about how many people let others talk them out of something they are passionate about, not because they don't care—it's the opposite. It's because they *do* care and they are scared for you.

I have no idea what will happen but I know I want someone waiting for me when I get to Philly. I went to a NA meeting the night before and met a guy named John W., who was interested in joining my Rockstar group. I had shared what I was doing in the meeting.

So I call him and say, "John, you hardly know me, but will you meet me in Philly and spend a few hours in the cold with me?"

He replies, "Yes what's the address?" I send it to him.

I walk out my door full of gratitude. The cold air hits and stings my face. No person should be outside in this type of night. It is beyond freezing.

I inhale the fresh cold air.

I look to the heavens, I whisper softly, "Please keep me safe, God." As I get into my car I say the Our Father. I pull into the city and into a parking lot and I start to live-stream from my phone, asking my followers for donations to help me get these people off the cold street.

My phone dies instantly. Apparently, iPhones die quickly in the cold. Who knew?

I go back to the parking garage and charge my phone for a few minutes. My old boss and friend Marie Greene messages me. "You want me to send Billy up with a blanket and a charger for you?"

I message back quickly, "OMG please!"

She says, "I would come, but you know Billy. He won't let me. I saw you live-stream for a few minutes and saw your phone die. All I had to do was look at Billy and he said, 'Okay, I'm getting my shoes on.'"

I start to laugh. That was just like Billy. He loves Marie. She's his everything. I text back, "Thank you Marie. I love you."

John W. gets there and sits with me a while. He tells me this is truly inspiring what I am doing. I thank him and say I would not have come without knowing I had someone with me. An hour later, Billy arrives. He gives me a look, "Hey you." I smile hugely when I see him. I am so cold. He plugs in my phone and wraps a blanket around me.

He says, "I am with you all night tonight. You know Marie—if I come home and you're still out here, she's going to try to come out here herself." He was 100 percent correct. That is just who they were. Really good people who cared.

"Bill, I don't know why I am here, but God struck a chord within me tonight and I don't know… but I care deeply for them."

He looks at me and smiles. "I get it." So, John W., Bill McAfee and I start walking the streets of Philly. I grab my phone and start live-streaming:

"My name is Carolyn Rim and I need your help. Some people froze to death in my city and more may tonight because it is so cold and that is why I want to help them. Please help me. I want to raise

$10,000 tonight. I will not go inside until the money is raised. I am freezing but I am here and I am committed. Please donate to this cause. Think about every person outside on this cold night, sleeping in the cold. Donate today and feel so grateful when you lay your head down in your warm bed tonight. Click here to can donate now."

I share the video out and into the Spark Your Rockstar group. Within two hours, we have raised more than $2,000. I cannot believe how many people care.

Peggy messages me: "Carolyn, there is something you need to know about your audience. We are not getting large donations. We are getting little donations from people here and there, and the messages that are coming in are remarkable. I am going to send you a few."

I look down at my phone and see the emails forwarded from those who donated. A list of people pours in and the comments just fill me with love.

Missy Loy: $10. Message: If I could give more I would. I hope this helps. We love Carolyn. Anything we can do to support her.

Carmel D'Arienzo: $25. Message: Keep going, Bella.

Ray Schwartz: $25. Message: Thank you for helping others and serving from your heart.

Scott Niolet: $200. Message: Go save em', kiddo.

A ton of people are giving from their hearts. Even Marie and Billy have donated. I cannot believe the support I am getting. At 12 a.m., John W. looks tired. He is fading. I tell home to go home. Bill is here now and we are good. I hug him. Bill and I continue onward into the heart of the city. We see people on benches under blankets.

WHAT IT FEELS LIKE TO BE *REALLY* FUCKING COLD

Sleeping outside in the cold is by far one of the hardest experiences of my life so far. My hands are on fire and burning. With the wind chill, it feels like minus 15 degrees and every time the wind blows, it sends a burning sensation onto my skin.

I have a blanket wrapped around me and to people walking by, I look like I am homeless. People are giving me disgusted looks as they walk by. Some don't even acknowledge me. I'm invisible here in the cold.

I have never been looked at like that, or ignored like that—and it is humbling to see even for a moment what a homeless person goes through.

Bill and I keep having to get up and move around to keep from freezing. I have people in my community staying up all night with me online and making sure I am okay and alive.

We meet people on the street. One man tells us he has lived on the street for years now. I ask him, "How do you do this every day?"

He looks at me and smiles gently, "God."

I am humbled and I get chills over my whole body. These are good people. Kind people. I brought a little bit of money to give to people and I give it to him.

We go into the subway station. I see people sleeping on cardboard boxes. I see people talking to themselves. I see things I have never seen before.

We continue to walk on and I find a big beautiful church and I see a red door there. I ask Bill to take a picture of me by it. It gives me comfort, this red door, the door I love and have opened so many times to connect with my creator. I am sitting in the freezing cold and I just start to cry.

Bill comes over to sit with me. He doesn't say anything. Instead, he just holds a space for me to cry. I say, "Thank you, Bill. This is hard. I have never cared about someone I haven't even meet. I am so cold. I am being judged. This night is gonna change my life forever. I swear I will never take my warm bed for granted. My house. My home."

He nods. He has tears in his eyes, too. He says, "You have changed a lot in the past two years, Carolyn. You should be proud of yourself. Marie and I are proud of you. We still watch over you."

God sent Bill out to me tonight, through Marie's heart. I feel love. I go live again and again throughout the night, asking for donations.

At about 7 a.m., I am literally falling asleep standing up. We have walked about three miles throughout the night to keep from freezing.

I tell Bill, "It's time, Bill. I need to rest and to go home, to my warm bed." I have a whole new perspective on life. I have never been more grateful for my home. We end up raising thousands and donations are still coming in. I am not quite at that $10K mark but I know I will get there. I drive home and I walk in my door.

I look at the sun shining through my windows. I fall to my knees and sob. I am so grateful. I get into my bed. I close my eyes utterly grateful for my life, my home, my family, my community, John, Bill, Marie, and God.

ONE PERSON *CAN* MAKE A DIFFERENCE

This goes to show you that one person, when their heart is in the right place, can make a difference. My family and a few friends told me that I was crazy and that sleeping outside wouldn't do anything but get myself sick. It is sad to say, but your friends and family may be the ones who try to convince you not to move towards what you feel passionately about. Why? Not because they are mean, or trying to hurt you, but because they love you and because of their own fears.

Next time you have a great idea, don't let anyone talk you out of it. If I listened to my coach, my sister, and my dad, I would not have gone and slept outside and I would not have raised all that money. The money I raised will get men, women and children out of the cold, sheltered and fed. Anything is possible if you believe it is.

YOU *can* and *do* make a difference in the world. With success, we must have some level of risk involved.

> *"It is sad to say, but your friends and family may be the ones who try to convince you not to move towards what you feel passionately about. Why? Not because they are mean, or trying to hurt you, but because they love you and because of their own fears."*
>
> *—Carolyn Rim*

Look at your life today and think about where you may have wanted to step forward and go for something but you allowed others to talk you out of it. Or how you *didn't* let others talk you out of something and you succeeded! It's through sharing our stories that we can empower and inspire others to reach for the stars and make the impossible possible.

BILLY MCAFEE FACEBOOK POST: FEBRUARY 14, 2016

Carolyn Rim is still walking the City of Brotherly Love spreading her love for people she doesn't know on Valentine's Day. On a quest to raise a small portion of money for the benefit people she's never met but cares so deeply for.

FEBRUARY 14, 2016

I made the whole night in the freezing cold. I am about to start driving home now! Wow. We did it. Thank you to John W. and Billy McAfee who made sure I was safe. I had people look at me like I was a piece of trash. I was so cold that at this point in this picture it was 3 a.m. and I didn't think I would make it. Then, with some motivation from Bill, I sat down for about 10 minutes. Then I continued walking the City of Brotherly Love spreading my love for people I don't know on Valentine's Day. On a quest to raise a small portion ($10K) of money for the benefit people I have never met but I care so deeply for. Happy Valentine's Day, sending you all love <3. This would not have been possible without you all. I am so utterly grateful for my home, my life and those people in it.

FEBRUARY 14, 2016

Last night was one of the most humbling nights of my life. I never thought I would sleep outside on the street in Philadelphia. I know many of you have been asking how much WE raised last night for the homeless. For those of you who don't know—I went into Philadelphia last night in minus 10-degree weather and slept outside to help get 150 homeless men, woman, children, off the street and into a shelter to be fed and clothed. I am so grateful and happy to tell you we raised thousands of dollars in one night. I am excited, exhausted and blown away by the donations, the love and everyone who shared and stayed up with me. I am grateful for Billy McAfee and John W. who stayed and protected me to make sure I was safe. I am praying this has a ripple effect into the hearts of others. Channel 10 will be doing a story on it this week. Very grateful. I still need to get to $10K by Tuesday—that's my goal. Here is the link donate. Remember no amount is too small. Every little bit counts. WE can make a difference. I am just one person but I can cast a stone that will create a rippling around the world.

FEBRUARY 15, 2016

Wow! WE raised over $8,300 and donations continue to come in! My goal is to get to $10K by tomorrow at midnight. I am finally starting to warm up and get my body temperature back to normal. It was the hardest night of my life mentally, emotionally and physically. It was also a very spiritual experience. I am not sure why I felt so strongly to do something as crazy as this. We spend billions of dollars of trying to find life on other planets but we cannot even take care of the life on our own. I want to thank the Spark Your Rockstar community and everyone else who donated.

I do not think I would have made it without Billy McAfee and Marie G McAfee and John W. and all the support and people staying up with me all night cheering me on as I live-streamed this. I have never been so unbelievably grateful for my warm home to sleep in. Thank you again!!

FEBRUARY 15, 2016

Eight years ago today, I spent 18 hours in labor with my little girl. Looking back now, I would not have cared if I had to spend 50 hours in labor—she would have been worth every second. I will never ever forget the first words out of my mouth when I saw her: "She is the most beautiful thing I have ever seen." I stared at this miracle, with her beautiful big ocean-blue eyes at the time. Happy Birthday to someone who I learn from, I laugh with, and who truly shines from within. Thank you KK for believing in mom—but even more important, for believing in yourself. Your laughter lights up my life. So many of my smiles begin with you.

FEBRUARY 19, 2016

Become grateful for everything you already have in your life. Then watch how quickly everything around you shifts. You have two different mindsets you can enter your day today with. One is lack and the other is abundance. When you are happy for another's success or joy, that's when you come from abundance. When you are feeling like "Why not me?" or "They're so lucky," you are coming from lack. Pick avalanches of abundance and join me with a grateful heart today. I freaking love seeing others succeed. The more I see others succeed the more I know it's possible.

FEBRUARY 19, 2016

Two things are certain. If you don't ask for what you want, then the answer will always be no. The Law of Attraction states that what you seek is also seeking you. It's like a boomerang. You shoot this desire you want out into the universe and then you must believe that it will come back to you. Want to know who you are? Open your heart and allow your heart to lead for a change instead of logic. Give yourself permission to dream big.

Chapter 20
West Palm Beach

"Be thyself."

—William Denton

I am waiting at the airport terminal #3 and I see her sitting by herself. The angel Carolyn Cole. As I walk over to her, I think about all the magic that has led me to right now. Even more blessings are about to happen, too. I can feel it in my heart.

"Carolyn Cole!" I yell, running up to her excitedly. "Hi!" She is laughing at my excitement. She is dressed in fashionable casual attire. We hug each other and then both sit down and chat.

"So, how are you?" she asks. I think about that for a moment. I have $186 to my name and am not sure when the next check will be coming in. I should be worried like crazy but I am not. All I feel is this incredible gratitude for all I have in my life, and for all the gifts that I know are coming to me. I quickly and honestly respond, "I have never been happier or more grateful in my whole life." Money didn't equal my happiness. My happiness is that I am living passionately on purpose in the present moment and as long as I continue to have faith, the universe

284

will continue to open doors for me that I have never dreamed possible.

I pull out my phone and go to the email I was sent last night. "Carolyn, look at this," I say. I show her the email I just received from the Tony Robbins offices:

"Hello Carolyn:

Tony and Sage are delighted that you will be attending Unleash the Power Within in West Palm Beach, Florida, March 10-13! They have asked me to make sure you have everything you need for your registration and participation in the event as their personal guests. If there is anything I can assist you with please don't hesitate to let me know. Tony and Sage are looking forward to seeing you!

Jonathan Cardozo, from the Office of Tony Robbins"

Carolyn is genuinely happy for me. I switch subjects and ask her about www.Boomtank.com, her business and her website. All is going really well. She is doing podcasts and starting all kinds of magic, helping men and women fall in love with themselves and connect with God. I tell her she is totally going to be the next Louise Hay or Oprah. She and I have this knowing. It's like I've met her before many times and have known her for many years, even though I just met her this past October, a few short months ago at Joe White's seminar Breaking Through the Barrier. I feel like I am part of her soul group, as if we are old friends perhaps from another lifetime.

Before the flight, I check my messages. One is from Mike Peppler, who is also going to be in UPW Palm Beach. He and his wife, Ginny, had become more than just clients. Ever since Mike came to Philly, it's like the Pepplers are just family to me now.

I tell Carolyn, "Mike Peppler thinks something really special is going to happen to one of the Rockstars but he said he could not tell me who it is!"

Carolyn says, "I believe that, because I can feel it too. Something very special is happening for us right now. I am going to stay open- minded this weekend and be open to the joy."

Once we are seated on the plane, I fall asleep. I don't know what it is about car rides and planes—they put me to sleep, as long as I am not the one flying or driving.

THE WEST PALM BEACH EVENT

Two hours later, we arrive in West Palm Beach. My heart is racing! I see the palm trees from the window of the plane. We get off the plane and we arrive, Wednesday, 2 p.m. On the shuttle to the hotel, I can't help but think how beautiful Florida is. What beautiful water. I'm so grateful for the present moment. All my senses seem turned on and tapped in to all the deliciousness of the moment.

My heart swells with gratitude for Tony Robbins and Anthony Conklin. I have 50 Rockstars who signed up for the trip too and at this UPW I will actually have my own Spark Your Rockstar group section.

Carolyn Cole and I arrive at the hotel and as we are checking in, I see someone in a UPW crew shirt. I have never seen him before but he is looking at me and I can tell he knows me by his excited expression

Carolyn Rim!" He runs up and hugs me! "OMG I love you! I've been following your story for two years now! I was in Dallas with you!"

I am taken back by this. I hug him back and ask his name—it's Bobby. It's been a year since my last UPW. Would everyone know me here? Would everyone be coming up to me?

Bobby continues, "Your story has spread through the Tony Robbins Community like wildfire. Husband leaves woman because woman wanted to follow dreams! Woman quits smoking! Woman quits job! Woman makes impossible possible!"

I laugh out loud. His headlines are my story. I introduce Carolyn Cole to him. He asks, "You all want a ride to the event?"

Carolyn Cole says, "Yes, just give us five minutes to drop our bags off." We drop off our suitcases in the room, I quickly change, and we are out the door.

When we get to the front of the hotel we see gentlemen have joined Bobby in the car. "Hey, you don't mind if I bring these guys too, do you?" he asks.

The more the merrier," I say. We get into the car and the man in the front, Mike Walecki, has a video camera and is filming us.

"So who are you and where you from?" he asks.

Carolyn Cole hides her face and says, "Not a fan of the camera."

I turn to the camera, smile and introduce myself and then the Bobby says, "Carolyn, tell him your story! Tell them who you are!" I have grown to love story telling. I love playing Mother Goose. I love telling my soul's truth. Stories help people remember and learn things. They are truly the key to awaken others.

"Well," I say, smiling, "it all started in a little cube two years ago, and I wanted to die at the time. No goals. No purpose or dreams. And then I went all in on me and I took out a $5K loan… and booked a ticket to Tony Robbins Unleash the Power Within event in Dallas… I quit smoking… I charged the stage… I was unwilling to leave without a mentor who had what I wanted…. and then I quit my job… and then my husband left me … and then I failed and lost a lot of money on an event and almost lost my house…."

I continue with my incredible story of how I have ended up here in this car.

Ten minutes later we pull up to the West Palm Beach Convention Center. The guy in the front, Mike, had tears in his eyes. The guys in the car hug me. Mike says, "Thank you. Thank you so *much* for not giving up."

Everyone in the car is so excited to get inside and register! We all get out of the car and walk into the event. It has been a year since my last UPW. I don't know what to expect, but my heart is open and I am enjoying this moment and this life!

As we go up the escalators, I see them. Some of the Rockstars who were in my group are right there! Ranjanna Mariia Hvenegaard, Lizeth Chica and her brother were there! I see them smiling big. They see me and Ranjanna points to me and yells, "CAROLYN!"

I pretend like I am running in really slow motion toward them. They laugh and hug me. We all walk into the main conference center.

As we do, I soon became aware that Bobby was telling the truth about my stories spreading like wildfire. Rockstar Red, a.k.a. Laurie, rushes up to me and practically tackles me. This is the first time I am meeting her in person. She has been a private client of mine and has done the past two Dares. Gorgeous green eyes and fire red hair—she is breathtakingly gorgeous inside and out.

Then I am rushed by another Rockstar. Soon a crowd of people surrounds me. Hugging me. It is as if time slows down for a moment. I have tears in my eyes as a line of people comes up to hug me. They are telling me how inspiring I am and how my stories changed their life.

"Carolyn! I have followed you for six months and you changed my life!" one girl says.

Another crew member comes up to me and says, "You are the next Tony Robbins, you know. Of course, in female form. My name is Todd Alexander and I have been watching you."

I say, "Nice to meet you, Todd Alexander. I think the world needs only *one* Tony Robbins, but I will be the *next* Carolyn Rim."

He laughs, "You got it, kiddo."

Others I do not know come up and share how my story has inspired them to change. I cannot believe all the love and affection I am getting. I am not sure what I expected, but I didn't expect *this*.

MORE THAN A MIRACLE

After an hour of hugging Rockstars and others, I go down to register for the event. Even Tony Robbins' staff are being so kind to me. I walk into the Diamond Lounge. My beautiful private client, Beth Komisar, is there and we hug. I see Scott Chamberlain, I run up and give him a huge hug. He says, "Hey you! Still a non-smoker, right?" YES!

Finally, I am standing outside. I see Dragan. Our energies just mesh well together. Dragan and Kelly have done so much to help my Rockstars get here. Hugs all around.

I am so excited for the event tomorrow I can barely sleep. I feel again like a little girl on Christmas Eve, an anticipation. Just sipping in each glorious moment. I finally close my eyes and slip away into the darkness behind my eyelids with a gentle smile on my face.

I wake up early the next day and am ready to go by 7 a.m. I have to be there at 8 a.m. to get in line and make sure the Rockstars have the best seats in the house. I speak with Pedro and Dragan and Kelly Phillips. The Rockstars are being well taken care of and are in good hands. Dragan texts me and says they made a miracle happen for me and that the Rockstars are to be really close to the stage! Right behind the Diamonds!

My seat, however, will be stage right. I even have a little sticker on my necklace. I am sitting in CSI, the section of Tony's family and friends. I am right in front of Tony the whole time. I walk outside to meditate. I visualize Tony calling on me for an intervention. I have seen our connection many times in my heart and mind.

Time to leave the hotel. I jump in a taxi with Missy, Ranjanna, Carolyn Cole and a few others and we are ready to get this party started.

I show up to the event, with 7,000 people there awaiting this incredible man, Tony Robbins. The 50 Rockstars are running up to me, hugging me and we all go in and start to take our seats. I make sure they are all set up in their section and then I turn and walk to the CSI section, Tony and Sage's special guest section. I feel so special and grateful for this.

What I had thought was such a disaster—my audio not working at the time—has turned into such a big incredible gift. God can turn our mistakes into our miracles.

LET THE DANCING BEGIN!

I sit in the front row with the star from *High School Musical*, Vanessa Hudgens. She is beautiful. I'm joined by a ton of other movie stars and famous people. This is where all of the movie stars and Rockstars sit. I chuckle to myself at the thought of how a Rockstar manifested this.

Then I hear, "LET'S GET THE DANCERS ON STAGE!"

The music gets louder and everyone is dancing and I am playing full-out today, baby! Nothing will stop this energy from flowing through me. We are six songs in, dancing and I am starting to sweat! Then I see him! He comes right out on stage and looks right at me. He points to me, then he grabs his heart and then he scans the room and starts jumping!

We start jumping too! The energy level goes higher and higher. Then Tony begins. The whole room is vibrant and bumping. He says, "Let me hear you!" The whole audience is roaring and screaming and just jumping out of their skins. Tony then says, "Go get 10 big hugs and 10 high-fives and then grab a seat!"

Everyone is giving high-fives and hugs. I feel so at home at these events. We all grab our seats.

Tony Robbins walks around the room and says, "Who here has been to UPW before?"

A bunch of hands go up but not everyone, so he says with a big wide grin, "Awesome. Fresh Meat. Let me ask you all, after the jumping, the dancing and the singing, I want to know: Who here is still depressed after *that*?"

Only a few people's hands go up.

Tony grabs a blonde woman in the back and asks, "What is your name?"

She replies, "Olga." She is about five-foot-eight, blonde hair, blue eyes, and slender. She's pretty but I can tell she has a lot of inner doubt and sadness. Tony grabs her by the hand and brings her up to the stage. He takes out his big black marker and his big white board and looks at her.

"Okay tell me," he says. "What do you need in order to be happy and successful?"

She says, "Well, I need to have a goal and a strategy to get there."

Tony says, "Okay, and where is there that you want to get to that will cause you to be successful and happy? How will you know when you are really successful? Is there a certain amount of business you need? Or children or finance or what?"

Olga continues, "All of the above. I need it all to feel happy and successful."

Tony says, "So tell me the details. You will be successful when you achieve what?"

Olga says, "When I am a certified financial planner and have a career in finance."

Tony says, "So all you have to do to feel successful is by being totally fulfilled by your job as a certified financial planner, and what else?"

Olga says, "I need to travel around the world at least twice a year."

Tony repeats this and writes down everything she says she needs to feel successful. He continues, "So, traveling twice a year all over the world and I am a great financial planner and I am totally fulfilled—anything else you need to feel totally successful?"

"Yes, I need to be healthy." she says.

Tony asks, "How will you know when you are healthy?"

Olga thinks for a moment and then replies, "Not be achy." Everyone starts laughing.

Then Tony says, "Not be achy. That is a highly technical term. So if I am not achy, I am fully fulfilled as a CFA, I travel around the world twice a year. Is there anything else you need to feel happy and successful?"

Olga says, "Yes a family of four."

Tony says, "Okay, so you need a family of four *what?*" Olga says, "Two kids and two adults."

Tony smiles and looks at her jokingly and says, "Two kids and two adults and do we need a white picket fence as well?" We all laugh. He puts the marker down and points to his mind. He says, "Everyone, I want you to watch what our mind fucking does to us. Her brain says I have to be a certified financial planner who is totally successful in my career. I have to make sure that I totally fulfilled every moment of what I do, I have to have two children and a partner and we need to travel at least twice a year around the world and then what? What happens when all that is done?"

Olga says, "Well I haven't figured that out yet."

Tony looks deeply into her eyes and says, "You haven't figured that one out. What if you got one child and they were totally healthy?"

Olga says, "Sure, I will take that."

Tony points at all the things he wrote down that she needs to be successful and then says, "You will take that? So the truth is all this shit, is pretty much bullshit." Tony looks at the audience and says, "Now I want you to watch this., Who here tells me, someone else, anyone, raise your hand tell me what do you think life is about, give us a different perspective of what it's about for you?"

WHAT WILL IT TAKE FOR YOU TO BE HAPPY?

I look up at Tony and when those words came out of his mouth I immediately raise my hand. I don't have to think; it is instant. He looks down and points to me. "Look here, ma'am yes, you, stand up, ladies and gentlemen give her a hand. What's your name?"

I say into the mic, "*Oh My God I have the mic!*" My Rockstars a few sections back, start cheering for me! "Those are my Rockstars back there! My name is Carolyn Rim!"

Tony smiles, "Where are you from?" I start screaming into the mic and cheering, "WOOOOOOO! I am from Philadelphia!" Everyone starts cheering and laughing as I dance a bit. Then we get back to business.

Tony says to me, "So, tell me what is life about for you?" I say, "Life is about loving and connecting."

Tony then asks, "And what has to happen, Carolyn, for you to feel connected and loved?"

I answer honestly, from my heart, "It's already happening, Tony." He says, "Okay, like what's an example then?"

I say, "Connecting with people from all over the world that are in my group."

Tony says, "Okay, and so do you need to travel twice a year to do that?"

I answer, "NO."

Tony asks again, "Do you need to have a partner to do that? Do you need to have two children to do that?"

I answer, "No! I am doing it right now!"

He laughs, "You are doing it right now? Well, what the fuck are you doing?" Everyone in the audience laughs. They enjoy our playfulness together.

In between my laughs, I say, "I am just having a really great time right now."

Tony asks the audience, "Does she look like she is really having a great time? Yes or no? And we can tell it's authentic for her, correct?" The crowd responds by cheering and clapping for me. Tony continues, asking me, "So what has to happen for you to connect and love is just—*be what?*"

I say into the mic, "Just *be here.*"

Tony says back, "Just be here and what else?"

I say it as if it's a silly question, "Just be me." Tony stops and looks around the room.

Then he says, "Be here and be me. That's a pretty good formula, Carolyn, because the oldest personal development information in the world is in a cave in Greece, and it says Love thy—?"

I answer, "Self."

He says, "Yes! But the second part is even more important. Most of us don't know ourselves. What we are going to find out next is the *real* you instead of the *conditioned* you, if you are up for it. Who's up for it? Say aye."

Everyone in the audience says, "Aye."

Tony continues, "You can learn to know yourself is do things spontaneously. If you do some shit and not think, that's the real fucking you. Now when you are drunk, we usually see the real you too. 'Oh, that was the alcohol,' you may say—no bitch that was you." Everyone again bursts out in laughter.

I say into the mic, "But I don't drink, Tony."

Tony continues, "I can see that, it's good that you don't drink because you are already *there.*" Everyone laughs, including me.

He continues, "But there is know myself and then here is the more important one we want to do this weekend: BE thyself. There is no fear, there is no effort, there is no stress when you are just being your true self and that's hard because most of us are born to adapt to get other people's attention or significance or love.

"And then we think we are the person we are trying to be, but inside it's pretty exhausting. It's not exhausting when you are being yourself. It's not difficult. In fact, you want to know what spirituality is?

"Find somebody who is totally comfortable with themselves and you will see a spiritual being. Because I want to tell you something, if you want to know what makes people and terrorists go murder strangers, I can tell you.

"It wasn't a person who is happy. Happy people don't hurt other people, happy people don't try to kill other people. Happy people are not trying to take advantage of other people, and unhappy people are people who are not being themselves, but trying to adapt to something within reach of you."

He turns back to Olga and he points to the list of things that need to happen for her to feel loved and successful, "So now, Olga, your challenge is not your life. Your challenge is, you have a blueprint that looks like this, that's very confusing. It has to be a very specific way before you can feel the way you deserve to feel."

He works with Olga a little while longer and tells her to call on a powerful state within herself and name it so it can be called out of her. She gives herself the name, "Glory."

Tony says, "Glory! Run up and down the aisle high-fiving everyone!" Olga's dancing, too! Everyone laughs with her!

FIREWALKING AND PITBULL

It's time for Tony to walk us through practicing the firewalk, and visualizing walking over the fire. But before we jump into that he says, "Ladies and Gentlemen, please welcome PITBULL!!" Seven thousand people jump to their feet and are screaming, and left and right people are so excited! I am right in front of Pitbull. Everyone else rushes the stage! This is a complete surprise to everyone in the audience!

Pitbull, the Cuban-American rapper, comes out and shares he's been listening to Tony Robbins in the car with his mom since he was a kid, and Tony changed his life. And then he blows us away with his rapping. The music starts and for 20 minutes straight Pitbull rocks the stage! Beautiful dancers surround him and he sounds and looks so amazing!

After Pitbull's performance, Tony comes back on to talk about the firewalk, but I have already decided I'm not going join in this time. I have firewalked probably six times in the last four months.

Between my firewalk in October and Joe White's firewalks, I don't need to do it again. The fire is already ignited within me. I *am* the fire. That's what Tony does—he sparks people to life and ignites their souls to who they really are. I stay until the end of the night and then tell my Rockstars to go ahead and do the firewalk and I will meet them back at the hotel.

DAY THREE

The third day, my mentor Joseph McClendon takes the stage, my main man and he rocks it as he always does, and the love continues.

Everywhere I go, I feel all eyes on me. Joseph makes me feel so special. One of the things I love most is connecting with people in the Rockstar group. I dance with them, hug them and just *be* with them. I love them.

When Tony comes back on, he keeps using me as an example, pointing to me and saying, "Look at Carolyn and watch how she has so much energy. Let's out-do her energy! Read? GO!"

Then he talks about identities. He points to me and says, "Carolyn is a generous soul. I have watched her with people she doesn't know. She is open. She is loving. She is warm. She greets others in a friendly way. I have never seen her with a frown. She plays full- on all the time, so from watching her, I generalized an identity for her.

"She is driven, she is passionate, she is loving, she is a sincere, she is caring." The cameraman puts my face on the big screen.

My Rockstars in the VIP Spark Your Rockstar Group section start to cheer for me. "WE LOVE YOU, CAROLYN! WOOOOOOO!"

Tony laughs, "She must have friends and some family here." I start to happy cry at all the nice things being said about me by my hero, Tony Robbins himself, and for all the magic I feel.

I take a deep breath in and I then say into the mic that is handed to me by the mic runner, "Those are my Rockstars back there cheering for me. I love them and I love you, Tony."

Tony jumps back on point and says, "So if we all believe that she is a loving, generous, beautiful soul who would give her heart to anybody, will that affect the way we interact with Carolyn?"

Everyone in the audience says, "Yes." Tony continues, "A little bit or a lot?" Everyone says, "A lot."

Tony says, "Yes. A *lot*. So the identity we hold for her is going to in turn affect the way we interact with her. How many of you are following this? Raise your hands and say aye."

The whole audience raises their hands and says, "Aye."

"Now what if we had a different identify for her? What if I had an identity for Carolyn that she is a manipulating bitch?" Tony gets this big grin on his face and points to me, saying, "I have been watching her front row with that little fake smile, she thinks she is going to manipulate me with that little smile. She thinks I am that stupid, I bet."

Everyone, including me, bursts out laughing. I am on the big screen cracking up. I keep thinking in my mind, this is amazing. I feel like he is playing in the universe with me. I am learning. I am having fun and I am being me, and Tony Robbins is not leaving me alone. I love it.

Tony goes on, "Now, if you wanted to believe that Carolyn is a manipulating bitch, which isn't true, that she has got this fake little smiley ass personality because she's got an agenda underneath, that she would screw anything to get what she wants, she will take advantage of anybody—and none of that is true, of course—but if you believed that it was true about Carolyn will it affect the way you interact with her? Yes or no?"

The audience says, "Yes." "A little or a lot?" Tony asks. "A lot," they say.

Tony then stands right in front of me and says, "Now, pay attention here and watch this. If Carolyn is your best friend, you love her, she is generous soul, remember the first identity—and Carolyn treats you really shitty, mean, harsh but you know in your belief system that she is a good person, and remember what a belief is, my friends? A feeling of absolute *what?*"

We all shout out, "Certainty!"

"Yes. That's all belief is: A feeling of absolute certainty about what something means. So, if you believe that Carolyn is your friend, she is generous, loving, kind soul and she treats you like shit, you will try to resolve it but if you can't resolve it what will you do in your brain if you have to leave and she has to go to work or something? What will you do?

"You will probably say to yourself, she is probably having a bad what?"

Everyone is keeping right up with Tony and they shout, "Day!"

Tony smiles and says, raising his hand, "Who here has ever had a day where you hoped someone rationalized your behavior?" Every single hand goes up.

"Okay. On the other hand, if we think Carolyn is a manipulating bitch but she hasn't treated us mean—No, no, she treats you real nice. What's the first question in your mind about Carolyn if she starts treating you real nice when you know she is really a manipulating bitch? What's the question, what does she—?

Laughing, the audience shouts, "Want!"

Tony then comes to a point that blows my mind and everyone else's. "I want you to notice, your relationship with Carolyn has nothing to do with Carolyn. It has to do with *the identity you have for Carolyn.* So think about all the relationships you have in your life. Our personal identities are in a constant state of evolution. We all contain the power to reinvent ourselves and create a new, empowered identity that expands what is possible in our lives. The key is to take conscious control of the beliefs we are creating about ourselves, so they can propel us toward what we desire most.

"Okay! Everybody stand up!" Tony commands us.

We all stand up. He tells us to massage people around us and wake them up. We have a dance contest and I feel like I am flying. People keep asking to take a picture with me, hugging me and telling me how grateful they are for me. Tony Robbins is watching, I see. Hours pass as we go through the Dickens Process. We cry. We scream. We dance.

Then Mike Miello comes on stage for a bit to talk about Business Mastery and Mastery University. They are two of Tony's elite programs and I decide I want to go, even though I am in a ton of debt. I am not getting financial help from Kaylee's dad with child support and handling the mortgage and all the bills by myself were about $5K each month. I am still learning how to manage things. I am making money but I have so many bills with the business. I am about two months behind in my mortgage as well. How the heck am I going to get $10K to go to this program?

On the break, I walk up to the man who is signing people up for both Business Mastery and Mastery University. In order for me to sign up, they need a credit card. Determined, I say, "I will be back tomorrow with the money." I walk away smiling because I knew in my heart something will happen and I would be able to go.

GRATITUDE THROUGHOUT THE NIGHT

I go back into the event and we continue expanding and growing. It's now 2 a.m. and we're still going strong. Throughout the night, Tony gets out his water gun and shoots everyone with it. We sing "Follow Me into the Jungle." I feel a connection with every soul in the room, as if we are one. We are this vibration of love, of massive energy, of making magic with these beautiful souls, beautiful music and beautiful lights. I feel like God is all around me but most important, I feel Him within me expanding outwardly. I have never felt so close to my creator before.

During the last visualization of the night, all I want to do is give Tony a hug and thank him. He says, "Maybe you are grateful for a synchronicity that happened and something amazing came out of it." I cannot just jump on the stage to hug Tony, so I just play full- out and allow the moment to unfold organically. I am in a state of flow with the universe. I am centered on the gratitude in my heart for this gift and for all my blessings. I am grateful for every moment good and bad because it had all brought me here.

At the end of the night, as 3 a.m. approaches, all the volunteer crew members are pulled on stage, as always, so we can thank them. Tony is standing in the front and he suddenly points to me and waves his hand for me to come on the stage. Stunned, I make my way towards the stage. Tony comes down the steps, wraps his arms around me and lifts me up. I whisper to him, "Thank you Tony, for saving my life."

He says back, "Know that I watch you, and I will continue to watch you." He hugs me for what feels like minute but is most likely just a few seconds. He puts me down and gently kisses my forehead as a father would do to a child. Then he jumps back on stage with his wife, Sage, and she smiles at me too. I have my camera out and I start happily filming all the crew members, who I have come to know and love like my own family.

What had just happened was nothing short of a miracle. A little later, as everyone is walking out, I can barely make it through the crowd. Everyone keeps stopping me, saying "You are the girl on camera! You are Carolyn Rim!" Missy Loy and Mike Peppler pretend to be my bodyguards. I just keep saying thank you. Thank you. Thank you. I have no other words other than thank you. I am smiling ear to ear.

Back to the hotel, I gently wash my face, brush my teeth, and still feel like someone is about to wake me from a dream. It's nearly 4 a.m. I say goodnight to Carolyn Cole and I close my eyes and seconds later I am asleep.

DAY FOUR

I wake up four hours later bright-eyed and bushy-tailed. I jump in the shower and I feel so good I start singing. "Come fly with me, come fly, let's fly away..." Nothing like a little Frank Sinatra in the morning.

Today is the last day of UPW. Joseph had given me a ticket to dance on stage at UPW NJ 2015 but I was unable to use it at the time and gave it to someone on Tony's creative team in the front section. She was grateful, but I was disappointed I didn't get to shake my ass on stage. I know in my heart I am going to dance on stage today. I know one of those pink tickets are mine.

Scott Chamberlain has asked me to share my testimony at the coaching break-out session, where people about 100 people have come to learn more about having a "Tony coach." The man who introduces says I have become like a legend in the Tony Robbins organization. I share with everyone that I would not be standing here if it were not for a Tony Robbins coach. I share my story, including the story of one session with Scott and how I am now a non-smoker. I tell them, with a Tony Robbins coach, anything is possible. Anything at all. I tell them, as long as their hearts beat, they are alive and they have a chance to make a difference. They all clap for me. I walk off stage and out of the room with tears in my eyes. I am so emotional. But these tears are not sadness. They are appreciation. They are love.

Then I walk into the main event. The announcer says, "Let's get those dancers on stage!" I walk to the front. Joseph looks at me from the stage, "Good morning to all the Rockstars out there!" Then during one of the videos playing of Tony, a security guard comes up to me, and hands me a pink dance ticket. He says, "Now, you better not let us down up there. We are all counting on you." I look over at Rocky, the beautiful redhead who is always there making sure everything is running smoothly behind the scenes. She looks at me and winks, "Make us proud, baby, and shake that ass!" I smile. I take the ticket. I feel like I've been handed a magic ticket— an ass-shaking, magical, pink unicorn dancing ticket.

During the day, I get a text from Mike Peppler. "Meet me outside the convention center." I grab my phone and walk out to the front. Mike and Ginny Peppler take me aside. Mike starts, "We want to lend you some money." How do they know I am in the hole? I only told Mike that I was struggling a little bit with money but definitely did not give any details.

Ginny smiles, "Carolyn, we have never done this for anyone but Mike says he got a message and we want to help you. We want to lend you $10,000." I seem to not be able to hold my body up any longer. I drop to my knees. This was such a weight lifted from me. I start to sob. How did they know? We are right outside the convention center and people are coming up towards us because it looks like I am in pain on the ground but I am not.

My mind is so blown that I cannot comprehend what's taken place. As I am on the ground, I am having trouble breathing. I center myself and then my tears turn to laughing. I can't stop laughing. Mike and Ginny are helping me up. They, too, are in tears and they both hug me. I say, "I am two months behind on my mortgage. If I don't pay them they could technically kick my kid and me out on the street. I owe the mortgage company $5K and just yesterday I told the man at the table that I wanted to go to Mastery University and so now I will be able to put a deposit on that."

Mike says, "I will wire you the money when we get back tomorrow, but no more messing around. You start charging what you are worth. You are too talented not to be able to charge much more than you are charging right now." I nod.

I look at the time on my phone and say, "It's almost time to end this event. I have a magical pink ticket to dance on stage. Let's go close this magical event with some magical ass-shaking, shall we?"

As we walk back into the event, I feel like I have stepped into another dimension. I am seeing the invisible, the little threads of energy all intertwined. I am ready to spread my wings and allow the energy within to send a ripple effect far and wide. I feel so much power manifesting within me right now that I feel if I said out loud, "I would like a van and a unicorn, please," five seconds later a unicorn driving a van would pull up and say, "You called?" I dance on stage with my mentor and 10 other incredible souls.

My mentor Joseph is running across the stage screaming, "She is shaking that ass!" I am dancing and laughing. He hugs me bye. When the event is finally over, I am walking out and saying goodbye to everyone and getting so much love from people.

BACK AT HOME: A NEW DAY, A NEW DARE, THIS NEW LIFE

Twenty-four hours later I am at home and creating a post about my 99 Day Dare. I decide to take out the fitness part of it and just stick to what I know, which is magic, meditation, and manifesting. I tell everyone about the 99 Day Meditation Dare, that I will be holding a free webinar in three days called How to Become a Sizzling Manifesting Rockstar with the 99 Day Dare.

Three days later I am on the webinar and 133 people signed up for

$197 for the 99 Day Dare. That was doubled from the last one, almost tripled. I made $26,000 in one night from one webinar. I no longer say I can't believe this. I just say thank you because I believe that miracles, magic and manifesting are my new normal.

A few days later, I decide I want to read to others. My friend Thomas—who is married, but we are friends—reads to me sometimes. I have not been read to since I was a child. It is such a form of love, and I want to give this love to others. As I have said, I love playing Mother Goose. I jump on live video and ask, "When is the last time someone read you a bedtime story?"

I read everyone *The 7 Spiritual Laws of Success* By Deepak Chopra and people are loving it. I am not going to hold back any of my love and magic. I am full throttle.

"Have faith in the invisible. Accept the gifts from the universe. Follow the whispers of your heart."

—Carolyn Rim

So, it seems my journey has just begun. I know who I am. I know why I am here. I am here to be a beacon of light and to be God's lighthouse of love. To be an example of the absolute joy we have available to us in every moment. I am here to love, to give, to dream, to create. Cheers to pixie dust, to magic. To Neverland. To all the lost boys still out there in the dark. Cheers to the people who choose to see the light in everyone. We are souls. This lifetime will flash by for us like a lightning bolt in the sky.

For now, I understand: I do not see the light. I AM THE LIGHT.

As always, my beautiful loves, sending you high-fives, hugs and pattern-breaking ass slaps,
Carolyn Rim

The following are posts from this time.

FEBRUARY 21, 2016

Some of the darkest moments in my life were preparing me for my best moments in my life. I am grateful for all my moments because they made me who I am today. Don't forget once and a while to connect the dots back in your life. You will see everything is a blessing and a gift—even your struggles.

FEBRUARY 22, 2016

One year ago today, if you had told me I would be leading people through guided meditations daily live-streamed, that I would be a published author, that I would hold my own events and retreats with people like Sifu Terryann and John Robertson, that I would sleep outside to raise money for the homeless, that I would be launching my own online courses, 99 Day Dares with Joseph McClendon, I would have told you that you were crazy!

You never know what you're capable of until you dig deep and go for it.

It hasn't been easy. (I assure you this was the hardest year of my life.) It takes a lot building a business and being an entrepreneur with many hats while still being a mom—but it's worth it, because I love what I do ...

Every day I get to wake up and do what I love. Think about where you were a year ago... Have you changed? Evolved?

Don't forget to look back and connect the dots. It allows you to stay humble, celebrate the wins and keep pushing forward. Nothing is out of your reach unless you believe it is.

Shout out to a few of my mentors and coaches who have helped change my world. And thank you to the people who believed in me, supported me, and taught me along the way.

I wanted to say thank you so much—you all have been angels along the way. I learned many lessons from you all. I will always remember the moments and smiles we shared together. Thank you for being part of my journey.

FEBRUARY 23, 2016

Too many people are so focused on the end result that they miss the magic in the moment now. When you worry about the future, you're missing the present moment. When you're reliving the past in your mind, you're missing the present moment. Be happy. Shift your focus.

Tonight: be grateful, even if it's just for your warm bed.

> *"Some of my darkest moments in my life were preparing me for my best moments in my life. I am grateful for all my moments because they made me who I am today. Don't forget once in a while to connect the dots back in your life. You will see everything is a blessing and a gift—even your struggles."*
>
> *—Carolyn Rim*

FEBRUARY 24, 2016

Go ahead—let your heart take you off the well-worn path. Let it lead you to heartbreak—let it lead you to failures—let it lead you to your knees. Imagine your heart blooming open like a beautiful red, vibrant rose. The world around you *is* a different place when you open your heart.

My heart has been broken many times—by people, by myself, circumstances. But I would much rather love deeply and follow my heart than not love at all because I am afraid it will get broken.

Today lead with a kind open heart.

301

"It's impossible," says pride.
"It's risky," says experience.
"It's pointless," says reason.
"Give it a try" says the heart."

—Unknown

FEBRUARY 26, 2016

I dare you to live your life fully. To have adventures. Be weird. Have fun and be crazy. Face your fears. Laugh out loud. Take leaps of faith. Be your own kind of wonderful! And never forget that *all you need is within you!* You have a powerful force within you that once unleashed can make any dream, vision or desire happen. Today I hold my event with 20 other beautiful souls! Cannot wait!

MARCH 1, 2016

I have had many amazing teachers and guides over the past year that I am so grateful for but the greatest lesson I learned was to stop looking for the answer in everyone else. The answer has always been within me. It never left.

We search constantly for the secret answer to life or the next big thing outside ourselves when really all we need to do is go within and connect to the magic within us. Bottom line—don't lose your inner spark just to make someone else feel better. You are who you are. Own it and rock it.

MARCH 2, 2016

This is from *The Desire Map: A Guide to Creating Goals with Soul,*

by Danielle LaPorte:

"Positive feeling states are a sign that we are in sync with our soul. Negative feeling states are indicators that we are out of sync with our soul. And we are going to get out of sync. We're going to forget about our magnificence a few hundred times a day.

"Some people will glimpse their own magnificence only a few times in a lifetime. Crushingly, some of us will spend the majority of our adult lives in resistance to our souls, in perpetual states of bitchdom and fearfulness.

"To those people I want to say: You've simply forgotten who you are— it's just a temporary situation.

"Getting off-track is not only natural, but it is also absolutely inevitable for every single one of us. It doesn't matter if you're markedly wiser than the majority, if you're in a beautiful selfless service to the world, an avowed monk, or a relentless reader of self-help books with years of therapy, yoga, and the aligned chakras to prove it.

"You're going to slip out of your soul zone and into the shadowy emotions of doubt, jealously, pettiness, vengefulness, and a whole cadre of other uncomfortable states of being. Getting off track is essential to our growth. Veering away from one's essence and steering back to it is how we accumulate insight into and trust in the nature of life. We learn more both about our personal and the universal landscape every time we take a wrong turn. And how do we know we've taken a wrong turn? Well generally speaking, we feel like shit. We feel exactly how we don't want to feel.

"How about reframing negative emotions as wake-up calls? Is frustration, or any other negative emotion useful or worthwhile? Hell Yes. Every emotion felt is valuable. The trick is to actually feel it and then to fully accept it. Judging ourselves for feeling less than outstanding, or for being adrift from our divinity for a minute or several months, only keeps us locked in those negative states. If we're condemning it, we're creating stuck-ness. When we wipe the residue of judgment off the lens, we can see where more positive options are waiting for us."

> *"My rage lite reminds me of what I truly desire: joy. It nudges me to laugh at myself. Sometimes it reminds me that the most loving act can be to just let it go. Sometimes it Spurs me to take action. My anger reminds me of peace. My sadness, of happiness. My fear, of faith."*
> —*Danielle LaPorte,* The Desire Map

MARCH 2, 2016

I dare you today to be joyous. Smile through the bullshit. Be yourself!

MARCH 2, 2016

Napoleon Hill advises that in life we must *forgive*, but we don't forget the lessons and then we live by the *self-confidence formula:*

"I fully realize that no wealth or position can long endure, unless built upon truth and justice, therefore, I engage only in transactions that benefit all whom it affects. I succeed by attracting to myself the forces I wish to use, and the cooperation of other people. I induce others to serve me, because of my willingness to serve others. I eliminate hatred, envy, jealousy, selfishness, and cynicism, by creating love for all humanity, because I know that a negative attitude toward others can never bring me success. I cause others to believe in me, because I believe in them, and in myself."

—*Napoleon Hill,* Think and Grow Rich

MARCH 3, 2016

Every night before bed and morning before I start my day... I read an inspirational story of someone overcoming the odds!

Success leaves a trail and today I am modeling excellence and success.

When I hear the word no, I know I am one step closer to my YES! Now, get excited and invest in yourself!! I dare you to get to know yourself and your passions, visions and goals!! Yes you can!! You must continue to visualize someone saying YES even if you have no all around you.

"If you don't make the time creating the life you want, you're eventually will be forced spending a lot of time dealing with a life you don't want."

—*Kevin Ngo*

MARCH 3, 2016

Exactly one year ago today, Tony Robbins was on stage telling my story. I could not believe my eyes as my picture and name appeared on the screen in front of 7,000 people. I didn't know what the word destiny or synchronicity meant until this day. I look back at this memory and for them I am grateful. Be grateful for the synchronicities in life.

MARCH 5, 2016

You must have faith in yourself and the world if you want to achieve your dreams. You must see it when no one else does. You must be able to take the hits. You see, I think each and every one of us has talent within us but we get so weighted down by the doubt and the misconception that we are going up against millions of people.

Go look in the mirror. Take a deep breath and smile because the only person you are going up against is yourself.

MARCH 5, 2016

In less than five days I will be in Fla. with 10,000 souls transported to a different planet for a few days. Sometimes... I feel like that song from Glee should start playing for me. "Don't Stop Believing! Ohhhhh!"

MARCH 8, 2016

I AM GOING TO GET VULNERABLE. THIS JUST IN!

America's Top Confidence Coach still experiences DOUBT? WTF? What a FRAUD! Coaches are not allowed to have doubt. Let alone share about them.

I sit here thinking it's not possible for me to experience doubt. I am America's Top Confidence Coach for God's sake. This doubt has not shown up in a long time, so why now?

Then I start to open my eyes. I see how everyone (even Tony Robbins) can still go through situations where they feel doubt. It may not be often and I am sure that all Tony Robbins has to do is get into a state and bang on his chest and BAM—he's back. That's great for him—but what about the people who it doesn't work for? It normally works for me... But for me, this time just slapping my ass and changing my state wasn't so easy.

I run through my morning to see what triggered this:

6 a.m. I ran a 99 Day Dare call with a group of people through a meditation.

7 a.m. I ran the community call with 30-plus Rockstars looking to me for advice and confidence.

8 a.m. I take my little girl to school and on the commute make her feel special, wanted and confident by knowing *I* am special, wanted and confident.

9 a.m. First coaching one-on-one session of the day—take her through

the process of reframing and believing in herself and knowing how truly fucking incredible she is and asking her not to give the key to her feelings to anyone else.

10 a.m. Second one-on-one and again, I need to be ON. Tap in. Tuned in. And Powered Up. She is really upset. Sad. Struggling. Her heart hurts. I listen and tell her not to make herself wrong about anything. You see, she thought she wasted time but our time is never wasted. We need to shift that into we learned and if we learn from our experiences, then time is never wasted.

11 a.m. I am thinking, why do I feel a sliver of doubt about tonight's webinar? Why? I just was the leader of five incredible calls! I have had the pleasure of leading more than 250 Live Zoom calls in the past year. After everything that happened over the past year, all the calls I have been the leader of, I still question my own greatness?

What the hell is wrong with me?

11:03 a.m. Here is where it gets interesting. I jump in my car—and I start jamming out but something doesn't feel right. The banging on my chest, slapping my ass, and jammin' out isn't working.

I pull over and this time for the first time, I *stop*. I breathe. I take a deep, refreshing breath in and expand my energy and I breathe out any energy that no longer serves me. I honor the doubt and the fear. I honor that part of myself that feels the doubt.

I imagine I am talking to that part of myself that no longer serves me. I say thank you for serving and fulfilling my needs. Even if it was in lower lying ways, doubt still served my needs through the years but it no longer serves me. I tell myself that Santa Claus is real. I tell that part of myself that the most amazing parts of me are the ones you can't see, hear or touch. But you can feel their presence and experience the energy. I go about it in a gentle way.

After all, it's my faith that anything is possible that keeps these amazing things happening to me.

Lesson: Banging on my chest didn't work today. So I decided to do the reframe in a calm way. I decided that I was just experiencing stepping into another part of me. A more evolved being. A more powerful part of my being replaces the doubt and the fear. I feel it in my core. I not only feel confident—I feel like I can bend the walls if I focus long enough. Just kidding. But seriously, I feel alive, amazing, and most important, I feel like me!

I am going to have a successful webinar tonight with more than 100

Rockstars signed up for the 99 Day SYR Dare! Why!? I already had 12 sign up so far and because anything is possible when you access the universal power within yourself, and by God, I am ready to move mountains with my energy.

> *"Go look in the mirror. Take a deep breath and smile because the only person you are going up against is yourself."*
>
> *—Carolyn Rim*

MARCH 9, 2016

Good morning world! I am ready to take a big bite out of you like the ripe juicy peach you are! Thank you for everything you have given me so far! I am so excited I am going as Tony Robbins' guest to West Palm Beach Florida today! I feel like the whole universe is cued up ready to give me anything I am willing to ask for!

MARCH 9, 2016

West Palm Beach bound!! Unleash the Power Within, here I come with the force of the universe behind me!

MARCH 11, 2016

LOL—so their first mistake was giving me a mic...

MARCH 13, 2016

You see my face? I didn't stop smiling for the whole day!

MARCH 13, 2016

I mean... I don't even have any words to describe this. I am just incredibly grateful to be able to share with Tony's audience my story of what his events and coaching do for people. If you don't have a Tony Robbins coach... Get one. If you haven't been to an event ... Get to one. That's where the magic started with me and continues for me.

MARCH 14, 2016

I danced on stage in front of 7,000 people and pumped them up! Honestly at this point, yesterday was so incredible that I would not be surprised if a freaking unicorn pulled up in a van and said, "You called?" Fourteen months ago, I decided that I am a reality architect and I will create my own destiny. Have you decided yet? Yes? No? Whatever the answer is for you... I dare you to join me April 1 on the new 99 DAY SPARK YOUR ROCKSTAR DARE. If you are sick and tired of settling for less than you know in your heart you are capable of... If you are ready to live with an open heart, and make dreams come true...

Only accepting 112 Rockstars into this next Dare... Claim your spot now and come spark your inner ROCKSTAR!

I look in my inbox and have more than 200 FB messages, tons of texts, emails, and comments...but it can all wait until tomorrow ... This little soul's smile lights up my whole world. Let this be a lesson to you, too! Look around. Who needs your love at this very moment? Go give them a smooch and a smile!

MARCH 17, 2016

When you get around the right people, at the right time, for the right reasons... You get magic results.

MARCH 17, 2016

People are signing up for the 99 DAY SPARK YOUR ROCKSTAR DARE and Orders are coming like crazy!! Joseph and I are taking on 112 people into this Dare (We are already at 73 people signed up so we only have another 40 or so spots left) and then it's closed for another three months! Knock! Knock! This is opportunity... Are you ready to tap into more energy than you ever thought possible? Have a powerful positive peer group? Have accountability partners? Wake up with vibrant energy? It's time to step up and make your move! Here is your chance! The price goes up tomorrow at 12 p.m.!

MARCH 18, 2016

I can't sleep. I am too excited to be alive. We have been born at the greatest time in history. It's time to step up. Allow this next line to vibrate and shake up your world.

"Make Your Fucking Move!"

MARCH 18, 2016

Don't fight the fear... Align with it. Grab it by the hand and say, "Shall we dance, darling?"

MARCH 18, 2016

I believe that one smile can change the world. Right now, smile, and let this energy empower and energize you! When you just BE YOU, I believe you empower others around you to do the same. Today... Smile.... Live in a beautiful state of mind and just be your amazing authentic self!

MARCH 19, 2016 BLOG POST

In the past month, I have made small shifts in my thinking that have created mammoth shifts in my reality. I am going to share some things with you and I want you to take notice to how you feel as I share them.

I am a keynote speaker and I also hold my own events. On April 8, I gave my Superman Physiology Talk to a whole school of more than 300 children. Then I was just asked to speak in front of 400 lawyers in Ohio in October and they want me to speak on The Power of Mentorship. I have a 99 Day Dare that didn't even officially open enrollment yet and it's almost sold out (30 spots left!). I was just hired to privately to coach three new clients. My inbox is full with messages to go through full of people who want to work with me. I am picking up incredible speed and I am planning my next big event! Why am I telling you all of this? Well... Because ...

The world will give you anything you are willing to ask for and believe you deserve. I have had this vision in my mind for years. I am on stage and the crowd is going wild. I stand in front of 10,000 people and I am smiling and grateful. I help wake up and shake their world.

You see, up until about a year and a half ago, I thought wanting what I wanted was selfish. I thought having my dreams come true was a selfish act. I would see others succeed and I would get incredibly jealous or say, "Oh, they are so lucky." It wasn't until I shifted my beliefs that the world outside started to change instantly.

Your beliefs and your thoughts shape the world around you. It's just that simple. Everyone tries to complicate this. I changed my belief about seeing people succeed and instead of getting jealous, I was excited and happy for them because if they could do it, that meant I could, too! I started to believe that I deserved my dreams to come true. I believed I deserved love. I started to respect others, and really see them for who they were.

At this past UPW, a few Rockstars joked with me that I would need security because so many people were coming up to me. They said my story inspired them to take leaps of faith into the dark on their own lives. At this seminar, I shared my story, and I allowed the world to see me for who I really was. I am just so grateful right now for my mentors. Without them, I would not be where I am. People ask me all the time, "How did you do it?" I tell them I listened to Tony Robbins when he said to find a mentor who had what I wanted. I asked ass-shaking rockstar Joseph McClendon to be my mentor. I keep moving forward despite others around me telling me to get a real job, that my dreams were impossible, and that I should really be more realistic. I stopped hanging around with anyone who told me my dreams were not achievable. I kept moving forward despite failures. I started to tell the story of my life the way I wanted it to be rather than the way it was! I remember though one thorn in my arm throughout the past year. That was my own self doubt in my abilities to help others.

Let me tell you, when you are doubtful about your abilities, everyone knows it. They can feel it. I was helping people all along the way, but it wasn't until I made the shift at my last UPW that I feel like my whole world changed instantly. I accepted the gifts that were in me. I thanked God for the gifts he had given me. I got on my knees and cried I was so grateful for my life.

Then it happened, I started to feel the incredible force that has been around me this whole time. All doubt was dissolved and replaced with faith. All weaknesses were instantly transformed into strengths. God, the universe, source, love, infinite intelligence, whatever you want to call it based on your beliefs. I could not hold this in my hands per se, I could not see it with my eyes, but I could feel it. It's pure love for me, for the world, for each soul. I embraced this force into my heart and then realized it had been there all along. It's the power that every soul has access to within themselves. I felt more elevated and alive than I ever have in my whole life. I just feel illuminated within.

I put this picture up because I am sending you love. Right now in this moment I am sending you love and smile in your heart.

The best advice I can give you is to have faith in the invisible. Just because you can't see it or touch it or hear it doesn't mean it's not there helping you towards your greatest self. Accept the gifts the universe has placed within you. Follow the whispers of your heart. And just remember when you are at your lowest point, surrounded by darkness, heaviness, bills, frustration, and not sure how you are going to make it... Remember... Victory is near. Don't give up like most, two feet from Gold.

Sending you hugs, Hugh gives, and pattern-breaking ass slaps,
Carolyn Rim
a.k.a., America's Top Confidence Coach

MARCH 19, 2016

Small shifts in my thinking have created mammoth shifts in my reality. I am going to share some things with you and I want you to take notice of how you feel as I share them.

The best advice I can give you is have faith in the invisible. Just because you can't see it or touch it or hear it doesn't mean it's not there helping you towards your greatest self.

Accept the gifts from the universe. Follow the whispers of your heart. And just remember when you are at your lowest point, surrounded by darkness, heaviness, bills, frustration, and not sure how you are going to make it, remember:

Victory is near. Don't give up like most do, two feet from Gold.

Sending you hugs, high-fives, and pattern-breaking ass slaps,
Carolyn Rim

MARCH 23, 2016

Minutes from now you will make a decision that could alter the course of your life forever—whether or not to join Spark Your Rockstar's 99 Day Dare. Many people ask me how I have so much energy. Many people ask how they can be the best possible version of themselves and create deeper connections with those they love, have more fulfillment in their lives, and just feel happier overall. THIS IS THE DARE THAT LITERALLY WILL REWIRE YOUR BRAIN AND AWAKEN YOUR HEART! So, are you ready to open the red door yet and see what sizzling dreams, answers and guidance are behind them for you? I dare you, I double-dog-dare you, I TRIPLE DOG DARE YOU to join me for 99 days! It is time to come home. Ready... SET... JOIN THE 99 DAY DARE! Come find out what's behind the red door for you! Go to:

www.SparkYourRockstar.com

ACKNOWLEDGEMENTS

Thank you to my little girl. She cried with me when I told her this was completed. She understood how much time, energy and effort went into this. She was my Why during this book. She pushed me more than I will ever know. She also taught me to laugh and roll down hills. She taught me about love and how to see the invisible again.

Thank you to my dad, John Anthony Rim, my mom, Karen Rim, my sisters, Marybeth Rim and Marie Ann Rim, my brother-in-law Brad Thomas, my brother Frank Rim and my sister-in-law Annie, who I always felt were only one call away to save the day for me. They took care of my daughter many nights while I worked on this! I want to say thank you to my nieces, Bea, El, Rosie, Grace, who believe in the invisible and the magic. Thank you for helping me see again. My heart is open and my eyes are wide!

Thank you to my editor, Heather Harris, whose dedication and heartfelt work were appreciated so much. She was the one who really helped me spin this into gold. She worked long days to help me complete the editing fast. She believed in me and my baby. She treated this book as if it were her own. Thank you! And thank you to Adam Spivak for the connection to her!

Thank you to the Spark Your Rockstar Community, all my friends and family, and followers who take this journey with me daily. Evolution is a choice and we choose it every day by choosing love. Thank you for pushing me to get this done! I am so utterly grateful for all your support and love.

Thank you to the people who believed in me, especially those who believed in me before I knew how to believe in myself. Thank you to all the people who helped me get here. My mentors, Tony Robbins, Joseph McClendon, Jairek Robbins, David Kauffman, Justin Ligeri, Dr. John Amaral, Dr. Kim Potter, Dr. David Mehler, and Anthony Conklin. I am so grateful for all the love, support and lessons I learned from you all. Thank you.

I thank my creator, God. Thank you for making me. I love my life and those in it. I am so blessed to be in this space and time. Forever grateful. Thank you.

Carolyn Rim
April 2017

ABOUT THE AUTHOR

Unicorn, Rockstar, Movie Star, Astronaut, Best-selling Author. Carolyn Rim assures us we can be, do, and have anything we want in this world. Her online courses, events, masterminds, 99 Day Dares, Facebook live videos and meditation programs have reached and transformed hundreds of thousands of people all over the world. She is an entrepreneur, a speaker, a leader, a mom, a rockstar and the force behind Spark Your Rockstar Community, an online community Facebook group with thousands of rockstars.

Carolyn is quickly becoming one of the most sought- after speakers and coaches in the world. Whether it's business, relationships, more fulfillment in your life or you just want unstoppable confidence in yourself, Carolyn Rim will help guide you to light the matches within and ignite the sizzle in your soul.

Get ready to be transformed. Carolyn uses energy work, meditation, visualizations, and neurolinguistic programing (NLP) to guide you toward creating unstoppable, unshakeable confidence in yourself, the world and your dreams.

Carolyn also holds live events for her community where she invites you to experience what she calls a Spark Your Rockstar Soulgasm! An orgasm in your soul! It is the ultimate unveiling of who you are. An explosion within where you can feel a vibration in your being so deep that you are awakened with intuition, guidance, and love! Most people refer to her events and courses as a "coming home" experience. Spark Your Rockstar has several events throughout the year that will help you put the sizzle in your soul and shake up your world with energy, transformation and love!

Carolyn Rim helps you awaken your own heart to who you really are! Learn more about Carolyn Rim and get free resources, tools, information on courses, events and meditations at www.SparkYourRockstar.com to help you create a life beyond your wildest dreams. Check out www.facebook.com/groups/sparkenergy/ and request to join thousands of people all over the world in the Spark Your Rockstar family today! Find out what it's like to have a positive powerful peer group of rockstars!

RESOURCES

Below is a list of some of the events I have attended and resources I have used that have helped me while honing in on my own rockstar soul style! And while these are some of my favorites (that I strongly suggest you check out and attend) my list is constantly growing and evolving.

So, if you would like a more all inclusive and up-to-date suggestions from me, please sign up to get all the hot-off- the- press details at www.SparkYourRockstar.com.

SEMINARS

Tony Robbins conducts his live Unleash The Power Within events with translation in seven languages. His seminars are great for anyone who wants more out of their life! I was reborn in Dallas, Texas in 2014 at my first UPW (Unleash The Power Within). I highly recommend it for anyone, any age, any time to get the energy, the love, and the tools to help make the impossible possible! When I first went to the seminar to see Tony, I felt so loved by him. I was in a room with 7,000 people but I felt like he loved each and every one of us. His energy transcends us and there is a humanity in the room that is hard to describe in words. What can I say? Get your butt to one of his seminars! Please check it out at www.TonyRobbins.com.

Joseph McClendon III, Ph.D., my incredible mentor, has his website at www.MakeYourFate.com. His unique brand of "Tell, Show, Do" teaching and coaching creates rapid personal change that effectively moves people to take more consistent action and go "Further Faster" with their personal and business achievements. As you know, Joseph has helped me tremendously in my abilities to go further faster!

Dr. John Amaral, D.C. is an energy healer who I have used and who has helped me tremendously in my abilities to heal and to tap into and harness energy. He helps you master the invisible forces that shape your body, life and destiny to fast-track your way to unshakable confidence, profound aliveness, and unlimited abundance. Feel free to check him out at www.BodyCenteredLeadership.com.

David Kauffman is my business mentor and has helped me truly understand how to take my business to the next level. He works with me to help with basic business practices, processes, and customer retention. He has an experienced set of eyes to look in from the outside and give me an honest view of my business. He can see things that may cause my business harm and offers solutions to the obstacles and issues I face. Don't let your business butt be naked! Get your butt covered by David! Please check him out at www.YourBusinessBasics.com.

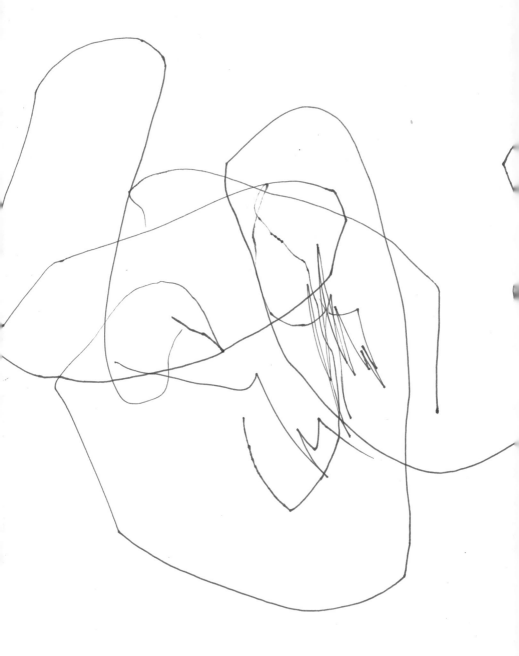

Made in the USA
Middletown, DE
28 March 2019